WOMEN IN PRISON

A Reference Handbook

Other Titles in ABC-CLIO's
CONTEMPORARY
WORLD ISSUES
Series

Books in the Contemporary World Issues series address vital issues in today's society such as genetic engineering, pollution, and biodiversity. Written by professional writers, scholars, and nonacademic experts, these books are authoritative, clearly written, up-to-date, and objective. They provide a good starting point for research by high school and college students, scholars, and general readers as well as by legislators, businesspeople, activists, and others.

Each book, carefully organized and easy to use, contains an overview of the subject, a detailed chronology, biographical sketches, facts and data and/or documents and other primary-source material, a directory of organizations and agencies, annotated lists of print and nonprint resources, and an index.

Readers of books in the Contemporary World Issues series will find the information they need in order to have a better understanding of the social, political, environmental, and economic issues facing the world today.

WOMEN IN PRISON

A Reference Handbook

Cyndi Banks

**CONTEMPORARY
WORLD ISSUES**

ABC-CLIO

Santa Barbara, California
Denver, Colorado
Oxford, England

Library of Congress Cataloging-in-Publication Data

Banks, Cyndi.
  Women in prison : a reference handbook / Cyndi Banks.
      p. cm.—(Contemporary world issues)
Includes bibliographical references and index.
  ISBN 1-57607-929-5 (hardcover)—ISBN 1-57607-930-9 (e-book)
  1. Women prisoners—United States. 2. Female offenders—United
States. 3. Reformatories for women—United States. I. Title. II.
Series.

HV9471 .B365 2003
365'.43—dc21

                                    2002154379

07 06 05 04 03 9 8 7 6 5 4 3 2 1

This book is also available on the World Wide Web as an e-book. Visit abc-clio.com for details.

ABC-CLIO, Inc.
130 Cremona Drive, P.O. Box 1911
Santa Barbara, California 93116-1911

This book is printed on acid-free paper ∞.
Manufactured in the United States of America

Contents

Preface

The United States maintains the largest prison system in the world and imprisons more people, both men and women, than any other country. This book focuses on women in the prison system and answers questions such as: How did women historically come to be sent to prison? How were they treated in prisons and reformatories? What kinds of offenses do women commit that end in their incarceration? How do women experience imprisonment? How do they cope with life in prison on a daily basis?

In the past it has been argued by those who study prisons that women prisoners were "invisible" because they made up such a small proportion of all persons imprisoned. Although women still comprise only a very small proportion of all prisoners, they are now more visible due to the many research studies that have been carried out since the late 1960s that have explored women's experience in the prison system and brought to light many issues, including the kinds of treatment available to women in confinement, how women are classified and disciplined by prison authorities, the effect of certain policy approaches like the so-called "war on drugs" and the "three strikes and you're out" legislation on the rate of women's imprisonment, and importantly, the differences that exist in the treatment of men and women within correctional systems.

My interest in this subject derives from my teaching at the university level in the areas of women in prison and gender and crime, as well as in my pedagogical practice that includes gender as a fundamental component in all criminology and criminal justice courses; from my own research into women and juveniles in prison and institutions; and from my published articles on punishment and incarceration generally.

This book contains a comprehensive history of women in prison, an in-depth examination of issues and controversies that affect women in prison, a chronology of events in the history of women in prison, and a list of persons who were influential in the history of women's imprisonment in the United States. This information is supplemented with the actual voices of women "doing time," who describe in their own words how it feels to be incarcerated. This feminist approach allows the reader to grasp more fully the experience of incarceration and the background of women who find themselves criminalized. Although women are guarded as prisoners, they are also guards themselves; I have therefore included a chapter on women performing the work of correctional officers and the issues that arise as women carry out these duties alongside their male counterparts. For those interested in pursuing these issues further, various sources of information are listed to enable students, researchers, and social activists to make connections and investigate particular aspects of this subject more deeply and thoroughly.

Any serious study of women in prison should begin with the history of women's incarceration in prisons and women's reformatories. This approach helps reveal the historical importance of gender in societal attitudes toward women in confinement: reformers attempted to "save" some women offenders and transform them into the "true woman" imbued with middle-class values and attitudes while women prisoners—languished, forgotten, and rejected by society—were considered "fallen women" and beyond redemption. The significance of this social and cultural history is that the same attitudes are reproduced today in modified forms as readers will see in the present issues and controversies studied. Most fundamentally, however, the material presented here shows how women's issues should not be subsumed under men's issues in any study of imprisonment, as once was the case. Women's crimes, their experience of incarceration, and their treatment needs are radically different from men's and should therefore continue to be the subject of discrete studies.

1

The History of Women's Prisons

The history of women in prison* in the United States is marked by a number of stages and developments that parallel, in part, the history of men in prison. In the first stage, from the time that imprisonment as a sanction was introduced in the colonies until the 1870s, all women prisoners were housed with men within the same prison complex. During the second stage, between 1870 and 1930, the conditions of some women prisoners changed after the women's reformatory movement succeeded in altering their living conditions and a new philosophy of redemption and training came into being. However, it is important to appreciate that for many women, custodial conditions did not change, and they continued to be housed in conditions similar to those for male prisoners. In the third stage (1931–present), women staff were hired to supervise women in prison and were appointed to govern women's institutions.

Imprisoning Women

The period between 1815 and 1860 was one of great social change in the United States due to migration from rural to urban areas, immigration from overseas, and the development of a market

---

*This history of women's prisons developed in this chapter is primarily based on Feinman (1984), Freedman (2000), Lekkerkerker (1931), and Rafter (1985), although other sources are also referred to.

economy, all of which greatly disrupted the lives of many men and women. Urban growth resulted in numerous social and economic problems for women, who occupied a marginal position in the economy due to limited opportunities for wage earning and lower salaries. These limited opportunities after the Civil War compelled many women to take up prostitution in order to survive, and many also resorted to property crime. Peculiar to women, however, were the many laws that regulated sexual conduct, such as adultery, lewd behavior, and idle and disorderly conduct. Conviction for such offenses resulted not only in punishment but also in labeling criminalized women as "fallen women," a stigma that once attached could never be removed. Other men and women refused to associate with such women or to employ them, and this could easily lead to further criminal acts when a woman tried to survive even though outcast and penniless.

"Fallen Women" in Prison

Political leaders of the time showed little concern about living conditions for women in prisons. This may have resulted from the low status of these "fallen" women, from their small numbers—that made their situation invisible—and from the general opinion that they were beyond reform. Male penal officials resented the extra demands that a few women placed on them and viewed hiring a matron to look after so few prisoners as a waste of money. Prisoners during this era were expected to work and earn money to support their institution, but female prisoners were regarded as unprofitable noncontributors.

This differential treatment of women had its roots in the perception that women criminals were depraved creatures who had denied their own pure womanly natures when committing crime. Male prisoners did not suffer the same perception and were regarded as still capable of redemption. Women's conduct was considered more serious than men's criminal conduct because of the belief that a woman who ignored her roles and influence as wife and mother actually encouraged male criminality. In addition, "fallen" women were considered disruptive to the harmony of society because they were a temptation for men to engage in sin. These perceptions of women were linked to the Victorian ideology developed during that era with its notions concerning the ideal woman as the angel in the house, and its insistence on women's role as the moral exemplar within the family, responsible for maintaining spiritual and moral values.

Women's Crime

During this period of history, women were significantly involved in the category of crimes against public order, including drunkenness, vagrancy, streetwalking, and petty larceny. Women were incarcerated for these crimes in local jails (penitentiaries were reserved for the more dangerous offenses of murder, arson, and burglary). Common thought was that women committed fewer crimes than men because of the strict sexual division of labor resulting from confining women to the home to carry out domestic duties. However, after 1840 the rate of imprisonment for women began to increase; in the New York courts, for example, convictions of women increased at a much higher rate than for men in the period 1847 to 1860. The greatest increase in women's rates occurred in the 1860s, when the female inmate population in Massachusetts and New York increased by one third while the rate of men's imprisonment declined by one half. This trend was attributable not only to the incidence of public order offenses—especially prostitution, which had become more visible during the Civil War—but also in crimes against other persons. It is likely that stricter laws and their intensive enforcement brought about this increase, although some commentators of the time believed the increasing practice of abortion to be a significant contributing factor.

Women's Imprisonment—Early Period to Reform

During the early period of women's imprisonment, men and women were housed in the same prison building. This thinking reflected the practices the colonists brought with them to the United States from their countries of origin. Gradually, women were separated from men, lodged within separate prison buildings either within the same prison or in separate institutions.

The early colonists followed British penal practice, and local jails were generally used to detain those awaiting trial or punishment. Punishment for both men and women involved not only imprisonment but visible forms of sanctioning, such as whipping, ducking, or being placed in the stocks or pillories. However, by the late eighteenth century, the United States became influenced by developments in penology in Europe, where capital punishment was being replaced with imprisonment. One impetus for this change was the reformers' belief that incarceration would encourage repentance. Incarceration would also isolate criminals from society, allow for supervision of their daily lives, and establish compulsory inmate labor.

After 1815, many states erected penitentiaries based on two competing models—the Pennsylvania system used by Quakers, which isolated prisoners in individual cells and required complete silence both day and night; and the Auburn model, named after a prison in New York that opened in 1817, where the inmates, although isolated in cells at night, worked together in silence during the day and were subjected to extensive scrutiny and surveillance backed up by a rigid system of discipline. Both men and women were imprisoned in penitentiaries, but the scant evidence available reveals limited imprisonment of women up until 1840. In 1850, for example, women made up only 3.6 percent of the total inmate population of thirty-four state and county prisons.

During the 1820s, women prisoners in the Auburn system were not subjected to the same disciplinary regime as men because the lack of specific accommodation for them made this impossible. Rather, the women were crowded together, often in one room, away from the male cellblock. Their quarters were overcrowded, and they were commonly subjected to harsh treatment and abuse. The death of one woman prisoner after being flogged in the Auburn prison in New York may have brought about legislation that in 1828 required county prisons to separate male and female inmates. In 1832 a matron was hired for the women's part of the Auburn prison. Along with the harsh and appalling conditions for women in penitentiaries came sexual abuse, sexual assaults, and illegitimate births, which were often systematic and overt.

The gradual segregation of women from men prisoners occurred in phases and patterns and varied from state to state. Broadly, there were three stages in this process. In the first, women were part of the general prison population and were confined in large rooms or in individual cells but were not segregated further. In the second, the women were placed in separate quarters within or attached to the men's section of the prison. During the third stage, women were relocated to a more remote place on or near the main prison grounds. The evolution of separate housing for women was most rapid in the northeast, slower in the Midwest, slower still in the South, and slowest of all in the West. (Even in the late 1970s, some states in the West remained in the second stage since they continued to incarcerate their few female prisoners in small units attached to male prisons.)

By the mid-nineteenth century, a number of states had hired matrons to supervise the female prisoners, but they seldom performed more than custodial duties. In many prisons there was only one matron to supervise all the female inmates, and she usually lived in the prison and was on duty twenty-four hours a day, six and a half days a week. The matrons were mostly older women, often widowed and forced to undertake this work through economic hardship. In some cases they were the wives of warders.

In 1835, the Mount Pleasant Female Prison at Ossining, New York, was established as the first women's prison in the United States. Although it was physically close to and administratively dependent on the men's prison, Sing Sing, it was housed in separate buildings and had its own staff. The Mount Pleasant Female Prison followed the Auburn plan with three tiers of twenty-four cells each and contained a nursery and workshop as well as two large separate cells for punishment cases. It was administered by a matron, who in turn supervised several assistant matrons. Women prisoners worked at tasks considered appropriate for the time, including button making, hat trimming, and sewing clothes for the male inmates. Women at Mount Pleasant were not disciplined as brutally as men (punishments included gagging but not the lash), and the most common punishment was confinement to one's cell with a reduction in food. In 1846 the list of violations that resulted in punishment included "noise in room" and "rushing from cell when the door was open," which carried punishments of twelve days in solitary confinement and chaining to the wall.

Women's Prison Reform
Early Period of Reform, 1840–1860

In the period between 1840 and 1860 reformers made radical changes to the physical conditions in some women's prisons, and they questioned the prisoners' label as "fallen women" and their assumed lack of capacity for reform. To a great extent, these reformers took their cue from the English women's prison reformer, Elizabeth Fry, who had entered London's Newgate jail in 1813 and met starving, drunken, and partly clothed women inmates. She subsequently wrote her treatise *Observations in Visiting, Superintendence and Government of Female Prisoners* in 1827, setting forth the principles that came to guide American women's prison reform. Fry, a Quaker, believed that women prisoners could be reformed, and so she devised methods for achieving reform through religious salvation, a structured daily schedule, and compassion, and stressed that women generally had a responsibility to aid their fallen sisters.

Nearly all of the thirty or so women in the United States active in prison reform during the nineteenth century came from middle- and upper-class homes, and almost one third were Quakers. Many also worked for other causes such as the abolition of slavery, temperance, and women's emancipation. Most had acquired the ideology of the "ideal" woman in school, and their socialization as moral guardians influenced their desire to obtain some "purposeful work" before marriage. This included teaching, missionary work, and religious instruction; some women reformers also gained experience as nurses and administrators.

During the 1820s and 1830s, reformers propagated the notion of salvation and brought to life movements for the redemption of sinners, temperance, and moral reform, as well as for the reform of the prison system. Women who joined this movement for salvation believed that even the most hardened sinners—and this included "fallen" women—could be brought to salvation. They considered the task of reforming women and children to be their special responsibility, and by 1823 the Quakers of Philadelphia had begun to visit women's prisons to offer instruction, a library, and sewing and writing classes to women inmates.

By the 1840s, Protestant missionaries in New York and even some male reformers were becoming concerned about the status and conditions of women in prison, especially about the sexual license that was permitted in institutions. The male Prison Association of New York asked women reformers to form a women's auxiliary called the Female Department, and those women who joined this organization followed Elizabeth Fry in trying to encourage religious feelings in the female prison population. An early leader of the Female Department was Abby Hopper Hopkins, who together with women like Sarah Doremus, Catherine Sedgwick, and Caroline Kirkland proposed a number of plans to assist women in prison, including a scheme for a halfway house that would provide shelter and prayer and prevent recidivism. Generally, they saw domestic training as the key to the women's salvation and believed this salvation would only take place in a "home" where the "fallen" women would reclaim their moral purity. Margaret Fuller, an outstanding early feminist and the editor of the *New York Tribune*, supported this proposal. She had visited the women's department at Sing Sing Prison in New York and concluded that the women there were victims who needed help to overcome the circumstances that had led them into crime. Fuller published a series of articles in the *Tribune* in 1845 exposing the conditions for women in prison and questioning the perception that these women were beyond redemption. Once the home for discharged women was opened, she led a campaign for funds to support it and promoted the acceptance of social responsibility for "fallen" women.

Along with the reformers' insistence that women in prison were not beyond redemption came their scrutiny of women's criminality. The reformers perceived many of the women as innocent victims of male seduction rather than designing temptresses, and they questioned whether, in view of their poverty, the women had any real choice in adopting a life of crime. In the 1850s this group of reformers rebelled against men's influence on their work and asserted their independence by forming the Women's Prison Association of New York in 1854. At this stage, the reform movement for women in prison limited itself to improving women prisoners' living conditions and to their moral renewal through prison visiting and the provision of halfway houses.

The Women's Reformatory Movement, 1870–1900

The women's reformatory movement was part of a broad current in penal reform that began soon after the end of the Civil War promoting the treatment or rehabilitation of the incarcerated. Many persons involved in penal reform had become disillusioned with existing custodial methods and practices and rejected the philosophy of retribution in favor of the new aim of prisoner reformation. The new penology was initially presented to a gathering of prison administrators and reformers in Cincinnati, Ohio, in 1870. The meeting endorsed a series of principles that shaped U.S.

penology for the next century. Among them was the classification of inmates as a preliminary step in designing the treatment plan for an inmate; this logically led to recognition that separate prisons were required for women prisoners. In fact, the meeting's Declaration of Principles stated explicitly, "prisons, as well as prisoners, should be classified or graded so that there shall be . . . separate establishments for women." This declaration gave the women reformers their basis for continuing to urge change in the treatment of women in prison.

Between 1870 and 1900, reformers advocated an alternative model for women's incarceration based on three principles: the separation of women prisoners from male prisoners, the provision of specific feminine care to women, and control over women's prisons by female staff. By the end of the nineteenth century, reformers had been successful in the states where they were most active—Indiana, Massachusetts, and New York—in that separate women's prisons were established.

After 1860, reform efforts expanded to a movement that sought professional status for women prison reformers through their appointment to prison boards and to the boards that governed institutions. The conclusion of the Civil War brought more women into the reform movement, and in the 1870s, Abby Hopper Gibbons joined with Josephine Shaw Lowell to campaign for women to run the separate women's prisons in New York. Lowell was from one of Boston's oldest families and had been active in charitable work. She investigated the situation of women in jails and argued for women's control of public institutions. In the Midwest, the Quakers began working for prison reform after 1860; their most active reformer was Rhoda Coffin of Indiana, who with Sarah Smith campaigned for a separate women's prison in that state. The Civil War had taught women that they could serve competently alongside men, and many had worked for the state as nurses and charity workers. After the war, they wanted to continue their work with social causes and, because of their experience, looked for public and professional roles from which to do this. A good example of this new interest in professionalism was Elizabeth Buffum Chace, a Quaker from Rhode Island who campaigned for female membership of prison boards. Thanks to her efforts, Rhode Island in 1870 passed legislation for a Board of Lady Visitors to inspect prisons housing women. Similarly, in Connecticut, the state Board of Charities formed a department with female members in 1876 to inspect jails and prisons.

In terms of national organizations, women became members of the National Prison Association (later called the American Prison Association, or APA) and the National Conference on Charities and Corrections. At its founding meeting in 1870, the APA called for women to be deployed in improving the prison system, and in 1875, Rhoda Coffin gave the first paper by a female member to the organization speaking about the importance of women's prisons being placed under the control of other women. As she put it, "a woman's prison should be entirely under the control of women, from the board of managers to the lowest officer" (Coffin 1877, 208).

The legislation that established women's reformatories permitted the incarceration of women for short terms for petty offenses for which they had previously been sent to jails rather than to prison. The laws also extended the time that women were required to spend in prison and, in doing so, created a category of female prisoner that had no counterpart among male prisoners. The reformatories for men held only felons, and men convicted of minor crimes such as drunkenness continued to be punished outside the state prison system and given only brief jail terms. Reformers overlooked the fact that they were creating a double standard that punished women more severely than men for committing the same offenses.

Treating Women Differently

By the 1860s, several new "women-only" quarters had been established in prisons throughout the country. American reformers continued to take their cues from English reforms for women prisoners; one such influence was the book *Our Convicts*, written by English prison reformer Mary Carpenter. Subsequent to observing the Mount Joy Female Convict Prison in Ireland, Carpenter published *Our Convicts* in 1864, arguing that women prisoners should be housed together in one prison where a merit system would regulate their treatment and privileges and female guards rather than male guards would be employed. Attracted to Carpenter's ideas, American reformer Elizabeth Buffum Chance met with Carpenter in London in 1872. Rhoda Coffin also visited Mount Joy and praised its representation of family life. At the same time that women reformers were urging separation of the sexes, male prison officials such as Zebulon Brockway, superintendent of the Detroit House of Corrections, began to support separation. In 1869, Michigan enacted the country's first indeterminate sentencing law, which enabled Brockway to hold women convicted of prostitution for up to three years on the theory that during this extended period of imprisonment the prostitutes might be reformed. This new sentencing tool was not applied to men. With this three-year sentence, parole became possible, and so the House of Shelter was created as a halfway house for paroled women, who would be given shelter there until their sentences concluded. The important consideration for Brockway was that residents of the House of Shelter would be under the maternal care of more mature, respectable women. He therefore engaged Emma Hall, a former Detroit public school teacher, as matron. Hall set up a merit system and formed a group with thirty female prisoners who lived as a family in well-furnished surroundings. She stressed spiritual study, domesticity, and academic improvement and pioneered the type of training offered in reformatories—propriety, decorum, and preparing women to lead a "good womanly" life. The House of Shelter closed in 1874 after both Brockway and Hall resigned from the Detroit House of Corrections.

The campaign for separate prisons was not without its difficulties. For example, in Massachusetts, implementing sexual separation required a four-year campaign by commissioners and private reformers. Reformers argued that women would remain incurably criminal unless they were separated from men and received a new form of treatment. They emphasized that this treatment would not be more lenient than previously but would be different. What they envisioned was a product of their own socialization. They believed that inculcating the women with their own Victorian middle-class values of true womanhood—purity, piety, domesticity, and submission—would transform them. It was important to them to treat the women as women, to recognize their femininity and encourage it to grow. Officials now recognized that women were more emotional and needed different management than men, and that they were more likely to respond to kind treatment than rigid discipline. The softening and nurturing influences would include flowers, farm animals, music, and visits to the infant nursery within the prison. Educating delinquent women to be women first was perceived as the prime task, and domesticity was therefore seen as the focal point for this teaching. For the reformers, the home became a symbol of transformation, able to restore womanhood to criminal women. Courses included reading, writing, and sewing together with Bible study, and a regime of piety was emphasized based on early rising, the banning of profanity and profane substances such as tobacco and alcohol, regular work, and on developing habits of neatness and industry. Both Josephine Lowell and Emma Hall advocated establishing homes where tender care would be provided and rejected the silent model of the penitentiaries. Thanks largely to Lowell's efforts, the Hudson House of Refuge opened in 1887 in New York as the first cottage-based adult female reformatory staffed almost entirely by women. It was filled to capacity within two years. The Western House of Refuge, opened in Albion, New York, in 1893, also followed the household model, and Bedford Hills in Westchester County, New York, opened as a reformatory in 1901.

In Indiana, Rhoda Coffin opened the Indiana Reformatory for Women and Girls in 1873. It was the first completely independent women's prison as well as the first to be administered and operated by an entirely female staff. Previously women had been kept in custody at the Indiana State Prison, and while visiting that prison, Coffin observed that male guards carried keys to the women's cells—with very adverse results for the women. There were also reports of sexual abuse involving bribing female inmates as well as inmate beatings in the presence of other guards. Also, on Sundays, the guards forced women inmates to bathe in front of them (Swain 2001, 202).

Coffin served on the board of the reformatory as its president. Like other female prison reformers, she believed that women were best suited to take charge of female prisoners and that only another woman could understand the "temptations" and "weaknesses" that surround female prisoners (203). The Indiana Reformatory expanded the theme of domestic treatment, allowing women to wear dresses and emphasizing refinement in decoration and furnishing. Again, though, the main activities were laundering, sewing, and knitting. The Reformatory received only adult felons and delinquent girls and did not use indeterminate sentencing initially. It made no attempt at reformation through the provision of education; however, the institution was considered an advancement of the model of the House of Shelter in Detroit because it was completely independent of any prison for men and those in authority were all females. As the first prison operated solely by women for women, the Indiana Reformatory was considered to have set the standard for prison reform in that state and in the nation, and Coffin received national recognition as the president of this pioneering institution (Swain 2001, 208). Coffin resigned her position as president in 1881, having encountered opposition to her leadership of the board resulting largely from disputes within the Society of Friends (210).

Female Staff and Management

Elizabeth Fry argued that it was essential to the proper order and regulation of prisons that female prisoners be placed under the control of officers of their own sex. American prisons adopted the practice of hiring matrons when women's departments of prisons were established in the first decades of the nineteenth century, but these matrons did not have the authority to reform "fallen" women and were not assigned to that task. In addition, male management staff usually supervised the matrons. With the increased number of female prisoners by 1870 and criticism of male custodians came justification for hiring more prison matrons. Also by this time, women were beginning to enter professions they considered natural extensions of their nurturing role, and correctional work joined the list of careers thought acceptable for women. Women reformers argued that female staff should be preferred because men contributed to women's delinquency, especially in view of their vulnerability to sexual abuse within prisons. For example, it was common practice for female prisoners to be searched by male guards, and these women were easy targets for men. Illegitimate births observed in a number of prisons were evidence of sexual activity, and in one state prison, a system of forced prostitution of women prisoners run by the guards was exposed. After examining this evidence, the reformers concluded that men did contribute to women's delinquency and suggested that the solution was to remove male influence altogether by separating female prisoners both from male prisoners and male officers or guards. The reformers were able to convince many of their cause by arguing that women's moral strength qualified them for custodial duties. However, some male correctional officials denied their claims, arguing that female warders would be too weak with the prisoners. In response, women continued to emphasize women's special skills to reform female prisoners.

Men also were reluctant to allow women to have control over separate institutions designed only for women, arguing that they did not possess the required skills and that a home for women ought to also include men. However, the argument that only women could teach the virtues that so-called "fallen women" required was persuasive, and the domesticity model was finally endorsed by male prison officials. By 1891, the APA acknowledged that female staff and management worked efficiently in Massachusetts and Indiana, and by 1900 the managers of women's reformatories had won their fight for female control: Every officer in these institutions, from the warden down to the lowest matron, was now a woman.

With these new prisons operated by female staff came female wardens like Eliza Mosher, who in 1877 joined the women's reformatory in New York as prison doctor. Cases of venereal disease, insanity, drug addiction, and the birth of illegitimate children overwhelmed her. In addition, she judged the superintendent of the institution as too severe in her discipline of the women (there were an average of ten cases of solitary confinement each day). Mosher resigned in 1879 but returned within a year, having been encouraged to accept the position of superintendent. In this role, Mosher attempted to improve conditions, including showing respect for the inmates by calling them women rather than girls, establishing a merit system, and hiring new staff members who could provide teaching and training. When she resigned in 1882 she was replaced by Clara Barton, who worked for the Red Cross and who continued Mosher's strategy of kindness and respect by giving women open access to her and attempting to deal with their problems and issues. Barton and Mosher were outstanding women of their generation in the progress of reform of women's prisons. Following in the footsteps of Barton, Ellen Johnson was appointed as superintendent and adopted an approach that organized the reformatory around the theme of training for self-control. She believed that rehabilitation resulted from the control provided by the prison routine in that it offered a structure for the women, and from the efforts of the inmates themselves. She introduced strict discipline but also appealed to the women's emotions. Generally, however, women's reformatories found it difficult to secure adequate and competent staff.

The standards set for women prisons in the 1870s and 1880s survived almost intact for the next 100 years, and differential treatment for women remained a fundamental cornerstone of women's treatment in prison until the emergence of a feminist approach in the 1970s.

Prison Design: The Cottage System

From the time of their conception, it was considered necessary for penitentiaries to symbolize incarceration through their physical structure, and so prison structures were massive and imposing, reflecting their objectives of isolation, discipline, and order. The usual design, based on Jeremy Bentham's panopticon of 1787, was that of a central building from which radiated wings of long hallways comprising tiers of cellblocks that could be viewed without obstruction by the warders. Cells averaged only fifty square feet, and prisoners were housed in isolation from each other and moved according to rigid schedules, always maintaining silence.

Reformers of the women's prisons did not want to duplicate these features. They instead sought an atmosphere that reflected the domestic ideals they were attempting to inculcate in the women prisoners. It is for this reason that many advocated the cottage system already in use in juvenile reformatories. If this system were not achievable for all women's prisons, women reformers wanted at least a diminution in the strict and rigid discipline and routine, and amelioration in the style of military discipline employed. Most male penal officials agreed that prisons designed purely for women did not need the same system of security and believed they should be homelike. A good example of the new style for women was the Massachusetts Reformatory Prison for Women, established on thirty acres of land thirty miles west of the city of Boston, suggesting a pastoral setting away from urban problems and temptations. In place of cells were private rooms ranging in size from fifty to ninety square feet, with iron bedsteads and white linens instead of the normal bare cot. If inmates conducted themselves according to expectations, they were allowed to decorate their rooms and have their windows unbarred. In the New York Refuges, also utilizing the cottage plan, the cottages were fitted out as much as possible like an average family home, and the cottages were assigned names instead of numbers to make them appear less like a prison. These institutions also contained chapels, workrooms, libraries, and infirmaries. Women were permitted to circulate within the public areas and cultivate the prison gardens. The presence of children assisted with the domestic atmosphere since at that time children were permitted to remain in prison with their mothers until the age of two years.

Some women's prisons did not follow this approach, instead relying on the traditional massive prison structure with wings containing rows of rooms. Space was often a problem in both styles of prison, as was overcrowding, so that women could not be separated into different offense classes.

Women's Crimes and Women Prisoners

Each state employed different criteria for determining whether a woman should be committed to its prisons; for example, the Indiana prison admitted only those convicted of felonies, whereas New York concentrated on young miscreants, and the Massachusetts Reformatory Prison focused on prisoners convicted of crimes ranging from "stubbornness" to murder. A consideration of the statistics maintained by several institutions from their opening until 1910 provides an overview of the female prison population and reveals that the majority of women were under the age of twenty-five, white, and native born. Nearly two thirds had been married at some time, although their family lives had been erratic, and most had received some formal education. Most had no previous convictions, but of those who did, the most common was for drunkenness. In two institutions, New York and Massachusetts, drunkenness and prostitution accounted for about half of the female prison population. The typical sentence was less than two years for a minor offense against public order, and the average stay was one year.

Based on a sample of inmates analyzed by Eliza Mosher, there were three classes of offenders. In the first category were those offending against public order, especially for drunkenness, who had a high recommitment rate and were generally regarded as victims and treated sympathetically by the prison staff. The second category included offenders against chastity, namely prostitutes and adulteresses, or lewd and lascivious women. This group included the "fallen" women to whom prison officials showed sympathy and regarded as prime candidates for reformation. It also included those committed for what was termed "stubbornness," referring to the inability of their relatives to control their behavior (for example, those who had run away from home). Only a few members of this group—the professional prostitutes—might be termed "criminal," and most had committed victimless crimes. In the third category were grouped the most dangerous offenders—those with crimes against property and person. Domestic workers tended to have been convicted of property offenses, usually petty larceny from employers, and factory workers committed crimes against other persons. The members of this group received the longest sentences and included habitual or professional criminals.

Retraining Women in Reformatories

Women's reformatory prisons were intended to retrain women through their sympathetic female staff, prayer, education, and an atmosphere of domesticity. Nevertheless, the underlying rationale of prisons—to control people—reasserted itself, and like traditional prisons, women's reformatories increasingly relied on discipline. This naturally gave rise to tensions between discipline and domesticity.

The kind of training provided to women inmates was varied. Reformers were keen to have women learn some skills they could use to secure an income and prevent recidivism for economic reasons. However, at this time, most women who worked in employment did so in domestic service; thus there was an emphasis on teaching domestic skills. The kinds of prison industry available to male prisoners were frequently not made available to women, and gravitation toward domestic skills was often supplemented only with outdoor work, such as working on chicken farms and in vegetable gardens maintained by the prison. In Massachusetts, a unique scheme indentured women to private employers for whom they provided domestic services. This was intended to bring women under the influence of "authentic" family life. Most of the homes selected were located away from the city of Boston in semi-rural areas, with the aim of reducing the perceived evil influence of the city on the indentured women. Most of the women released in this way completed their service without incident; in this respect, the scheme resembled a form of parole.

In reformation aimed at women's characters, the notion of the ideal woman guided the prison staff. Virtues of purity, domesticity, and piety were those most valued. At the same time, there was a concern to engender self-sufficiency for women to avoid recidivism; this approach acknowledged reformers' concerns about women's dependence leading to crime. Staff taught these values by themselves assuming the role of a loving but strict parent who forgave past errors but insisted on obedience. Spiritual services were provided by chaplains who visited prisons and wrote letters for those unable to write and conducted daily religious services. Overall, the domestic strategy offered women a supportive atmosphere, especially when contrasted with the hardships of joint incarceration with men.

As mentioned earlier, however, discipline and rules were also considered of prime importance. This resulted in the banning of certain perceived unwomanly vices, such as smoking, and sometimes the prohibition of newspapers other than religious publications. Ellen Johnson in the New York reformatory disapproved of idle unsupervised talk among prisoners and, as a result, suspended recreation periods, substituting them with special events such as spiritual meetings. Johnson's successor, Frances Morton, explicitly rejected the kindness approach and cut out all recreational hours on the basis that they were detrimental to good order and discipline. Instead, she stressed obedience and relied more on the principle of establishing total control over the women's lives rather than on any notion of sisterhood with the women inmates.

The merit system placed the burden on the women for maintaining their status within the prison. When indeterminate sentences were first introduced at the end of the nineteenth century, merit became paramount in the determination of sentences. As an incentive to good behavior in prison, reformers had long advocated setting a maximum and minimum range of sentence, but for women it brought a new source of tension and stress. Punishments for rule infractions remained severe even in the reformatories, and solitary confinement and a diet of bread and water were imposed on women who were disrespectful, talked at meals, or attempted to escape. Disciplinary sanctions varied among the facilities, with some maintaining corporal punishment and using means of restraint such as handcuffs and straitjackets. Nevertheless, most women's prisons relied on the merit system to keep order and maintain control.

It is difficult to reconstruct the experience of prison for women at that time; most documentation of their experience comes from prison officials and reformers rather than the women themselves. Institutional records mostly document favorable comments from the inmates and according to the records, women inmates generally complied with prison rules and tried to make themselves into the dutiful daughters that staff expected. This process was assisted by the condition of the women when they arrived at the prison: The women often were already humbled and humiliated by their life experiences, including sexual mistreatment. On arrival, they were stripped of their identities and in the process of being classified, they were placed in solitary confinement for a time. The complex merit system regulated all details of their lives, and there is some evidence to suggest that whatever resistance might have existed gradually gave way in the face of the overwhelming power of reformatory values, and the women eventually became passive recipients of whatever training was imposed on them.

A Progressive Approach, 1900–1920

Social, Economic, and Psychological Approaches to Women's Crime

By the end of the nineteenth century, the process of reforming women's prisons had reached a point of stagnation. Between 1890 and 1910 the original activist reformers, women like Gibbons, Coffin, and Chace, died, and the women who took their places were officials and part of the system rather than agitators and activists from outside it. Within a decade, however, a new spirit came to invigorate the reform movement. The new generation of reformers did not necessarily accept the philosophies of its predecessors, and at the same time, the newly established discipline of criminology was questioning criminality generally and emphasizing not the ideals of womanhood, but the social and economic backgrounds of women implicated in crime. The new reformers were exceptionally well educated, many having attended women's colleges and earned advanced degrees. This was especially true after the 1890s, when the University of Chicago first admitted women as graduate students. Having been trained in social science, social work, law, and medicine, these new women reformers placed less reliance on religion and the conversion of "fallen" women. Instead, they viewed the women prisoners more in terms of professional clients or research subjects. It was during this period that innovations in penology brought in new preventive social services, as well as probation and specialized courts, such as those for juveniles.

The new criminologists were interested in establishing a scientific basis for crime; they focused less on emotion and character and more on amassing and analyzing data concerning crime and criminals. Physical and mental factors were thought to be implicated in criminal activity, and intelligence tests were used as tools for assessing criminality. The new women reformers were able to gain access to the captive prison population of women to test their theories and to collect data. Some institutions, like Bedford Hills in New York, established positions for psychologists and set up clinics and laboratories to study the inmates and generate data. The new science of psychology gave impetus to the diagnosis of women as psychotic or psychopathic, and to a notion of specialist treatment for those with psychological problems. Inevitably, this had an effect on prison programs and training regimes. As well as the psychological approach, researchers and criminologists began to focus on the economic context of crime, asserting, for example, that social forces played a major role in female crime, including the channeling of women into prostitution.

Seventeen women's reformatories came into being during the Progressive period and in the years immediately after it, with reformatory construction concentrated in the Northeast and Midwest. Reformers emphasized the need to rescue women from local jails and state prisons as well as the need to protect society, an issue usually expressed in terms of their preoccupation with prostitution and venereal disease. In fact, campaigns for women's reformatories were allied to campaigns against prostitution, so that the former was seen as a solution to the latter.

Preventive Approaches

Having identified the causes of women's crime as social and economic rather than bad character and moral sin, the new reformers did not see prison as a solution to those issues. In addition, the new reformers rejected the notion of women having a separate sphere from men and did not subscribe to the traditional reformatory goals. As a result of these new approaches, the new prison superintendents adopted a strategy of more sophisticated classification systems for inmates and more education and diversified training so as to better equip women to deal with their economic issues after release. Around 1910, widespread concern about prostitution came to a head and facilitated the expansion of women's prison reform. In contrast to the earlier reformers, who had stressed the redemption of "fallen" women, the new reformers concentrated their efforts on preventing their "falling" at all. New women's organizations reached out to women already involved in prostitution and to those in danger of becoming involved, as preventive services. A closely related development was the recruitment of women police. Between 1910 and 1925, over 150 cities appointed female police officers whose duties centered on the protection of women and children. Now the Women's Prison Association (WPA) urged probation or fines for convicted women rather than imprisonment, and women's courts were set up in some states mainly to provide a more dignified arena for trying morality cases.

Anti-Institutional Approach

These experiments outside the prison were aimed at the social causes of crime and helped to instill an anti-institutional outlook for women's prisons. Katherine Bement Davis and Jessie Donaldson Hodder in New York and Massachusetts, respectively, pursued this strategy. They attempted to follow two lines of innovation: to emphasize the cottage system and break down the institutionalism of prison in that way; and to expand training and reduce the emphasis on domesticity to include nontraditional work and training. Davis became the first superintendent of Bedford Hills, which opened in 1901. It was located on 200 acres in rural Westchester County, had no fences around it, and was modeled on the cottage plan. Each cottage had a flower garden, a kitchen with good linen and china, and single furnished rooms for the inmates that they could decorate as they pleased. Davis wanted her residents to learn about the law, not as something abstract, but as a factor in their lives, and she began a series of talks on the law, democracy, and civics. She also believed that an essential aim of prison ought to be early release on parole and that this emphasis required different training methods. She hired academic instructors in addition to providing vocational training such as carpentry, bookbinding, and painting. In spite of these efforts, women released from prison continued to find themselves in domestic positions because the opportunities available to them in other forms of employment were still limited. Davis also focused on the physical well-being of women inmates and introduced outside recreation in open areas, exercise, gardening, and farming.

Like Davis, Hodder brought innovation to women's prisons, though she focused on the nature of the institution as adverse to the interests of the prisoners. She went so far as to seek a special state appropriation to fund a new building; if this was not possible, she recommended the building be abandoned. Her goal was to change the women's prison to an industrial training institute for women and to make the reformatory a laboratory for the study of criminology, but her requests for funding were frustrated. She was able to achieve limited success in diversifying training, in organizing physical fitness classes, and in introducing training in farming. The influence of Hodder and Davis was felt in other new institutions, such as the women's prison in New Jersey, opened in 1910, which adopted an anti-institutional structure from the outset, using the cottage plan with specialized cottages and introducing inmate self-government in 1914.

Although these reforms broke down the domestic pattern of institutions and allowed women more freedom and opportunity to learn useful things, they did not succeed in fulfilling the reformers' aim of fostering self-sufficiency for women so that they could live outside the institution without dependency. In some states, reforms were not adopted at all, and in the case of Bedford Hills, Davis noted that because of its good reputation, it was increasingly used as a dumping ground by the New York courts for the most difficult cases, including the mentally defective, drug addicts, and those suffering from sexual disease. This resulted in serious overcrowding, adding to tensions within the institution, so that by 1915 Bedford Hills held 100 more inmates than its capacity. By 1919 the inmate population at Bedford Hills was composed mainly of recidivists, and it ceased to be the showcase institution that Davis had struggled to establish. Finally, in 1921 the state appointed a male superintendent.

The Period after 1920

Regional Differences

By the end of the reformatory movement in the early 1930s, regional differences were apparent in the women's prison system reflective of the reformatory movement's impact in those regions. In the Northeast, where the movement had been strongest, every state except New Hampshire and Vermont had a reformatory, and they tended to exclude custodial aspects to a greater extent than reformatories in other states. In the Midwest, seven states had established reformatories, but four did not set up reformatories at all, and reformatories there generally failed to exhibit a high

degree of zeal for reform. The South established only a few reformatories and produced only weak institutions. In the West, the
only women's reformatory was located in California; it constituted that state's sole prison for women until the 1960s. Generally,
most states continued to hold women in male prisons. For many
states, and for the reformatories themselves, funding was the
major problem. States could not afford to finance the reformatory
plan, and reformatories needed substantial secured funding to
operate their institutions. The reformatory was an expensive and
inefficient operation ideally requiring a number of cottages, each
with its own cooking and dining facilities and staff, a chapel,
classrooms, administrative quarters, staff accommodation, a farm
with buildings for animals, and so on. No other adult penal institutions demanded such resources.

Separate women's prisons had been generally accepted by
the end of World War I and were considered useful in enforcing
social control both during and after the war, when many women
were imprisoned for prostitution. This necessitated a new building program for women prisons, most of which abandoned the
reform aims and instead focused on custody and detention. The
first federal women's prison was opened in 1927, the initial impetus for it being the increase in the number of women imprisoned
for federal offenses in the years after World War I, after laws were
passed outlawing narcotics, the prohibition of alcohol consump-
tion, and the federalizing of automobile theft. It was located in
West Virginia on a 500-acre cottage-style campus. By 1940,
twenty-three states had established separate women's prisons,
but by 1975, sixteen states still lacked such prisons. Despite efforts
for change, the training offered in women's prisons remained sexually stereotyped as vocational training schemes were rejected in
favor of traditionally feminine skills.

The Demise of the Reformatory

In nearly all the early reformatories, an initial period with a small
population of inmates and good relations between staff and prisoners was replaced with overcrowding and rising tensions.
Prisoners flooded in when judges were willing to send petty
offenders to reformatories, parole failures began to accumulate,
and ultimately, administrators began to blame inmates for the
failure of the reformatory ideal. By the 1930s, felons made up a
significant proportion of the inmate population at reformatories.

At about the same time, many states elected to close down women's units attached to men's prisons and to transfer their populations to reformatories, with the effect that women's reformatories ceased to exist in all but name. For example, the women's unit at the New Jersey state prison in Trenton was closed down in 1929 and the inmates were relocated to the reformatory at Clinton Farms. In the same year the Ohio Reformatory was redesignated as an institution for felons only, and petty female offenders were excluded from the state's prison system altogether. Consequently, in state after state the original reformatory inmate population of petty offenders was either diluted by the intake of felons or pushed out altogether and sentenced thereafter to local jails. In effect, the criminal justice system returned to the practice that had existed before the reformatory movement.

The crash of the stock market in 1929 and the ensuing Great Depression also played a major role in the demise of reformatories. Quite simply, states could not afford to continue to hold petty offenders for these lengths of time. As the male prison population increased, wardens in those prisons pressed for more space for prisoners, provoking decisions to close down female units and transfer those female populations to reformatories so the space could be made available for male inmates. The Progressive movement also ended, shattered by World War I and the subsequent move toward a conservative philosophy in penal matters. The reformatory movement essentially had nowhere else to go—it had sustained itself for some sixty years and, for the most part, had achieved its goal of separate prisons for women.

Custodial Prisons for Women, 1870–1935

Concurrent with the reformatory movement, women's prison units of the custodial type continued to develop separately throughout the country. Even after the advent of the reformatory system, custodial women's prisons became more numerous, and in the South and West particularly, they shaped the nature of women's imprisonment. They were populated by felons rather than petty offenders, and therefore did not attract the attention of reformers. They continued along the lines laid down in the nineteenth century, slowly growing and sometimes developing into separate prisons for women. During the period 1870–1935, three kinds of state-run custodial prisons existed: units attached to male prisons, prison farm camps in the South, and independent prisons that were nonreformatory in style. Of the three kinds, the unit attached to a male prison was the most common.

Women in these custodial prisons, many of which were old and dilapidated, suffered extreme neglect along with overcrowding. The women were not a visible inmate population and were often left by the warden to the charge of low-level staff. Women held in units attached to male prisons were often transferred, sometimes being shifted to larger quarters; for example, in 1926 Missouri transferred its convicts to a nearby farm. Work programs were common in these prisons, but most prisons offered no other training or education programs, their aim being nothing more than to keep the women in custody and keep them busy.

Reliance on the custodial model varied regionally. Female prisoners in the Northeast and Midwest were more likely to be sent to reformatories, whereas in the South, the custodial model dominated. In many respects the South represented the worst in women's custodial units because there was a disregard for inmates' health and a failure to provide programs or to protect inmates from violence. Female inmates were charged with hard labor, mainly in laundries and clothing factories. In addition, prisons in the South lacked proper sanitary facilities and were frequently overcrowded, and medical attention was only available for the most serious cases. In the West, little attention was paid to systematic penal development until well into the twentieth century. Outside of California, the Western states incarcerated their women inmates in, or close to, their male penitentiaries.

Between 1876 and 1909, the Arizona Territorial Prison at Yuma housed both men and women in conditions that reflected the discomforts of the frontier at the time (Jeffrey 1969, 13). Of the 3,000 prisoners housed at Yuma during this period, only 1 percent were women, but, according to Jeffrey, the women prisoners were the source of as much trouble and received more publicity than the male inmates. Reportedly, all superintendents at Yuma found the women to be a "terrible nuisance" in a men's prison (1969, 74).

The situation at Yuma was paralleled in California between 1910 and 1933, when female prisoners were housed in male prisons at San Quentin and Folsom (Bookspan 1991). In fact, in California, legislation enacted as early as 1851 provided for female prisoners to have a separate building from male prisoners to avoid sexual contact between them, but it was not until 1933 that the growing number of women convicts led to the establishment of a separate California Institution for Women near Tehachapi (1991, 69). As was often the case when women prisoners were housed in men's prisons, efforts were made to gain early pardons and paroles for the women. For example, the first woman convict entered the Missouri Penitentiary in 1842, and as early as 1844 a citizen's petition asked for her release on the ground that she had just given birth in the prison. With winter approaching and no separate women's wing available in the penitentiary as well as no heating in the men's cells, a pardon seemed the only solution and was accordingly granted by the governor (Butler 1997, 78).

The California State Prison at San Quentin was originally designed to contain nine cells for women in a building separate from the men; however, the few female convicts sentenced there during the 1850s were not kept separate in their activities from the male inmates (Bookspan 1991, 70). There were reports that at least one guard regularly slept with a female prisoner and that a guard captain had sexual relations with a female inmate. Despite detailed reports from prison superintendents and others, no mention was made in such reports or other published documents of the small group of female prisoners at Folsom Prison, California, where the first female inmate arrived in 1885 (Bookspan 1991, 72). At San Quentin, a journalist visiting the prison in 1867 reported on the conditions of the three women he found there at the time of his visit, noting that they were confined away from the men and left their quarters only on Sundays, when the men were attending church services (73). Apparently the women received better food than the male inmates because it was issued from the officer's mess. However, the women were kept idle, and there was no matron to supervise them. Another journalist, reporting in 1888, noted that the women prisoners were idle and that due to their long sentences and lack of activity, he believed they would be totally unable to make an "honest living" after release (73). The neglect shown in California to its female prisoners in the nineteenth century was reflected elsewhere in the West since many states built no facilities for women at all during the nineteenth century and through most of the twentieth. In fact, as late as the early 1970s, Idaho was still contracting with Oregon to house its female convicts, and Montana and North and South Dakota were contracting with Nebraska (73).

At San Quentin Prison the women's quarters comprised a "bear pit" fifty feet by ninety feet in dimension with a cell building forty feet by twenty feet taking up the middle of the space. The women's activities were located in the perimeter of this space, but the women were never allowed out for exercise or air in case they might communicate with the men (Bookspan 1991, 75). In 1919 legislation was passed in California to establish the California Industrial Farm for Women at Sonoma. This institution was located on 645 acres, of which no more than thirty were arable. It was not until 1922 that Sonoma Farm received its first inmates from county jails and San Quentin, but in 1923 the main building was burnt down and the legislature declined to provide funds to rebuild (79).

At San Quentin, overcrowding in the women's quarters at the end of World War I brought a sudden increase in the inmate population, so that the numbers increased from thirty-four in 1921 to fifty-one in 1923 (81). Women reformers in California had by 1925 successfully gained an appropriation for a new separate women's building at San Quentin. It was to be a three-story construction housing 120 prisoners, located outside the main prison wall and completely separate from the men's facilities. This building was completed in late 1927, by which time 127 women inmates were relocated there and were occupied in manufacturing flags for use at government offices throughout the state. Engaged in this traditionally female activity, the women were expected to gain a sense of pride that would bring about their reformation (Bookspan 1991, 82). As well as tending to a fully equipped laundry, the women busied themselves with housekeeping and food preserving and contributed to what was considered by the administrators to be an outstanding model of domestic efficiency. However, the state appropriated no funds for teachers for the women prisoners, and programs offered by the women's department depended on there being instructors available among the inmates themselves. Thus, for example, inmates taught the nursing course and typing and stenography, and an inmate beautician gave instruction in cosmetology. Neither the teachers nor the students received any financial compensation.

Although these improvements for the women prisoners at San Quentin were welcomed, they did not fundamentally shift the focus of male neglect of female prisoners (Bookspan 1991, 83), and the goal of women prison reformers in California remained one of achieving a separate reformatory for women administered by women correctional officers. In 1929 the state passed legislation to establish a separate institution for women, and a 1,600-acre site was purchased in the Cummings Valley of the Tehachapi Mountains. This prison, according to its board of trustees, was not intended to be punitive but corrective, modeled after the federal prison for women at Alderson, West Virginia (86). At this prison, the cells were really private rooms (ten feet by eight feet), colorfully painted, which the inmates were permitted to decorate and personalize. The initial male administrators of the California Institute for Women showed no interest in pursuing the education and training programs the board of trustees had envisaged for the institution. However, after the appointment of a female warden in 1934 and the creation of a board of trustees composed entirely of women, women were permitted to be treated differently than similarly convicted men (91).

In Wyoming, the Territorial Penitentiary opened in 1873 and housed both male and some female inmates despite its longtime lack of cells or toilet facilities for women (Butler 1997, 65). The first female convict was admitted in January 1873 and was housed in the female department, an airy room on the second floor in the southwest corner of the prison. The room was barely furnished and included two beds with straw-filled mattresses and night stands (Brown 2001, 26–27). The prison regime required all prisoners to rise at 5:30 A.M. Monday through Saturday and clean their cells before being called to breakfast. Dinner was eaten at noon, followed by rest or exercise; supper was at 6 P.M.; and prisoners were back in their cells by 7 P.M. On Sundays, prisoners were allowed thirty additional minutes of sleep and an additional half hour to clean their cells. The first female inmate apparently refused to "keep quiet" and was locked away in the "dark cell." This cell could be sealed against the light by closing a small eye-level port through which bread and water could be passed. There were strict rules against prisoner communications; violation would result in confinement in the dark cell for twenty-five consecutive hours. In another case, a female inmate was caught writing notes and in possession of "unauthorized lead pencils" and was locked in her cell and given nothing but bread and water from 9 A.M. that day until 4 P.M. two days later (110).

The Wyoming State Penitentiary succeeded the Wyoming Territorial Penitentiary in 1901. Women were now housed in a chamber fifteen feet by eighteen feet in dimension that contained three individual cells. Authorities allowed the women prisoners to wear whatever clothes friends and relatives provided. Unlike the men who worked in the prison factory, labored in the fields, and tended livestock, the women were confined to their ward where they ate, mended, washed clothes, and slept. Any fraternization with male inmates was severely punished and might result in loss of "good time" as well as in confinement in the dark cell (Brown 2001, 122).

In Illinois during the nineteenth century female prisoners were incarcerated in men's prisons at Alton, Joliet, and Chester. As the numbers of women in prison increased, prison administrators were confronted with the problem of managing the female prisoners within a male institution. In 1896 a separate women's prison was established at Joliet across the street from the male prison (Dodge 1999). In Illinois between 1831 and 1859, only fifty-nine women were incarcerated, in contrast to over 3,000 men. The first penitentiary in Illinois was located at Alton in 1830, and at its highest capacity in 1858 it confined over 600 men and one dozen women. This prison and its convict body was leased out for an annual sum, and the lessee was responsible for providing for the physical and medical needs of the convicts. In exchange, he received any profits he might earn from using or contracting out their labor (Dodge 1999, 3). After 1867, the state took over management of prisons but continued leasing out convict labor to private contractors.

Prison reformer Dorothea Dix inspected the conditions at Alton and condemned them, noting that the site of the prison was so uneven that the walls were continually falling down while rainstorms caused rivers of mud to flow through the basements of the buildings. Standard features of prisons of the time—a prison yard for exercise, hospital, chapel, and library—did not exist, and no chaplain or even Bibles were available.

Not until 1842 was the presence of women at Alton publicly noted. In their biannual report, the Committee on the Penitentiary noted that two female convicts were being housed in the cookhouse in the daytime and in the cellar at night (Dodge 1999, 4). The prison inspectors were perturbed by the warden's decision to house females alongside men and wanted a female department because of the impropriety of confining them in cells adjoining male prisoners and of employing them in the same shops with the male prisoners (Dodge 1999, 4). However, a female department, separate from the men's prison, was not approved during the 1840s. This may have been connected to the perceived inability of women convicts to reform. Over one half of the female inmates at Alton were foreign-born immigrant women, mainly Irish, though after 1890 African American women constituted the majority of the female population. A large number had worked as domestic servants and later been convicted of larceny, and others were professional shoplifters and prostitutes who had robbed their clients (5).

It was not until the 1850s that women became a constant presence in the Alton prison, with an average of six women out of a daily population of 300 to 600 men. Finally, in 1852 a two-story hospital building containing six cells and workrooms was converted into a female department. The prison inspectors were not only concerned about the propriety of housing men with women but also warned of the "pernicious" influence of the women on the good order of the men. In 1845 they wrote that "one female prisoner is of more trouble than twenty males," and over the next thirty years it was women who were identified as the focus of disruption in the prison in all official reports (Dodge 1999, 6).

Why were women considered a source and cause of disruption? Clearly prison administrators and guards were frustrated in their efforts to manage and control the women who required additional supervision. One researcher has argued that the perceived disturbance by women was the outcome of middle-class expectations of feminine behavior so that foul language, drunkenness, and immodesty were viewed as being far more disruptive when displayed by female convicts (Dodge 1999, 6). Another cause of frustration was the women prisoners' demand to be treated as individuals and to receive individual care and treatment. The issue of threats or punishments that might be imposed on women prisoners was also problematic, and the official discipline reports show that female convicts were not flogged, that being the standard punishment for male convicts. In fact, it was only in the 1870s, when women were separated in isolated attic quarters and supervised by a female matron, that prison administrators believed they had them under control (7).

One issue concerning women's imprisonment was what should be done with pregnant women. In 1855 prison inspectors at Alton noted that the prison had no hospital or nurse, and no official policy was developed for dealing with pregnancies despite a committee recommendation in 1857 that all pregnant female prisoners should be immediately released (Dodge 1999, 8). As an alternative to this proposal, a new warden wanted a nursery established within the prison, but in the end a policy evolved in which pregnant women prisoners were pardoned and released. After 1860, the existence of pregnant women was no longer mentioned in prison reports, suggesting that such women were being pardoned and released as policy dictated.

Pardoning women prisoners, and some men, seems to have been a common practice in the 1850s, and at Alton nearly one half of the women and almost a quarter of the men were pardoned and served less than their full sentences. At that time, the average sentence for women was 1.6 years and the average time a woman served in prison was less than a year. Many pardon petitions were supported by the same lawyers and judges who convicted the women and by members of the community who had previously shown no interest in their cases. In one case, a judge in Chicago told the governor that he had misjudged a woman's case, explaining that he had imposed the maximum sentence of six years for larceny, believing her to be a professional thief (Dodge 1999, 9). Now however, he believed that she had stolen only out of desperation and to support her children. She was granted a pardon. The pardon files show how women who had been unsuccessful at avoiding conviction were able to present new evidence and convince officials that their case had mitigating circumstances. Such circumstances included those of the crime itself, pregnancy, illness, good conduct in prison, and age. However, after 1860 the rate of granting pardons declined; the rate specifically for women decreased from 46 percent in the 1850s to 15 percent in the 1870s, stabilizing at only 5 percent through 1910 (10). This decrease reflected the development of systems allowing for good time and parole but may also have been an indication of hardened attitudes toward female offenders—by that time, longer sentences were being imposed on women, with average sentences of seven years being awarded in the 1860s and sixteen years in the 1870s.

Joliet Prison in Illinois housed approximately 700 women between 1860 and 1896, when a separate women's unit was built (Dodge 1999, 10). The original design of Joliet provided a 100-cell internal female prison located within the main prison yard with its own surrounding wall. The women's prison was two stories with fifty cells on each floor and was adjacent to a large two-story building known as "the female workshop." The women were completely isolated from the male population by the surrounding wall, a segregation that seemed a suitable arrangement to prison officials. However, a list of prison rules in 1861 specified that no male guard would be permitted to converse with any woman prisoner, which suggests that the segregation was not as absolute as it appeared. During the early years at Joliet, the warden's wife may have supervised female prisoners, but after 1869 a female matron was employed. The state abolished the lease system at Joliet in 1867, and the following year, the new warden recommended the construction of a female unit to be located completely outside of the male prison enclosure. In line with complaints at Alton Prison, the warden wrote that the female department required extra care and attention and was a great annoyance to the management. The chaplain agreed with the warden that "no degree of vigilance secures the great mass of prisoners from the pernicious influence of these females" (Dodge 1999, 12). Significantly, it was the women prisoners who were perceived to be the agents of depravity and not the male inmates. In 1870, the female prisoners were removed from the prison and relocated in the fourth-story of the warden's house. The chaplain reported that while this move was to be applauded, the best solution was still to remove them entirely.

As was the case at Alton Prison, the proportion of African American prisoners at Joliet increased concurrent with a decline in Irish and foreign-born prisoners (Dodge 1999, 13). In the 1850s African American women made up only 2 percent of prison commitments in Illinois, but in the years after the Civil War they constituted 25 percent of all commitments even though they made up only 1.1 percent of the state's population. It seems that most of these black women prisoners were former slaves who had recently entered the state, and nearly half of them were teenagers sentenced along with two or three others, suggesting that groups of black migrants were coming under increased surveillance.

In 1896 a separate Joliet women's prison was constructed. The women spent their time under a regime of strict silence, doing contract knitting and light manufacturing as well as mending and sewing for the male convicts and guards. One prison photographer described the women as sitting facing their windows all day long with "great piles of stockings in their laps" (14). He reported that "the women keep their eyes bent on their work" and that the work was "monotonous" and "a dreary routine" (Dodge 1999, 14).

When Illinois's third prison was constructed in Chester in 1878 the architectural plans called for the construction of a female department similar to that in Joliet, located inside the male prison and surrounded by a high stone wall. However, the female department was never constructed, and the few female prisoners were kept in a cellar at night under one of the workhouses, employed in making clothing for the male convicts. In 1882 the prison commissioners recommended a separate female prison be constructed, but this was ignored, and in 1884 the female prisoners were relocated to the warden's house and a matron engaged to supervise them. The warden at the time calculated that using two knitting machines, the female convicts had produced some 4,800 pairs of socks for the male convicts; had made underclothes, coats, and pants for the guards; and performed all the laundry work in the warden's house (Dodge 1999, 15). As at Joliet, the main concern of the prison administrators was the profitability of the women prisoners, not their care and treatment. In similar fashion in 1887, the state assembly resolved that the commissioners at Chester should remove the female convicts to Joliet to save expenses and secure economy.

In Texas, women prison reformers working during the period 1918 to 1930 sought to advance a program that would rehabilitate convicted felons and ensure that women had more say in prison reform and administration (Lucko 1990). In 1918 the Texas prison system contained a penitentiary housing about 400 prisoners, male and female, at Huntsville, but of the vast majority of the inmates, some 3,750 were located on fifteen farms owned or leased by the state. In 1874 the warden of Huntsville, Colonel A. J. Ward, allowed men and women to share bunk houses, where naked unwashed inmates slept on corncob sacks, and where women inmates roamed the yard carrying their infant children conceived and born inside the prison (Butler 1997, 135–137). Ward and his staff imposed many forms of punishment on the prisoners including beatings, hanging women in the stocks so the tips of their toes barely met the ground, and forcing them to ride "the wooden horse," which consisted of a pick-ax handle embedded into an upright post that the prisoner had to mount and sit astride while her ankles were fastened to rings embedded in the ground and her head tied to the post. Prisoners were forced to dangle on this wooden horse without moving and typically passed out (136). In 1910, African American women at Huntsville spoke of routine punishment by the lash.

The Texas prison farms were run as plantations using gang labor to raise cotton, sugar cane, and other crops in an attempt to make the prison system self-supporting (Lucko 1990, 4). Conditions on the farms were horrendous, including crowded and dilapidated housing with filthy bedding covered with vermin and insects. At one farm, guards often hung prisoners from chains in a manner that left their toes barely touching the ground. Employees routinely beat prisoners and allowed prison dogs to attack them. State law permitted prisoners to be whipped with a leather strap or bat.

In response, women prison reformers in the Texas Federation of Women's Clubs demanded humane treatment of all state convicts and asked that the governor appoint a woman to the Board of Prison Commissioners and that women have exclusive control over female prisoners. The women reformers wanted to rehabilitate criminals rather than hold continual investigations that exposed awful prison conditions but offered no solutions (6). Beginning in 1921, women reformers in Texas assisted in abrogating a proposed contract between the prison system and a private manufacturer for the purchase of garments produced at Huntsville and supported a ban against chaining prisoners (Lucko 1990, 10). In 1926, Elizabeth Speer was appointed executive secretary to the Texas Prison Board, giving women reformers an influential voice in the prison system. From 1927 to 1929, the board under Speer's leadership attempted to implement reforms that would limit corporal punishment, discourage the mistreatment of prisoners, and encourage education in prisons. Despite these attempts, the Texas prison system remained dependent on its plantation farms and continued to use brutal forms of discipline (13). By 1947 a campaign by the Texas State Council of Methodist Women brought about improvements in prison facilities, and in 1972, a prisoner's lawsuit resulted in the 1980 *Ruiz v. Estelle* ruling that required a substantial transformation in the state's penal policies (14). In effect, therefore, the federal judiciary brought about the alternative correctional policies advocated fifty years earlier by the women reformers.

In the 1860s, male and female prisoners in Arkansas were required to share cells and common waste buckets. Nevada's prison system got underway in 1862, but five years later the prison site had no water supply for bathing and no wall of any substance around the property (Butler 1997, 65). In Missouri, there was no intent to incarcerate women with the men in the penitentiary and so no female quarters were included in the building. In the end, an area designated as a female department was considered so inadequate that wardens agitated for it to be abolished (66). In Kansas, the correctional authorities had no state female facility and incarcerated women convicts in the men's penitentiary. By 1883 its administrators had formulated rules and regulations for the management of those female prisoners. During an investigation into punishments at the Kansas State Penitentiary, matrons of the female ward reported that as late as 1910 guards routinely used strait jackets, handcuffs, and gags as punishments for female inmates and that one warden had rings placed in the walls of the female ward so that prisoners' arms could be extended as a form of punishment (Butler 1997, 137). Ultimately, in 1916 Kansas, under pressure to reform, transferred the female inmates to an old house about one mile from the penitentiary, where the women stayed until the opening of a female industrial farm in 1917 (Butler 1997, 66).

In the West generally, women were never easily accommodated within the structure of any prison and were always greatly outnumbered by male inmates. The majority of women imprisoned in the West had committed crimes against property that were minor in nature and might better have been accommodated in a local jail (Butler 1997, 99). Nevertheless, women were sent to penitentiaries for minor and nonviolent crimes. Vice charges brought against women could also result in incarceration, especially if women crossed racial lines. For example, in 1881 Sallie Wheeler, an African American mother with four young children who was the only support for her family, was fined $250 after a conviction for fornication with a white man (102). Unable to pay a fine of that magnitude, she remained incarcerated until officials directed her release to care for her children. In the case of Ella Anderson, a Texas prisoner convicted of adultery with a white man and sentenced to a convict labor camp to work off a fine of $300, the camp contractor had fixed the female convict labor rate at $30 a year, leaving her facing a ten-year sentence for adultery (102). Her partner in crime was more fortunate, serving only five years because the contractor priced male convict labor at $60 per year.

Incarcerated women in the West encountered considerable violence in the male penitentiaries, beginning with their transport there. For male prisoners, the transportation routine involved a group of convicts being bound around the neck, wrists, and ankles and from waist to feet, forming a human chain and hobbling along in line escorted by deputies (Butler 1997, 133). Women were treated in much the same way and on intake were stripped naked for guards or male trustees to examine their bodies. Jailors would record every physical feature of a female prisoner including height and weight, body scars, and detailed descriptions of complexion, eyes, ears, and nose. Although not a standard requirement for women, one humiliating procedure used sometimes was the threat of head shaving, a routine practice for male inmates (134). As the women moved into the inner prison, they continued to wear civilian dress, although some prisons required the women to wear a regulation striped skirt with apron. Women laborers at the Texas farm camps were barefoot and obliged to wear skimpy shifts.

Prison Farm Camps in the South

Some Southern states adopted the practice of leasing female convicts out to individually owned farms to work or to publicly owned prison farms. In the beginning, these camp arrangements were ad hoc solutions to the problem of coping with a multitude of prisoners in the aftermath of the Civil War. For example, the state penitentiary might have been destroyed during the war, and if it still stood, was incapable of accommodating the enormous number of African Americans sentenced to hard labor for petty offenses after the war. In effect, penal servitude substituted for slavery.

As mentioned earlier, in Texas at the turn of the century, female convicts were sent to a private farm about seven miles from the main state prison at Huntsville. The farm owner provided food and clothing for the female inmates and each year paid the state for their labor. Usually, black women worked in the fields, and white women served as domestics. As might be expected in a camp arrangement, living quarters were primitive and there were no medical facilities. In post–Civil War Georgia, female prisoners were leased out; legislative investigators subsequently found women chained to men and occupying the same bunks, and they revealed instances where the farm lessee had whipped women.

There is no doubt that the farm solution to the prison population marked a low point in penology for both women and men. Convicts sent to farms were required to work long hours in the fields and maintain a set pace of work, and they were subjected to the use of the strap or to harassment by guards and their dogs if they lapsed in their efforts. Unlike administrators in the northern states, those in the South were uninterested in treating or rehabilitating inmates. Rather, their overriding concern was to exploit the labor that prisoners represented for reward. In line with the philosophy of slavery that had so recently shaped life in the South, it seemed natural to many officials to transfer to the prison system the techniques that had been employed in the system of slavery.

Independent Prisons for Women

During the period 1870–1935, six independent custodial-style prisons were established for women: Four operated in reformatory states and received women considered unsuitable for the reformatories, and two were the only female prison in the state. Although independent given their separation from men's prisons or by legislative act, they did not enjoy the freedom in penal matters that the reformatories did and were closer in style to the custodial women's units attached to male prisons. Most were erected at minimal cost and for reasons of administrative convenience and certainly not with reform in mind. Establishing these independent prisons in the custodial style meant little more than renaming an already existing institution, usually one considered no longer suitable for male convicts. In these prisons, women received treatment much like that accorded to men in male prisons. However, unlike the men's prisons these institutions seldom employed a full-time physician, chaplain, or teacher and provided fewer programs for inmates. Matrons headed these prisons but were subject to the direction of male administrators in the correctional system.

In only one case—that of the State Farm for Women at Valatie in New York—did this pattern vary. Farm administrators attempted to found a new type of custodial unit for older women who were repeat but petty offenders and were assigned to the farm rather than being sent to local jails. The Valatie Farm contained 315 acres and housed about sixty inmates in two cottages. The founding legislation required that all officers at the farm would be female, but an exception was made when the nature of the work was said to necessitate the employment of men. This was interpreted to mean that the warden should be a man. All sentences served at the farm were indeterminate, with a maximum of three years, but the farm received a total of only 146 inmates, most of whom were between the ages of thirty and sixty at the time of commitment, white, and native born; most had been convicted of drunkenness. There was little employment for the women save some farming and sewing, and funds were always short. By 1918 the farm had been turned over to the health authorities for use as a treatment center for women suffering from venereal disease, and all remaining inmates were paroled.

Race and Racism in State Prisons Holding Women, 1865–1935

Before 1865, black women were imprisoned in the Northeast and Midwest in numbers far out of proportion to their representation in the general populations of these regions. In the South, however, few blacks, whether male or female, were held in state prisons before the Civil War because it was the responsibility of owners to discipline slaves and only freed blacks were eligible for public punishment. After the Civil War, racism continued to influence prisoner populations, and the proportion of blacks in prison, male and female, increased steadily in the Northeast and Midwest to an extent that now even the previously white prisons of the South became full of newly freed blacks. Even in the West, where there were few prisons and a much smaller population, blacks were imprisoned in proportions that far exceeded their representation in the general population.

Historically, the prison system has incarcerated disproportionate numbers of black women. For example, in Tennessee over 70 percent of the women committed to the Tennessee Penitentiary during the period 1860–1887 were black; this figure increased to 90 percent at the turn of the century, declining to 65 percent in the years 1926–1934. Yet, during the period 1860–1930 the black population in Tennessee fell from 26 to 18 percent of the total state population. Ohio's black population increased from 2 to 5 percent during the period 1890–1930, but the proportion of black women incarcerated in that state increased from 26 to nearly 52 percent. Only in the Albion reformatory in New York did the black female inmate population coincide with the proportion of blacks in the general population in that state.

As for the treatment and conditions of black men and women in prison, as a rule, the higher the proportion of blacks in a prison population, the lower the level of care. However, white women

were treated better than black women even in mainly black institutions. In the South, where some women prisoners were leased
out while others were retained in custody, those leased out were
nearly always black. Of forty white women held in prisons by the
southern states in 1880, only one was leased, as compared to
eighty-one out of 2,220 black women. It is clear that the burden of
leasing fell more heavily on black women and that race was at
least as important as sex in the decision to lease a female prisoner.
In the penitentiaries and plantations of the South, black and white
women were segregated in housing. Prison administrators in
Georgia decided that black women made excellent field hands
based on their perception that these women were accustomed to
that kind of work. White women, in contrast, were assigned to
housekeeping and sewing.

In the reformatories of the North and Midwest, the situation
was somewhat better since racial segregation among women
inmates only occurred if there were sufficient black women in the
prison population. Thus, for example, so few black women were
committed to the Nebraska and Maine reformatories that segregation was impracticable. However, where there were sizeable
populations of black women, segregation was the rule. Racial discrimination also affected programming in prisons. Since most
prison staff were white, they designed programs for white interests and concerns and ignored all other interests.

Female incarceration rates continue to reveal racial and eth-
nic disparities. As of December 31, 2000, the Bureau of Justice
reported that black females, with an incarceration rate of 205 per
100,000, were more than three times as likely as Hispanic females
(with a rate of 60 per 100,000) and six times more likely than
white females (with a rate of 34 per 100,000) to be in prison
(Bureau of Justice Statistics 2001).

The Women's Prison System since 1935

Academic research into women in prison began in the 1960s, providing a wealth of information about the condition of women in
some prisons. Following a nationwide survey of women's prisons
in 1966, one researcher described the women's prison as typically
small and patterned on the cottage model. Of the thirty prisons
surveyed, two thirds had populations of less than 200. Most had
less than 150 staff, and many were located in the Northeast. The

age range of women inmates was sixteen to sixty-five, and the majority of prisons used simple classification tests for the assignment of inmates. Of those surveyed, about 18 percent were termed custodial, 32 percent custody-oriented, 17 percent mixed, and about 22 percent treatment-oriented.

By 1971 there were two federal prisons for women, and thirty-four states had completely separate prisons for women. Most women's prisons are designated medium-security, and therefore a single women's facility must house women convicted of a wide range of offenses. This contrasts with men's prisons, where security grading ranges from minimum to maximum or even supermax prisons for the most dangerous offenders. Males are increasingly employed as guards in women's prisons; by 1988, only 65 percent of correctional officers at female prisons were female.

In 1971 Texas established the first co-corrections prison. This was essentially a return to earlier times, as the prison held both male and female inmates who, although housed in separate buildings, shared some or all of the prison programs and services. Five such institutions opened in the 1970s, and by 1977, fifteen state institutions of the same kind were operating; however, in a reversal of policy, by 1984 only six states had such facilities.

In the 1980s, the number of women in prison in the United States tripled. Most of the increase in the female population is accounted for by minor property crime such as theft, and by drug and public order offenses. Due to the explosion in women's imprisonment, there has been a growth in building women-only prisons and in adding women's units to male prisons. Despite this increase in their incarceration, women still make up only about 7 percent of all those incarcerated, with considerable variation across states. For example, as of December 31, 2000, Oklahoma imprisoned women at the highest rate, 138 per 100,000 women in the population, followed by Mississippi, at 105 per 100,000. This compares to a rate of only seven per 100,000 for Massachusetts and fifteen per 100,000 for Minnesota (Bureau of Justice Statistics 2001).

Sources

Bookspan, Shelley. 1991. *A Germ of Goodness: The California State Prison System, 1851–1944.* Lincoln: University of Nebraska Press.

Brown, Larry. 2001. *Petticoat Prisoners of Old Wyoming.* Glendo, WY: High Plains Press.

Bureau of Justice Statistics. 2001. *Prisoners in 2000*. Washington, DC: Bureau of Justice Statistics, Department of Justice.

Butler, Anne M. 1997. *Gendered Justice in the American West: Women Prisoners in Men's Penitentiaries*. Urbana: University of Illinois Press.

Coffin, Rhoda. 1877. "Systems of Discipline Suited to a Female Prison." In *Transactions of the Fourth National Prison Congress Held in New York, June 6–9, 1876*. New York.

Dodge, Mara. 1999. "'One Female Prisoner Is of More Trouble Than Twenty Males': Women Convicts in Illinois Prisons, 1835–1896." *Journal of Social History* 32 (4): 907–930.

Feinman, C. 1984. "An Historical Overview of the Treatment of Incarcerated Women: Myths and Realities of Rehabilitation." *Prison Journal* 63 (2): 12–26.

Freedman, E. 2000. *Their Sister's Keepers: Women's Prison Reform in America, 1830–1930*. Ann Arbor: University of Michigan Press.

Jeffrey, John Mason. 1969. *Adobe and Iron: The Story of the Arizona Territorial Prison at Yuma*. La Jolla, CA: Prospect Avenue Press.

Lekkerkerker, E. C. 1931. *Reformatories for Women in the United States*. J. B. Wolters, Groningen, etc.

Lucko, Paul. 1990. "The Next Big Job: Women Prison Reformers in Texas, 1918–1930." Unpublished Paper, Texas Historical Society.

Rafter, N. 1985. *Partial Justice: Women in State Prisons 1800–1935*. Boston: Northeastern University Press.

Ruiz v. Estelle. 1980. 503 Federal Supplement 1265.

Strickland, K. 1976. *Correctional Institutions for Women in the U.S.* Lexington, MA: Lexington Books.

Swain, Ellen. 2001. "From Benevolence to Reform: The Expanding Career of Mrs. Rhoda M. Coffin." *Indiana Magazine of History* 97 (September): 190–217.

2

Problems, Controversies, and Solutions

Most issues relating to incarcerated women did not come to light until the late 1960s, when major research studies concerned with women's incarceration began to be conducted. It is significant, for example, that there is no mention of women prisoners in the massive "Report on Crime" completed by the President's Commission on Law Enforcement and Administration of Justice in 1967. The earliest research on women in prison focused on female prison subculture, especially the aspect of sexuality, rather than on living conditions. In contrast to women in prison, there has been an extensive examination of issues concerning men in prison beginning in the 1940s.

A number of reasons have been advanced for this neglect of the study of women in prison, including the fact that women constitute only a small proportion of the prison population and are therefore almost invisible, that women generally are incarcerated for less serious crimes than men and therefore do not command the same research attention, and that incarcerated women are less likely than men to resist their imprisonment through acts such as riots and disturbances and therefore do not attract attention by the authorities or the media. In addition, prisoner litigation has been mounted almost entirely by men, and where women have brought suits, they have focused almost entirely on obtaining parity with the conditions in men's prisons and have not dealt with the particular problems and issues affecting women.

The following discussion presents a picture of women's situation in prisons. The context and background of these issues are presented along with various points of view. In this way it is possible to develop a fuller appreciation for the female prisoner and her concerns as well as issues of public policy affecting women and crime and the consequent societal responses to women's criminality. It is helpful to first identify the broad issues that affect women in prison to help frame the following discussion. They are women's criminality, the experience of imprisonment, criminal justice policy issues, health and medical issues, and legal challenges (for example, equal protection).

Women's Criminality

In order to fully appreciate the issues that arise from the incarceration of women it is first necessary to gain an understanding of women's criminality, that is, the kinds of offenses that women commit, their reasons for offending, and the nature and extent of female crime. Historically, women's crime has not been treated with the same seriousness as men's crime, and men have always been seen as the "real" offenders. This perception is attributable to the fact that women generally commit fewer crimes than men and women's crimes tend to be less serious in nature.

What does the data on arrests and crimes tell us about women's criminality? Overall, it shows that women most often commit offenses against property, are guilty of fraud, or incur drug offenses. Furthermore, it shows no differentiation by gender according to arrest rates for the first four types of offenses among the top ten: larceny-theft, assault, drug violations, and driving under the influence of alcohol. In other words, women generally commit the same kinds of offenses as men. Data on arrests in 1998 from the Bureau of Justice Statistics (Greenfeld and Snell 1999) show that almost 22 percent of arrests in that year were of women, that about 17 percent of all violent crimes arrests were of women, and that aggravated assault committed by women had the highest arrest rate, 20 percent. In relation to serious offenses of murder, manslaughter, robbery, and rape, female arrests made up just over one tenth for these categories except for rape, where the rate was 1 percent. Almost 29 percent of property crime arrests were of women, and the highest incidence within this category was larceny-theft. For the crimes of burglary, motor vehicle theft, and arson, female arrests made up between 13 and 16 percent of all arrests. For the sixth, seventh, and eighth in the top ten offenses, males and females share the same offenses, namely, disorderly conduct, violations of laws relating to alcohol, and aggravated assault. For men, burglary and vandalism were ninth and tenth on the list, but these do not appear at all on the list for women. However, the crime of fraud, the fifth most common offense for women, did not make the top ten list for men (Belknap 2001).

Some have argued that the feminist movement in the early 1970s influenced women to commit more offenses, but most research demonstrates that crime rates for women mainly remained the same from the 1970s until the present, except in the cases of less serious property crimes and crimes involving drugs, which have both increased. In terms of gender stability—that is, whether there are gender differences in the extent and nature of offending and whether these differences have changed over time—most research studies have found that differences have remained fairly stable over time. At points where rates have tended to converge, this can largely be explained by four factors: changes in law enforcement practices so that women are the targets of increased police enforcement of laws; the worsening economic position of women, making them vulnerable to a higher rate of arrest; technical factors such as changes in data collection methods; and inflation in the small base of women's crimes. If there is any closing of the gender gap it is due to a convergence in less serious property crimes and possibly for drug abuse.

Though either sex is capable of committing the same offenses, the law sometimes can be enforced in a way that is adverse to women. For example, laws against sex work tend to be enforced against female prostitutes rather than male prostitutes because police tend to think of women in this role rather than men. In the case of battered women who commit crimes against their batterers, offenses they often carry out under duress, extreme stress, and pressure, the women may take the entire blame for the violence. Selling drugs can also result in women becoming targets and accepting culpability even though they may unknowingly commit the crime at the instigation of their male partners, or may commit the crime by helping their male partners to avoid risks to themselves or their children.

In 1998 women committed 11 percent of all homicides in the United States, and in that year the murder rate for women was the lowest recorded since 1976. Overall, the murder rate for women has been declining since 1980 (Greenfeld and Snell 1999).

By far the majority of homicides are committed by men, and when women do commit this offense, their victims tend to be their male partners—boyfriends, husbands, or ex-husbands. In cases where women kill their male intimates, women are often acting in self-defense after a long history of abuse in a particular relationship.

The typical female inmate is a racial minority aged twenty-five to twenty-nine, unmarried but with one to three children, most likely the victim of sexual abuse as a child and of physical abuse as an adult, with current alcohol and drug abuse problems, multiple arrests with the first arrest taking place around fifteen years of age, a high school dropout, on welfare, unskilled, with a history of holding mainly low-wage jobs (Fowler 1993).

Race and Women's Imprisonment

More than half the women imprisoned in the United States are African American or Hispanic. For the year 2000, Bureau of Justice Statistics data reveal that 83,668 women were imprisoned, of which 44 percent were African American and 12 percent Hispanic (Bureau of Justice Statistics 2001). This stands in contrast to the fact that African American women make up only 13 percent of the U.S. female population and Hispanic women only 12 percent. The rate of imprisonment for African American women has escalated dramatically and coincided with a growth in the number of women sentenced to imprisonment for drug offenses. In the five-year period from 1986 to 1991, the number of black women incarcerated in state prisons for a drug offense rose by 828 percent. In the year 2000, drug offenders accounted for the largest source of the total growth among female inmates of all races. The chances of receiving a prison term after being arrested for a drug offense increased by 447 percent between 1980 and 1992. Well over three times as many black women have contact with the criminal justice system than do their white counterparts. Research reveals that the increase in the number of women in prison for drug offenses is far steeper for Hispanic women and for African American women than for white women. It follows then that the so-called "War on Drugs" has had a dramatic effect on the incarceration patterns of these women. The trend of locking up successive generations of women is creating a generation of parentless children and has reinforced the stereotype of the absentee African American parent. The most obvious policy change that could reduce the number of African American women in prison is decarceration of drug-related offenders, but current sentencing practices do not generally support this policy.

In contrast with African American and Hispanic women, American Native and Alaskan Native women tend to be forgotten because they make up such a small proportion of incarcerated women and tend to be located in certain states only. Nevertheless, as the only indigenous women serving sentences of imprisonment, they have special needs and concerns not shared by other women prisoners. Both groups are disproportionately imprisoned by comparison to their proportion of the population. Male and female Alaskan Natives, for example, make up 16 percent of the Alaska population but 34 percent of the adult inmate population in that state. American Natives in South Dakota make up 7 percent of the state population but represent 26 percent of all inmates male and female; and in Nebraska, the Native American inmate population has ranged between 3.1 and 4.4 percent in recent years, which is approximately three times the number of Native Americans living in that state (Grobsmith 1994, 154, 155).

The cultures of indigenous women continue to play an important part in their lives and, in fact, those women who may have lost contact with their native culture often return to it for solace and support in coping with their imprisonment. For example, both American Native and Alaskan Native women seek access to spiritual teachers and ceremonies in the same way that nonindigenous women may turn to religion for solace. Some prisons are now prepared to allow sweat lodges to be built within the prison, and some permit the use of native substances in cultural ceremonies. As well as this kind of contact with their culture, indigenous women also have special needs in their interactions with prison staff and other prisoners that flow from their cultural specificity. For instance, research has shown that staff often hold stereotypical images of both American Native and Alaskan Native women and usually receive no special training that would alert them to their different value systems, modes of behavior, and expectations (Banks 2002). Indigenous women living in rural areas prior to incarceration may have been leading a traditional subsistence lifestyle (this is especially likely for Alaskan Native women), and the act of confinement itself presents them with an emotional challenge that other women from urban areas may not face. Lack of English speaking skills or experience with structured lifestyles like that in the highly regimented prison environment present further obstacles to adjustment for these women. Perhaps most importantly, indigenous women often maintain close relations with an extended family unit, and relationships with members of that unit are a central and fundamental part of their lifestyle and culture. Being deprived of that contact constitutes for them a particular hardship (Banks 2002).

Women and Capital Punishment

Historically, the notion of executing women offenders generally has been accepted in the United States. Though executions of female offenders rarely occur, there have been 520 confirmed executions of women since 1608; this represents about 3 percent of all executions in the country (Streib 1995). Fewer executions occur now than in the past, and women accounted for only 0.5 percent of all executions in the United States in the twentieth century. Several patterns emerge from a study of the crimes committed by executed women. Generally, their crimes were not especially heinous in nature, and collecting insurance was the main motivation for the murders they committed. In most instances, a male accomplice assisted the women. During the 1970s women received only twenty-one death sentences, but this increased dramatically during the 1980s and 1990s, when forty-five death sentences were imposed. Women make up 1.5 percent of the total population on death row on average, and their ages range from twenty-one to seventy-eight years with the majority between twenty and twenty-nine years of age. Sixty percent of females on death row are white, 33 percent are black, and Hispanics account for the remaining 7 percent.

Women awaiting execution are subject to the same constraints and poor conditions as other women prisoners, including isolation from their families. Death row is segregated from the general prison population; prisoners interact only with correctional officers, though they may visit and talk to other death row prisoners if housed in the same cell unit. There is a high rate of reversal on appeal—about 97 percent—for women sentenced to death. The prevailing political rhetoric of "get tough on crime" policies is reflected in the increase in the number of executions over the past twenty years and in the willingness of the public to accept the appropriateness of execution for women. In a 1992 study conducted by the National Coalition to Abolish the Death

Penalty, research revealed that female prisoners on death row are mainly from poor socioeconomic backgrounds and are therefore obliged to rely on court-appointed attorneys, many of whom have no experience in handling capital cases; that the women are sometimes mentally ill; that they are often mothers; and that they are usually from families where physical or sexual abuse occurred, which later contributed to their continued victimization in other abuse relationships (Nelson and Foster 2000).

Female Youthful Offenders Confined in Adult Prison

In 1996 more than 13,000 juveniles were detained in adult prisons. Violent youthful offenders are being held in prisons in ever-increasing numbers (Fleming and Winkler 1999, 1). An example of the legislative response to the increasing use of adult prisons for youth is provided by legislation passed in Washington state that defines the requirements concerning juvenile offenders confined in adult prisons. The law provides that an offender under the age of eighteen who is sentenced to the Department of Corrections must be placed in a housing unit separated from adult inmates and may, if necessary, be placed in administrative segregation for his/her safety or security. The department also must provide an education program for offenders under the age of eighteen, which must enable him/her to obtain a high school diploma or GED.

Female offenders in Washington state are placed at the Washington Corrections Center for Women in existing facilities that have been adapted for this special purpose. A youth offender program team is formed, consisting of a program manager, two teachers, a unit supervisor, a counselor, a recreation specialist, a teacher's aid, a school psychologist, a principal, and correctional officers. Youthful offender schedules are based on existing adult schedules. Among the special programs provided, girls are offered offense cycle groups, anger management groups, victim awareness groups, and a cognitive behavioral group (Fleming and Winkler 1999, 3). The offenders are housed in single-cell units separated from adult offenders and meet with counselors for at least an hour a day. Youthful offenders have separate shower and toilet areas, may order canteen items with the exception of tobacco products, and have a separate visiting area. Stringent measures are taken to keep the youthful offenders separate from adults. For example, they are moved through the institution ten minutes before adult offenders are moved so as to prevent any contact with adult offenders.

The Experience of Imprisonment

Starting from the 1940s, researchers began to investigate the ways in which men "did their time" in prison, but it was not until the mid- to late 1960s that attention was given to the experience of imprisonment for women. Researching and explaining women's experiences of life in prison has illuminated many of the issues and problems that incarceration has posed for women and generated a better understanding of the prison experience. Studies continue to be conducted and ultimately contribute toward the search for possible alternatives to imprisonment of women. From the beginning, these explorations of life in prison found that the world of the women's prison was quite different than that of male inmates because personal relationships within the prison and connections to family and loved ones outside the prison tended to shape the culture of women's prisons.

The first few studies of women in prison focused on the social structures that emerged in prison. These were based on the family and traditional gender roles as well as on coping with, and adapting to, prison conditions. As an example, one study conducted in the early 1970s identified three forms of adaptation by women in prison; these were termed "the Square", "the Cool," and "the Life" (Heffernan 1972). "The Square" denotes a woman tied to conventional norms and values whereas "the Life" encompasses a more criminal identity based on acts in the outside world judged as criminal, such as prostitution and drug use. "The Cool" uses control and manipulation within the prison as a strategy for doing her time.

One recent study of the largest women's prison in the country argues that the environment of the women's prison is shaped by pre-prison experiences, by traditional gender roles, and by the manner in which women form relationships within the prison as coping strategies (Owen 1998). Nevertheless, women still must adapt to the structure, rules, and demands of the prison and formulate for themselves a structure that helps give them some control over their lives within an alien environment. In essence, women are able to survive the prison experience and do their time by formulating a routine and by establishing close personal relations with certain other prisoners.

Apart from these specific aspects of the prison environment, research studies have brought to the surface the wide range of adverse features that make up life in women's prisons. These include the stigma of incarceration, loss of freedom and consequent claustrophobia, endless and mind-numbing boredom of daily routine in confinement, strict limitations imposed on movement, states of nervousness and anxiety engendered by being constantly under the scrutiny and supervision of others, physical and emotional problems that go with withdrawal from substance or drug abuse, absence of an advocate to deal with concerns and needs, total lack of privacy and consequent tension that may erupt at any time between persons who have not chosen to be confined in a small space together for many hours of each day, endless lineups to be counted and checked, being punished for violations of what seem to inmates like minor rules and which are always coercive in nature, the fear of being segregated in isolation as punishment or for medical observation, always being under the control and power of others and therefore subject to abuse of that power, unending noise and clamor that accompanies the custodial environment, the dependency that prison promotes and encourages, and perhaps most importantly, never being sure of your release date and being always conscious that others who control you often have the right to influence that point in time.

Prison Subculture

Prison subculture is concerned with the way prisoners adapt to the conditions of imprisonment and how their individual values and norms are employed or affected by incarceration. In effect, the prison subculture comprises the daily life of the prison and includes how women organize their time each day, how they interact with other prisoners and with staff, and the overall state of affairs constituted by the prison environment. Like any new experience, entering a prison involves learning about prison as a place in which to live, its preexisting culture, and coping with this strange new environment. Women learn to adapt and cope in different ways, but always within a general code of conduct, the primary rules of which tend to follow those in men's prisons. This code requires that a woman should "do your own time" and "protect the inmate interests." The code points to the need to regulate standards of behavior so that inmates do not interfere in the business of others and yet take care of each other. Studies suggest, however, that aspects of this code have changed over the years and that, for example, there is now a distinction in women's prisons between those who regard themselves as inmates and those who see themselves as convicts (Owen 1998). The latter follow the code closely, but the former are less willing to maintain close solidarity against the staff and the prison regime of rules and regulations and will, for example, be more willing to inform on other women inmates to staff. This situation stands in strong contrast to men's prisons, where snitching or "ratting" on other prisoners is not tolerated at all.

Importing Traditional Gender Roles

Researchers argue that women cope differently with the prison experience than men in that they adjust to the experience by forming close relationships with other prisoners whereas men tend to isolate themselves. Like all general statements this can be challenged with counter arguments that, for example, prisoners of both genders tend to congregate in racial groupings for support and solidarity in relation to other prisoners and as a form of protection against staff abuse. However, a number of researchers have identified specific forms of association between women inmates such as groups based on housing assignments, homegirl networks, and prison family/kinship networks, and, in the case of Hispanic women, a subdivision according to nationality and language spoken.

One focus of research on association among women in prison has been the issue of women forming close emotional and even sexual bonds with each other while doing their time. Early studies argued that the informal social order of the women's prison is based on identities imported from outside, so that traditional gender roles of mother, wife, or daughter are repeated within the prison environment, and family structures emerge that assist women in coping with the prison experience and create trust and solidarity among the prisoners. Some rather dated research suggests that pseudo families are formed in women's prisons, but research that is more recent tends to suggest that such families are a logical outcome of women's socialized roles as homemakers and as key persons in family relationships (Ward and Kasselbaum 1965; Giallombardo 1966; Owen 1998). It would not be surprising, therefore, to find women developing family-type structures in prisons for social support.

A very recent study of women in a Midwestern prison suggests that the subculture of women's prisons might be changing (Greer 2000). Specifically, there were indications in Greer's study of several kinds of relationships including friendships between offenders, of sexual relationships between offenders, and of a lack of kinship networks. Generally, the study found that all interpersonal relationships were tainted with perceptions of dishonesty, paranoia, and hostility. Friendships with other inmates were conducted on the basis that any person engaging in such friendships did so at her own risk, and many women adopted a position of loners (448). In other words, the women inmates made a conscious decision not to seek friendships, and this was reflected in women referring to "associates" and not to "friends" when asked whether they had formed any friendships. Several women believed that the transitory nature of relationships in prison prevented forming friendships because such relationships take time to develop and temporary relationships did not grow into anything more substantial.

In relation to kinship networks or families within the prison, Greer's study found that most of the women interviewed did not engage in family relationships, which might be said to approximate kinship networks, but some did establish very loose arrangements that might include referring to other women by terms of endearment such as "mom" and "grandma." Generally, the women suggested that structured, formal family roles did not exist in this particular institution (Greer 2000, 460–461).

Owen's previous study in California suggested that pseudo families do not necessarily carry with them associations of lesbian conduct, and studies seem to suggest that while some women enter prison as lesbians already, others assume that status only while incarcerated, and still others maintain that status after their release, having "come out" as lesbians while incarcerated (Owen 1998). In Greer's study, though the women interviewed noted that there were a number of reasons for maintaining a sexual relationship, a high proportion considered the primary reason to be "economic manipulation," referring to women who participated in sexual relationships as a means of improving their economic standing as "canteen whores" or "commissary whores" (Greer 2000, 454). As one woman put it, "a lot of people do it for money. Here it is a money thing. It is not about people's feelings or it is all [a] game really and so, people when you are broke and only get $7.50 a month and somebody may get $250 a week or month . . . it begins to be attractive to you" (455). However, some of the women interviewed in Greer's study were involved in sincere and committed relationships and saw a great difference between these stable and caring relationships and those that existed between persons who "play games" for canteen privileges (457). Other women thought that loneliness and the need for companionship were reasons for some women to take part in sexual activities; related to this notion and found in previous research, is the fact that sexual relationships help women to do their time with the least degree of psychological discomfort. In other words, the excitement involved in a romantic relationship in prison can mitigate the harsh realities of correctional life.

The fact is that the experience of prison will likely intensify emotions for women, and relations between them in prison may be more emotional than sexual. It is significant that one study discovered that the strict policy against homosexuality applied in women's prisons is more likely to encourage than discourage such relations and that sometimes women are penalized or punished simply for forming close relations with their fellow inmates (Mahan 1984). This in turn may lead to women avoiding any close relations at all with other women, thereby exacerbating their feelings of isolation during incarceration.

Race

It seems that race is much less of an organizing factor in women's prisons than in men's, but some research has indicated strained relations between white and American Native women (Ross 2000), and there exists a unique issue for Spanish-speaking women who know no other languages but are forbidden to speak Spanish. This means they incur sanctions not only for speaking a forbidden language but also for violations of prison rules that they can neither read nor understand.

Self-Mutilation

Women seem to self-mutilate in prison at a high rate. Forms of self-mutilation observed in women's prisons include slashing or carving the body, head banging, burning, and tattooing. Some theories attribute these acts to the tendency of women to internalize anger in contrast to the rather more open approach that men take in assaulting prison staff or other inmates (Dobash, Dobash, and Gutteridge 1986). A variation of this theory has women directing their anger at themselves in the absence of any other targets. Other theorists believe that self-mutilation is generally a means for incarcerated women to experience feelings of "something" as opposed to the deadness and nothingness that incarceration and loss of liberty engender (Morris 1987). Some see childhood sexual abuse among women as a precipitating factor in self-mutilation, arguing that the act of inscribing tattoos on the body is a means for women to lay claim to their own bodies (Heney 1990). Other explanations for self-injurious behavior of this kind include the view that it is a coping strategy arising out of childhood abuse by which a woman disassociates herself from her body, a tactic often used to survive actual abuse in childhood (Faith 1993). In one survey, prison tension was given as the rationale for slashing. The slashing itself was said to produce a domino effect because a woman might become emotional when her prison friend slashes herself and copy it, and other women might in turn repeat this act. Self-mutilation has been classified as a health rather than as a security issue on the basis that women who engage in it often insist they feel the absence of anyone to talk to about their issues and problems in the prison environment. This would suggest that the greater presence of counselors would help to alleviate the problem.

Separation from Families

Separation from the family is a crucial issue for incarcerated women. As emotional and probably also financial providers, women experience both guilt and stress when separated from their families through incarceration. They are more likely than men to be concerned about custody arrangements for their children during their imprisonment and whether their children are being adequately supervised and nurtured. Data indicates that four out of five women and three out of five men entering prison are parents, but almost all imprisoned women have custody of their children prior to their imprisonment, as compared to fewer than half of men (Koban 1983). It follows, then, that women are much more likely to suffer stress than men because of the hardship of being separated from their children. Studies reveal that grandparents, usually maternal grandmothers, are the most likely caregivers for children whose mothers have been imprisoned. Giving custody to close relatives while incarcerated often lessens the likelihood of contests over custody upon the woman's release (Belknap 2001). Stress factors for women in prison arising out of their family role include fear of the effects their absence will have on their children's development generally, and practical matters such as children having to change schools or endure financial constraints due to the absence of a working mother. They may have continuing concerns about their children's welfare when they are placed with relatives, but problems affecting the children often have to be tolerated since the only alternative for incarcerated mothers may be having their children institutionalized. The dislocation caused a family when the mother is incarcerated has been demonstrated to be a likely factor in youth delinquency, and several researchers have found that incarceration undermines parental authority. As well, studies have shown that as the children of inmate mothers grow older they may become more resentful and angry about parental absence. The Department of Justice estimates that nearly two million children have parents or relatives who are in prison or in jail (Butterfield 1999).

Studies concerned with the separation of fathers from the family through incarceration apply equally to imprisoned mothers. They suggest that the father's absence from a child's life may cause psychological and developmental disruption, including social and cognitive problems (Hughes 1982; Rosenfeld et al. 1973). Children may experience denial, anger, guilt, and sadness about the parent's incarceration and may develop behavioral problems at home and in school as well as emotional stress and depression following their father's incarceration. In many cases parents fail to fully advise their children of the father's incarceration, which may in turn produce confusion and feelings of rejection in the child (Fishman 1983; Sack 1977; Swan 1981). Wives of incarcerated men have reported problems with their children during incarceration, including increased antisocial behavior and aggression, truancy from school, and disobedience at home (Sack et al. 1976; Fishman 1990; Gaudin 1984).

In addition, mothers sent to prison are faced with the problem of telling their children about their incarceration and the reasons for it. Although young children may not be told because of an inability to understand, this in itself will contribute to maternal anxiety. Some mothers try to hide the fact of their imprisonment, encouraging other family members to speak of them as though they are on vacation or away at school, but most prefer to tell their children they are in prison and provide some reason for it (Baunach 1982, 161). Although there are risks of rejection in this approach, most women inmates believe it is best to tell the child directly rather than leave this to strangers or acquaintances.

When mothers return to their families after serving a term of imprisonment, they must face the problem of reestablishing their role as mother. They may find that their children have learned to survive quite well without them; they may be rejected by their children because of their inmate status; and they must also face the problem of finding employment, housing, and generally finding their way into the world outside the prison. Sometimes failures in these areas may be taken out on children or create pressure to revert to crime, especially in the case of single parents (Baunach 1985 in Hawkins 1999, 138).

In the federal courts, the fact that a convicted woman cares for others, especially her children, has been eliminated as a relevant consideration for departing from the mandated federal sentencing guidelines. In the past, family responsibilities mitigated sentences in order to keep women out of prison. Now the impact of these guidelines has been to increase the number of women in prison and to ensure that women who are imprisoned spend more time there (Raeder 1993). For example, the average federal prison sentence for drug offenders increased from thirty months in 1986 to sixty-six months by 1997 following the application of sentencing guidelines (Sabol and McGready 1999).

Prison Visiting

Fishman's study of wives visiting their husbands in prison has suggested that wives, in effect, "do time on the outside" (Fishman 1990) while their husbands are inside. This notion is prompted by factors such as the hostility shown by guards to visitors, and the guards' attitude that visiting wives are no different in character and conduct than their incarcerated spouses. The regulations that govern visits in many prisons cover matters such as days allowed for visits, the time permitted, the degree of physical contact allowed, and the items that can be brought into the prison. Not surprisingly, there is a strong emphasis on security, especially in prisons that are graded at the higher end of custody. There are often written rules detailing when prisoners and visitors may kiss or embrace, where they may sit, how children are to behave, and how loudly they may address each other. There is usually a strong emphasis on the prevention of contraband entering the prison, and all visitors are searched on entry, going through a metal detector and having all bags and packages searched. Strip searches of visitors may also be ordered.

In a recent case in the U.S. Court of Appeals, a number of inmates sued the Michigan Department of Corrections, claiming that restrictions on prison visiting violated their constitutional rights (*Bazzetta and others v. Michigan Department of Corrections* [1998]). The facts were that in 1995 the department had issued new regulations limiting those who could visit prisoners. For example, the regulations banned visits from minor brothers, sisters, nieces, and nephews; all visits by a prisoner's children when parental rights had been terminated; all visits by former prisoners who were not immediate family; and permanently banned visitors for prisoners who had twice violated drug abuse policies. The new regulations were made in response to a growth in the prison population in Michigan and a consequent increase in the number of visitors, who were perceived to constitute a problem for department officials in that supervision became more difficult, and smuggling of drugs and weapons more prevalent and difficult to stop.

The court noted that there were two kinds of visits, contact and noncontact. Contact visits allowed physical contact between prisoner and visitor whereas noncontact visits require the prisoner and visitor to sit in separate rooms but observe each other through a clear window and speak via a telephone. The court found that prisoners do retain a limited right to freedom of association even while incarcerated, specifically in the form of noncontact visits with intimate associates. The court analyzed each of the new regulations and considered the basis for their justification as argued by the department. In terms of banning visits of minor brothers, nieces, and nephews, the court considered this to be an "exaggerated response" to the perceived problems that had arisen in prison visiting and held that the regulations were not attempts to manage visits so much as to end them altogether. Regarding the suggestion that new regulations were required to deal with smuggling contraband, the court found that the department offered no testimony to support such claims and, moreover, noncontact visits would prevent smuggling in any event. The court also criticized prison officials for stating their opposition to visits of children on the ground that this would cause the children to become "too comfortable with prisons." The court pointed out this determination was for the parents to make, not the prison officials.

Significantly, the department's argument that letters and phone calls were adequate alternatives to visits by minor relations was not accepted, in part because the court reviewed evidence that 40 to 80 percent of inmates were illiterate and unable to compose letters. The court also held that phone calls were unsatisfactory, being of only short duration and monitored by correctional staff. Similarly, the court refused to endorse the ban on visits by natural children where parental rights had been terminated, finding that the department offered no adequate reason for this ban that did not relate to a legitimate penological interest. Too, the court ruled that the blanket ban on visits by former inmates was an exaggerated response. As for the ban based on violation of drug abuse policies, the court found there were no proper criteria for lifting this ban, which could only be removed at the discretion of prison officials, who did not have to explain their decisions. Importantly, the court also held that the permanent ban on visitors violated the constitutional prohibition against cruel and unusual punishments and the protection of due process. In its conclusion the court wrote,

> Instead of crafting policies that would legitimately meet the very real need to maintain order in prisons, the department has implemented a series of haphazard policies that violated these rights and did real harm to inmates in its care. It then defended these policies not with reasoned arguments, but with misdirection and demands that federal courts blindly defer to corrections officials . . . in the present case, the regulations fall below minimum standards of decency owed by a civilized society to those it has incarcerated.

Conjugal Visits

A few states allow family members of specified inmates to have overnight visits, called conjugal visits, and permit some inmates to be released on furlough, to be spent in their home with their family (Carlson and Cervera 1992, 38). The major purpose of such visits is to enhance family ties and thereby assist in the prisoners' adjustment after release (Howser et al. 1983). There have been concerns about such programs based on perceptions of community safety, the fact that the prisoner is released from incarceration, and moral views about conjugal visits themselves. It is significant that many countries view marital relations as a right and not a privilege and see conjugal visits as promoting family solidarity and contributing to the security and good management of the prison itself (Balogh 1964). In 1992, seven states operated these programs, which allow for parents, spouses, children, and specified family members to visit with the inmate (Goetting 1982).

Conjugal visits take place in specially designated areas, usually trailers; their duration is seven to seventy-two hours and their frequency is two to three months (Goetting 1982). Stringent conditions must be satisfied in order to earn the privilege of a conjugal visit, including a legal marriage, a relatively long sentence, and no eligibility for parole. It is essential that the inmate has maintained a good disciplinary record in the prison. Some research indicates that those who participate in such programs have improved discipline records and are less likely to be returned to custody than those who do not participate.

The issues that arise from conjugal visits include the limitations on physical space available and the eligibility requirements. In addition, prison administrators are concerned about contraband and security, and in policy terms, there is some question as to whether common-law marriages and girlfriends or boyfriends should be included (Goetting 1982; Balogh 1964). As a result of these concerns, furlough programs have been set up as an alternative to conjugal visits. The former are considered easier to administer and provide for greater eligibility. Generally, a temporary absence from incarceration on furlough will be granted from four hours to thirty days, with the average length of absence being forty-eight to seventy-two hours. Furloughs may be granted for family visits as well as funerals and medical reasons. Generally, eligibility is based on the inmate having served a minimum part of his or her sentence; being close to release date or parole eligibility; having a good disciplinary record; and not having been convicted of violent or sex crimes. Home visits on furlough are considered to be more "natural" than conjugal visits, which can take on an air of artificiality, especially in view of the use of trailers within the prison to accommodate the visits. The evidence suggests that furloughs and conjugal visits can aid in keeping families together and that the rate of recidivism is lower for those maintaining family relationships during incarceration (Howser and MacDonald 1982).

One alternative to furloughs and conjugal visits for prisoners and their spouses is procreation through artificial insemination. In a recent case in the U.S. Court of Appeals, a male inmate in the California prison system filed a complaint in the federal court alleging that his constitutional rights were being violated by the prison not permitting him to provide his wife with a sperm specimen that she might use to become artificially inseminated (*Gerber v. Rodney Hickman*). The petitioner's claim was dismissed by the district court, which ruled that an inmate had no constitutional right to procreate while incarcerated; the Court of Appeals affirmed the district court's decision. The facts of the case indicate that the inmate, a forty-one-year-old man, was serving a sentence of 100 years to life plus eleven years. The inmate and his wife wanted a baby, but the California Department of Corrections prohibits family visits for inmates sentenced to life without parole. In its analysis of the issue of fundamental rights in prison, the Court of Appeals noted that prison walls do not negate the protections of the Constitution and that a state could not, for example, ban inmate access to mail or prohibit access to the courts. Nevertheless, as the court stated, imprisonment does result in the loss of significant rights, and prisoners retain only those rights "not inconsistent with their status as prisoners or with the legitimate penological objectives of the corrections system" (3).

As far as the right to procreate is concerned, the court noted that because incarceration removes an inmate from society, this necessarily involves a separation of the inmate from his spouse and family and that during the period of confinement a right of intimate association is necessarily foregone. The court noted a number of other rights that incarcerated persons could not claim to exercise while incarcerated, including contact visits and conjugal visits. The fact that prison officials may choose to allow some inmates the privilege of conjugal visits does not carry with it any constitutional rights to such visits (4). A majority of the court dissented, ruling that procreation, in the sense of the right to have a child, is not fundamentally inconsistent with incarceration, relying, among other things, on the fact that the Supreme Court has ruled that the fundamental right to marry does survive incarceration even though it may be subjected to substantial restrictions (8). The dissenters noted also that no law in

California authorized the prohibition against procreation imposed by the prison warden and that the Department of Corrections authorized denial of the inmate's request under a regulation that limited medical services for inmates to those based on medical necessity (9). It is significant that the process and procedure sought by the inmate involved him providing a semen sample to his lawyer either personally or by mail; this in turn would be delivered to a laboratory, which would perform the artificial insemination. Analyzing this process, a group of dissenting judges could see nothing inconsistent with incarceration in producing semen and mailing or handing it to a lawyer, and pointed out that once the package was outside prison walls the prison no longer had any legitimate interest in it. Accordingly, given the procedure the inmate intended to follow, there was no reason to refuse his request. In the view of the dissenting judges, the inmate was not asking for release to go home for a conjugal visit or for a conjugal visit within the prison. His request would not affect his confinement at all. It would appear that the majority decision was aimed more at the goal of isolating prisoners, and as one judge pointed out, it would not be right for prison administrators to

> supplement the punishment imposed by the legislature because they believe doing so would enhance deterrence and retribution. By cutting off the [inmate's] fundamental right to procreate, prison authorities have enhanced [his] punishment beyond that authorized by statute and consigned [his wife] to a childless marriage. (15)

The issue of a prisoner marrying while incarcerated was tested in the superior court of New Jersey, Appellate Division, where an inmate appealed against a prison administrator's denial of her request to marry a noninmate *(Vazquez v. New Jersey Department of Corrections)*. According to department regulations, an inmate must request permission to marry at least ninety days before the proposed marriage date, and any such request to marry is to be considered by a marriage committee composed of a chaplain, social work supervisor, correctional staff officer at the rank of lieutenant or above, and other staff designated by the superintendent. Standards for approval of a request to marry include that the inmate has made a satisfactory adjustment to the correctional facility, that the marriage does not present a security risk, that the intended spouse is not presently incarcerated, and that the inmate is able to comply with state law requirements governing marriage. In making its decision, the marriage committee may consider such factors as the inmate's maturity, emotional stability, and length and type of sentence.

In this particular case, the inmate, Judith Vazquez, was serving a life sentence and requested permission to marry a man she had known for well over twenty-three years. The marriage committee interviewed the inmate and the potential spouse and recommended denial of the request to marry on the grounds that "this marriage would not be in the best interest of either party or the institution" (3). The basis for this statement was the length of the inmate's sentence; the apparent belief by both parties that her sentence would be reduced; a suggestion that the potential spouse might have knowledge of the crime for which she was convicted; and the vagueness of their prior relationships, which the committee found could not be documented. During questioning by the committee, the inmate was very nervous and the potential spouse was described as "very sarcastic," suggesting that he did not even understand why the correctional department was involved in the decision. In conclusion the committee noted that the parties had only been in touch for the past six months and had been visiting each other only for the past three months. Accordingly, the committee did not feel there was an established relationship for marriage. The administrator accepted the committee's decision, and the inmate then argued that this refusal to allow her to marry violated her constitutional right to marry and was an abuse of discretion.

The New Jersey Superior Court noted that the right to marry is subject to restrictions as a result of incarceration (4). Nevertheless, inmate marriages, like other marriages, do express emotional support and public commitment, and that marriage also has spiritual significance. In addition, eventually most inmates will be released and therefore inmate marriages are founded on the belief that they will ultimately be fully consummated. Referring to the Supreme Court decision in *Turner v. Safley* (1987), which invalidated part of a regulation stating that permission to marry would only be given if there were "compelling" reasons, the New Jersey Superior Court noted that the New Jersey regulations concerning inmate marriages still contained a blanket prohibition against approving the marriage of an inmate to another inmate despite Turner's decision that such marriages cannot be totally prohibited. Accordingly, the New Jersey regulations did not properly reflect the constitutional position. The court found that the decisions of the marriage committee and administrator failed to identify any security or other concerns that would justify denial of the request to marry. The court considered that the fact that the potential spouse may have been "sarcastic" before the committee in responding to what the court called "overly intrusive questioning" did not mean that he constituted a security threat to the institution. The court was critical of the "excessive paternalism" shown by the committee in its conclusion that the parties did not have an established relationship, ruling that this conclusion was totally unrelated to any legitimate security or other concerns.

Location of Women's Prisons

Women's prisons are usually sited in isolated locations; consequently, women are often a considerable distance from friends and families. This often means that women in prison lack family support because of difficult visiting conditions. The location of women's prisons is affected by women's low rate of imprisonment: Since there are relatively few women incarcerated in each state, administrators usually erect only one prison for women in each state, and all convicted women are incarcerated there. A number of prisons built on the cottage design were, in the past, specifically located in rural areas because it was thought during the time of the women's reformatory movement that women ought to be kept away from the attractions of urban areas. Therefore, historical circumstances operate to isolate incarcerated women from towns and cities. In one study, the main reason given for infrequent visitation or no visitation at all by inmate mothers' children was the distance between the child's residence and the correctional facility. In that study, over 60 percent of the children lived more than 100 miles from their mother's place of incarceration (Bloom and Steinhart 1993).

Prison Programs for Women

Generally, because so few women are imprisoned, few educational and other programs are made available to them. Indeed, their smaller numbers and relatively short periods of imprisonment are used to justify this deficiency. Additionally, women have historically been viewed as unworthy or incapable of training or treatment. Other justifications for a lack of treatment options have included women's status as nonbreadwinners and as not needing employment upon release. Generally, one can expect that programming in women's prisons will reflect the gender biases in the broader society, especially the notion that a woman's role is to function as housekeeper and caregiver in the home. It is significant that the American Correctional Association (1990) has found that fewer work assignments are available to women in prisons, and those that do exist are not classed as prison industries with associated skills that can be marketed after release from prison. Women prisoners often have limited access to prison libraries and to vocational and educational opportunities. Only about half of women's prisons have law libraries for prisoner use, which means they enjoy only restricted access to the courts.

In general, programs for women fall into five categories: institutional maintenance, including clerical work, the food service at the institution, and general cleaning and maintenance of the grounds; education, mainly focused on remedial education; vocational training, which emphasizes stereotypical jobs for women such as cosmetology and sewing; treatment, including Alcoholics Anonymous and Narcotics Anonymous; and medical care (Wilson 1994 in Winifred 1996). In a survey of existing vocational and technical training programs for women, conducted by the American Correctional Association, a number of states failed to respond, and Hawaii, Nebraska, North Carolina, West Virginia, and Wyoming reported that they had no technical or vocation training programs for women (Winifred 1996, 2). Almost 94 percent of the programs surveyed gave entry-level job skills as a stated goal. Several states reported problems with old or aging equipment, especially sewing machines and computers, and others identified constraints including limited funding, an inability to hire staff willing to work with offenders, a low inmate pay scale, and low inmate self-esteem. Many recommendations were made by the states, including the certifying of prison programs by state boards or industries, equal pay for men and women in comparable inmate jobs (female inmates are paid on a lower scale than males, often receiving only half the amount paid to men), increased interaction with community employers, encouraging women to enroll in nontraditional programs, and the provision of new and updated equipment (2).

In Belknap's study conducted at a state prison, sixty-eight female prisoners were surveyed about access to programs and programming needs within the prison (2000, 113). Over half of those interviewed were African Americans, and two identified themselves as American Indian; almost two thirds reported having dependent children. The survey asked which programs and activities the women participated in and which programs they would like to participate in if offered. Two thirds of the women had participated in high school or GED courses, and more than a third had taken at least one college course. Just over one quarter had taken part in vocational training, over half had participated in recreational activities, and four fifths had participated in other types of programs such as twelve step, self-awareness, parenting, domestic violence, and stress management (114). The need for drug programs was emphasized by the fact that almost half the women were active in twelve-step programs such as Alcoholics Anonymous or Narcotics Anonymous and one quarter took part in other drug programs. Concerning programs the women wanted to participate in but could not get into, 16 percent of the women wanted to take part in twelve-step programs and over one quarter wanted to gain access to other drug programs. One fifth wanted to take part in domestic violence programs. The study suggests that female prisoners would like to have had easier access to many existing programs and wanted new programs offered to them as well (119).

Most lawsuits brought by women since the 1970s have tried to compare women's access to job assignments, pay for work, vocational programs, recreation, and living conditions relative to men. In the 1980s, legal suits challenged conditions that permitted women to receive vocational training in work such as sewing while male prisons in the same state received training in a multitude of skills such as electronics and carpentry. In programming, the ideology of the reformatory—that women should be taught to be "proper women" and trained in domestic tasks for the home—seems to still prevail in prisons for women. There is a reluctance to afford women the opportunity for gender equality in terms of training and acquiring vocational skills, and many programs for women remain focused on the home and on training in domestic skills. Women in prison lack education, and figures show that less than one third of all imprisoned women hold a high school degree at intake (American Correctional Association 1990). It is not surprising, then, that both prisoners and staff rank education as the most valuable resource for women during their imprisonment. In a report to Congress in December 1999, the United States General Accounting Office (GAO) identified programs for women at federal facilities that teach skills such as business technology, dental hygiene, carpentry, tool machine set up and operation, bus driving, and forklift operation (United States 1999a). These programs were gender-specific for female prisoners whereas, for example, programs identified by the GAO in a survey of women's prisons in California and Texas focused on standardized or equal treatment of male and female prisoners. The Federal Bureau of Prisons adopted a gender-specific policy in 1997 for programming in women's prisons and is promoting a gender-specific policy in all state departments of corrections, but much remains to be done.

Classification

Classification within prisons for both men and women governs decisions about issues such as eligibility and access to treatment and educational programs, housing assignments, selection of cell mates, safety, access to worker status, and fairness and appropriateness of almost all inmate processing decisions during the period of incarceration. Importantly, classification appears to greatly influence how an inmate is informally regarded and perceived by both staff and other inmates. In many women's prisons, there is generally no segregation of prisoners by risk, so that, for example, women imprisoned for murder are mixed with women in prison for check fraud or for minor misdemeanors. This is in contrast to men's prisons, where classification systems are fully developed and sophisticated tools of prison management. This failure to segregate means that the mentally ill and the more serious offenders are not separated from the less serious offenders, as is routinely done in men's prisons. The absence of any system for women prisoners is often the outcome of the small number of women incarcerated and, in most states, of housing women in a single prison. Associated with this issue is the absence of specialized treatment, again justified by reference to the low numbers of women incarcerated. The few classification systems in women's prisons that do exist are generally designed for male prisoners and have been applied as if they were gender neutral. They assume, therefore, that the same classification factors are equally appropriate for both male and female inmates. However, evidence suggests that this assumption is questionable, for research data suggest that women present quite a different profile of needs and risks than male inmates. In addition, women have been shown to have different social, medical, and psychological needs.

Correctional administrators have expressed the belief that systems tend to overclassify females and place them in higher custody levels than are warranted. Generally, local correctional staff have wide discretion in determining which method of classification to apply, if any, in a women's prison; thus, local culture, politics, values, and the training background of local decision makers determine which method is selected. This absence of consistency in definitions and procedures, as well as goals, across different organizations and jurisdictions can obviously work to the disadvantage of women, who may suffer from the absence of a discrete system for their needs and may be subjected to ad hoc and arbitrary decision making. A further complicating factor is that there tends to be an excessive use of discretionary overrides by staff engaged in classification work, reflecting their disagreement with the classification procedures. In effect, staff may replace the supposedly objective assessment process with their own intuitive judgment as to classification. In one study, the override rate in a women's prison was as high as 40 percent, which is more than twice the usual rate and far higher than that for male inmates (Brennan 1998).

Associated with the classification issue generally is that for classification to be effective, housing and treatment options must exist in a particular institution, and yet housing and programming options for women are frequently lacking. In the case of housing, commingling women prisoners without classification can, from the administrators' point of view, result in the undermining of correctional goals such as safety, order, and the least restrictive form of custody. With crowding and inadequate housing comes the breakdown of whatever classification systems do exist and a reversion to the category of "space available," meaning that a woman inmate is held in whatever space is available regardless of security and custody factors. Generally, research has challenged the notion that women prisoners need to be housed in conditions of such extreme security given their very low risk of escape, of violence, or of serious violation of discipline, as compared to male detainees (Brennan 1998). Yet, women continue to be housed in high-security arrangements, possibly causing them psychological damage through the perception given to visitors that these women are dangerous and need to be kept in conditions of strict confinement. Women may also be denied access to whatever programs exist in the institution as a result of the tendency of risk systems to overclassify them, because being placed in a higher classification of risk than is warranted often serves to deny or limit access to treatment programs. Access to treatment may also be denied or restricted when the classification system underestimates or fails to record the real treatment and programming needs of a woman inmate.

Discipline

The regime in women's prisons is characterized by elaborate systems of rules and regulations, policies, and procedures designed to order and control their behavior in confinement. This wealth of regulations makes it possible for women prisoners to be sanctioned for conduct that might be considered minor but which still violates disciplinary codes. Compared with men's prisons, women's institutions often have more rules about conduct as well as rules that are pettier in nature (Pollock-Byrne 1990). However, even when the rules in both prisons are broadly identical, women seem to be subject to stricter supervision than men and are often punished for behavior that would not be sanctioned in men's prisons, such as cursing, failing to eat all the food on one's plate, and sharing shampoo. Essentially, women are subjected to a greater degree of surveillance than men, leading to findings of more rule infractions. This intensive surveillance seems to be a carry-over from historical times, reflecting the broad societal belief that women should conform to gender stereotypes of obedience, submission, and dependence. Therefore, successful adaptation of women to the prison regime is measured by the extent to which they conform to this stereotype of the compliant woman. A study of Texas prisons in 1994 found that women were far more likely than men to be cited for infractions of prison rules, especially those minor in nature, and to be far more severely punished for them (McClellan 1994). For example, women received citations for drying underwear, talking while waiting in line, displaying too many family photographs, and for failing to consume all of their food at mealtimes. Rule infractions for possessing contraband included possessing an extra bra or pillowcase, a borrowed comb, or candy. Sharing shampoo in the shower or lighting another prisoner's cigarette were classified as "trafficking." Other examples include "walking on the grass, rattling doors and yelling, failing to return towels, or having torn sheets" (Glick and Neto 1977, 42). Prison regimes that punish women in this manner have been characterized as treating the women like children, in effect infantilizing them. As Freedman (2000) points out, the family model applied to female inmates historically resulted in women prisoners being referred to as "girls," and in modern times, prison guards have continued to view female inmates as children with the result that women are seen as inherently dependent while men are given adult status. Similarly, correctional officers, like parents, will often show an excessive concern with women's cleanliness, and displaying minor vices, such as smoking, may result in cleaning work as punishment. For example, a rule statement in a Wisconsin women's institution read:

> It is our policy that if you smoke you will be expected to wash your room walls once every other month. If you do not smoke you should wash them once every three months. (Gibson 1976 in Hawkins 1999, 125)

Women Prisoners and Prison Staff

Prison staff historically and in the present day have consistently perceived female prisoners as more difficult to work with than male prisoners. This has led to a tendency for correctional staff to exhibit their discomfort or dislike of working with women prisoners or to avoid working in women's prisons at all. This preference for working with male inmates applies to both male and female correctional staff at all levels and ranks and seems to date back to the very beginnings of women's prisons. For example, a prison matron writing in the 1860s described female inmates as being "harder to manage . . . more impulsive, more individual, more unreasonable and excitable than men; will not act in concert and cannot be disciplined in masses" (Muraskin 2000, 239). Recent research has revealed that male and female staff do not necessarily have the same justification for their preference for male inmates (Pollock-Byrne 1986). Male officers express their concern over the perceived difficulties in supervising women and the fear of being accused of rape as well as the need to modify their normal behavior when supervising women inmates, such as being careful of their language and being more circumspect in the possible use of force. The reasons female officers give for their preference in working with males include the perception that male inmates are more likely to treat the women staff with respect, and to the appreciation they believe is shown them by male inmates, which, in their view, makes their work more comfortable. Both male and female staff consider women inmates to be more demanding and to complain more often and as more likely to refuse to comply with orders and directions. Some officers interviewed in one study did, however, express appreciation for the challenge of working with female inmates even though they agreed they were more difficult to control and supervise. Generally, the research shows that both male and female staff perceive women prisoners as possessing certain attributes that make them more difficult to work with. Echoing the comments of the prison matron in 1861, they stated that women prisoners showed defiance, exhibited open displays of emotion, and were seen as seeking gratification.

The import of this research is that women and men prisoners are indeed different in their persons and personalities and that these many real differences can appropriately be catered to by management and supervisory approaches that recognize difference and account for it. Typically there has been a lack of specialized training for staff employed in women's prisons, as once again, it was assumed that there were no differences between men and women prisoners in terms of treatment and conditions. Generally, it seems that most correctional training focuses on instruction in the skills of security and in handling inmates to prevent disorder, and there is a heavy concentration on the policies, rules, and regulations of the particular correctional service. After this type of formal training, officers must learn on the job how to manage inmates and interact with them on a daily basis within an actual prison environment; it is only then that officers learn the occupational culture, including all the stereotypes that have been developed about differences between male and female prisoners.

Sexual Abuse in Prison

Though the exact number of sexual assaults committed against female and male prisoners is not known, surveys estimate more than 290,000 inmates of both sexes are sexually assaulted each year. In 1995 the Department of Justice estimated 135,000 rapes of female inmates throughout the country (Bureau of Justice Statistics 1995). A report by the General Accounting Office to Congress in June 1999 focused on four jurisdictions containing the largest correctional systems for female offenders and found that despite training programs and legislation criminalizing such conduct, sexual misconduct was still occurring, with more than 500 allegations of staff sexual misconduct being made in these jurisdictions over the period 1995–1998 (U.S. General Accounting Office 1999b). According to the report, most allegations were of verbal harassment, improper visual surveillance, improper touching, and consensual sex. During the 1990s the Justice Department brought proceedings against the states of Arizona and Michigan, alleging systemic sexual misconduct by male staff against women inmates. In both cases, settlement agreements were entered into requiring those states to revise training, strengthen investigative techniques, and oblige male officers to announce their presence when entering areas where female inmates might be in a state of undress. There is good reason to believe that the majority of assaults on women inmates are not reported to correctional authorities. An example of this reluctance to prosecute assaults against women occurred over a five-year period between 1990 and 1995, when seventy-six sexual misconduct complaints were filed by inmates at a prison in New York, the state's largest prison for women (Williams 1996). Ultimately, fifty-six of those complaints were not pursued, mainly because the inmates refused to answer questions about incidents when questioned, but fourteen cases were proved. The outcome was the transfer of six officers out of the prison, with one officer receiving counseling. Cases of abuse may go unreported because of the woman's fear of repercussions, or because there is a perception that correctional officers are more credible witnesses than a woman incarcerated for criminal conduct. A number of states have laws that criminalize sex between inmates and correctional staff, and in New York state, legislation classifies all sex relations between staff and prisoners as rape, but in spite of this assaults continue. Anecdotal evidence suggests that a fine line is drawn in prison between consensual and nonconsensual sex, and female inmates are always liable to be punished for making an accusation at all. In one case, for example, immediately after alleging sexual abuse, the woman prisoner was transferred to a maximum security facility out of her current minimum security and was beaten and harassed by guards there (Holmes 1996). Sexual abuse can also take place under the guise of security, as in the case of the strip search normally conducted on all new inmates.

Explanations of women prisoners' vulnerability to sexual abuse tend to center on the notion that their presence in prison proves to male staff that they are no longer members of the "gentle sex," and for this violation of gender role expectations they are liable to harsh treatment, including sexual abuse. The institutional culture of the prison emphasizes security and discipline, but in contrast, correctional staff are also required to give prominence to treatment. Inevitably, tensions arise in the relations between guard and inmate. Guards have both legitimate and coercive power, and in situations where these roles are confused, abuse of power, including using coercive power in sexual assaults, can occur. It was found not to be unusual for male staff to force women into performing sexual favors in order to have their basic needs met, such as seeing visitors and obtaining food (Henriques and Gilbert 2000). Significantly, there is a greater degree of sex integration in women's prisons than in men's prisons—this despite the fact that female prisoners are much more likely to be abused by male guards than male prisoners are by female guards.

In recent years, following a landmark case brought by male inmates in a Florida prison, female inmates have brought suit in class action proceedings on behalf of women alleging sexual harassment and abuse by prison guards (U.S. General Accounting Office 1999b). In cases brought by women in California, Georgia, and the District of Columbia, out of court settlements were reached. Often these cases resulted from advocacy undertaken by groups that have taken up the cause of female inmates being sexually assaulted, such as the ACLU Prison Project and the California Prison Focus.

There are practical means of avoiding assaults against women prisoners: having body searches of women inmates conducted by two officers, one of whom must be a woman; and ensuring that correctional staff training includes their role in preventing rape and sexual abuse. However, in relation to privacy rights, the courts have recognized only limited rights holding in *Forts v. Ward* (1980), that the privacy rights of women inmates do not extend to protection against being viewed by male guards while sleeping, so long as suitable sleepwear is provided and they are allowed to cover their cell windows while changing clothes. In *Jordan v. Gardner* (1993), a circuit court found that the psychological impact of clothed body searches by male prison guards of women inmates with histories of sexual abuse amounted to an infliction of pain contrary to the Constitution (Farrell 2000, 202).

Rape services should be provided to women in prison just as they are to women on the outside, and correctional staff ought to always be punished for assaults and rape through the criminal justice system and not simply internally within the correctional system. On May 30, 2002, the *Boston Globe* reported that officials had agreed to pay $10 million to settle a class action lawsuit instituted on behalf of some 5,400 women who were routinely and illegally strip-searched over a four-year period at a local jail (*Boston Globe* 2002). The settlement followed the ruling by the U.S. District Court that the city of Boston and Suffolk County had engaged in a blanket strip-search policy. The practice followed by the local sheriff's department was that women arrested and taken to the county jail were subjected to the same treatment as female inmates awaiting trial because they were ordered to strip naked and bend over while a female officer searched their vaginas and rectums.

Criminal Justice Policy Issues

The actions of lawmakers and the policies of the federal and state governments can affect the situation of women in prison and particularly the rate at which women are imprisoned. Changes in justice policy, such as declaring a "war on crime" or a "war on drugs," affect law enforcement authorities when demands are made for them to be more proactive in catching criminals. Changes in sentencing practices may have the effect of increasing the size of the prison population or extending the time spent in prison for various offenses. The rate of imprisonment of women has increased substantially, largely due to the current "war on drugs" and mandatory minimum sentencing policies. On December 31, 2000, 91,612 women were housed in federal and state prisons in the United States (Bureau of Justice Statistics 2001). This compares with 1.2 million men. Over one third of all female prisoners were held in the three largest jurisdictions of Texas, California, and in the federal system. Since the 1970s, there has been a rapid growth in the number of women (and men) imprisoned, as the criminal justice system has become more punitive, placing ever-greater reliance on incarceration as the appropriate response to criminality. Since 1990 the number of female prisoners has increased 108 percent, and the female prison population has increased at an average rate of at least 10 percent in seventeen states.

"Three Strikes and You're Out"

In the 1990s legislation was enacted that imposes minimum sentences for repeat offenders in response to a perceived wave of violent crime. In particular, California has pioneered legislation that provides for "three strikes and you're out," intended originally by its proponents to target violent male offenders and keep them behind bars for repeat offenses. Despite its supposed emphasis on violent offenders, in California the vast majority of second- and third-strike inmates have been sentenced for crimes that involved no element of violence. There is general agreement that the legislation has led to absurdities in sentencing. For example, in one case an offender received a sentence of twenty-seven years to life for attempting to sell stolen batteries to a retailer. The loss to the owner of the batteries was $90, and the offender, who was disabled, was collecting disability pay at the time of the offense (Austin and Irwin 2001, 208). By 1997, twenty-six states and the federal government had enacted "three strikes" laws. As with much legislation, no account was taken of gender in designing the three strikes model due to the perception of the policy makers that men's and women's crime can be equated. This ignores the gendered nature of female criminality and the different family responsibilities of men and women.

There are a number of reasons for opposing the use of this type of legislation against women. For one thing, women offenders are not the type of offenders the legislation is aimed at, yet they are caught by it anyway. The legislation is intended to keep violent offenders imprisoned, but the majority of women are not violent or predatory offenders; they are property and drug offenders. As well, women often commit property or drug offenses to ensure the survival of their families and because of their poverty. Women tend to shoplift and write bad checks; they do not rob liquor stores with sawn-off shotguns. Nevertheless, they may be caught by versions of the "three strikes" legislation that does not limit its penalties to violent criminals and consequently may be incarcerated for long periods. Some argue that there is also a moral objection to three strikes legislation, in that it penalizes future conduct on the assumption that a person will commit further offenses and should therefore be locked up based on that prediction. However, legislation like this can overestimate the likelihood of future criminal conduct by women and can incarcerate women not deserving severe punishment.

Although the incarceration of female drug offenders has increased, the proportion of women imprisoned for violent offenses declined in the 1980s, dropping from 48.9 percent of all women to 41 percent in 1986 and to 32.8 percent by 1991 (Casey and Wiatrowski 1996). It is estimated that one half of women incarcerated for a violent offense killed abusive partners or spouses. For women involved in robbery, there is support for the argument that many were not active participants in the crime but were dependent accomplices to male partners. Clearly, women are not predatory violent offenders who are suitable for mandatory twenty-five-year three strikes sentences, such as those that apply in California to offenders with three felony convictions, regardless of the nature of the third conviction. The effect of imposing a twenty-five-year sentence on a woman with children is to sever the mother and child bond for the rest of the child's formative years. The purpose of three strikes legislation was to incapacitate persistent violent offenders, but the question must be asked whether those who formulated the legislation really considered the effects this law would have on women offenders or simply promoted yet another measure intended to "get tough on crime" with no regard to gender at all.

The "War on Drugs"

The so-called war on drugs has really been four recent political initiatives, with the initial one declared in 1972 by President Richard Nixon. Others followed in 1982, 1986, and 1988. The goals of each movement were broadly the same: to reduce individual drug use, to stop the inflow of drugs into the United States, and to reduce drug-related crime. In 1986 and 1988, antidrug legislation changed the focus away from large drug dealers and from the treatment of drug abusers toward users and street-level dealers, especially those involved in dealing and using crack cocaine. The 1986 and 1988 legislation resulted from media attention to the issue, with continual reporting about the use of crack cocaine. The media identified crack cocaine as a national epidemic, and it in turn became a major issue in the elections of 1986. Legislation enacted in that year laid down the parameters of the current "war" by prescribing mandatory minimum penalties for drug trafficking based on the amount of drugs involved, and by making a distinction between possession of cocaine and crack cocaine, with a minimum of twenty-five years imprisonment for possession of five or more grams of crack cocaine. In contrast, an offender found guilty of possession of powder cocaine would only be liable to a mandatory minimum sentence of five years if the amount of cocaine exceeded or equaled 500 grams. The legislation was firmly aimed at social control and included provisions that eliminated probation and parole for certain drug offenders and allowed for the forfeiture of assets. Fundamentally, drug abuse had been perceived and defined as a national security issue, and the "war on drugs" was portrayed as a matter of national survival. After 1986, however, media and public attention drifted away from the issue of drug abuse. The subject reared its head again in 1988 with the passing of more legislation that enhanced penalties and established the office of the "drug czar."

Historically, women have always been greater users of drugs such as sedatives and tranquilizers than men. This fact cuts across class and race: middle-class, working-class, and upper-class women all turn to drug use for similar reasons, including depression, low self-esteem, and personal trauma, such as physical and sexual abuse by men. There is no doubt that the "war on drugs" was the impetus for the policy shift that has greatly contributed to the increase in the imprisonment of women in the United States. During the 1980s, the arrest rate for women with drug violations increased at about twice the rate of arrests for men for the same violations. In 1991 one out of every three women was in prison for a drug offense, compared with only one in ten in 1979. Overall, drug offenses made up 55 percent of the national increase in women prisoners in the period 1986 to 1991 (Casey and Wiatrowski 1996). The "war on drugs" has been described as "a war on women," particularly women of color (Chesney-Lind 1995; Bloom and Chesney-Lind 2000), since one of the effects of the legislation is that more women have been brought into the criminal justice system, producing a tremendous increase in the number of incarcerated women. The background of most of these offenders is, as one woman judge put it, from the "lowest, most easily arrested rung of the drug crime business" (Bush-Baskette

1999, 224). There is a general consensus among researchers and professionals working in the drug abuse field that harsh sentencing has little or no effect on the prevalence of drug offenses and that such practices do not serve as a deterrent to such offenses. The question must be asked whether imprisoning large numbers of women, most of whom are mothers, is an appropriate response to street-level drug use and abuse when other options such as treatment or the imposition of sanctions within the community might better serve the general interests of the women and of society in general.

Boot Camps for Women

Boot camps for women constitute a special form of incarceration. Since the 1980s a variety of boot camp-style programs have been developed that require participation in military-type drills, strict discipline, and physical challenges (Clark and Kellam 2001). According to the *Criminal Justice Year Book*, at the beginning of 1998 some thirty-three states and the Federal Bureau of Prisons operated forty-nine boot camp facilities, sixteen of which included female participants (Clark and Kellam 2001, 1). Research on the subject of female offenders in boot camps has been limited, but MacKenzie's 1996 study assessed several programs using surveys and interviews (MacKenzie and Donaldson 1996). The study concluded that in light of their provision for early release, women should have equal access to boot camp programs, and that such programs could be tailored to fit women's special needs. It noted that only a small number of women participated in these programs in each state and that women were often precluded from programs because of their eligibility requirements, which were originally developed for men. Also, there were high dropout rates among women, with explanations of health problems and high levels of stress provoked by the physical demands of boot camp programs. The study found that given their small numbers, women felt isolated and vulnerable to harassment in the male-dominated programs. Further, the military regimes and harshness of the male drill instructors might have adverse effects on women who had been in abusive relationships with men.

Angela Gover and others (1999) describe the regimen at a boot camp as beginning with a predawn reveille, the inception of a ten to sixteen hour day. During the day, inmates must address staff as "sir" or "ma'am," ask permission to speak, and refer to themselves as "this inmate." Frequent punishments for minor rule violations often involve physical exercises such as pushups or running (Gover, Styve, and MacKenzie 1999, 385). After dressing, inmates will march to an exercise yard and engage in an hour or two of physical training, followed by drill and ceremony. At breakfast, inmates must stand in front of the table until commanded to sit and may not speak while eating. The meal is followed by a march to work sites involving hard physical labor, such as cleaning state parks or highways. At the end of the working day, inmates return to the compound and take part in more drill and exercise, followed by a series of evening programs and dinner. For those who complete the program, an elaborate graduation ceremony occurs and awards are given for achievements in the program.

MacKenzie and Donaldson (1996) studied six boot camps with female participants and found that the women inmates had difficulty with the physical demands of the program and experienced emotional stress due to the majority of staff and inmates being male. This leads some researchers to argue that it is inappropriate to place female boot camp inmates with males. After a review of the results of adult and juvenile boot camp research, Sherman and others (1997) concluded there was no evidence that the military style atmosphere, structure, and discipline of boot camps reduced recidivism as compared to other forms of punishment. Similarly, although there was no evidence that boot camps actually changed offenders, there was some evidence that they could be used to mark those offenders who would have difficulty in completing probation or parole.

In an attempt to balance the military aspects of shock incarceration in boot camps with therapeutic programming, a Shock Incarceration Program has been developed for women in New York; the first women entered the six-month program in December 1988 (Clark and Kellam 2001, 2). The program is the largest in the country, with 120 beds for participants and a further twenty beds for intake, reception, and orientation. The program models a therapeutic community approach including drug and alcohol abuse treatment, education, and training in life skills as well as exercise, discipline, and military drills. It includes 500 hours of physical training, 780 hours of substance abuse treatment, and 260 hours of education aimed at high school equivalency. Women also receive vocational training, focusing on skills such as upholstery repair, building maintenance skills, and toy repair (3). The focus on academic achievement is borne out by the fact that from 1988 to 1999, 86 percent of program participants who took the GED test passed, a rate considerably higher than that in prison facilities. Each year about one third of all new female admissions to the Department of Correctional Services in New York are eligible for the Shock Incarceration Program, subject to a screening process. In that process, females are less likely than males to qualify because they are often found to suffer serious health conditions such as hypertension, diabetes, or tuberculosis. They may also be precluded from admission because of mental health needs.

Female offenders are less likely than their male counterparts to complete the program; more than 66 percent of men complete the program, compared to 57 percent of the women (Clark and Kellam 2001, 4). The difference is due mainly to women's medical needs, which made women almost twice as likely as men to leave. Nevertheless, as a proportion of New York's incarcerated population, women are well represented in the program: Though they comprise 8 percent of the program's population, they make up less than 5 percent of the total prison population in New York.

In an attempt to assess the success of the program, the New York Department of Correctional Services surveyed women who had completed the program between 1989 and 1995 for a period of three years after release and compared their rates of return to prison to two other groups from the same period; that is, women who were eligible but did not enter the program, and women who dropped out of the program (Clark and Kellam 2001, 4). The assessment showed that women who completed Shock Incarceration were substantially less likely than the other groups to return to prison within three years, and in fact nearly eight out of ten graduates of the program avoided a return to prison.

The promoters of Shock Incarceration contend that a properly designed boot camp has the potential to build women's self-esteem, and women participants have credited it with promoting their sobriety and success. Since 1989 nearly 2,000 women have graduated from the New York program, which has offered a viable alternative to longer sentences for women offenders. In terms of its physical impact, shock incarceration in New York emphasizes a gradual increase in standards of physical conditioning. The program is available in New York to women with varying physical conditions (Clark and Kellam 2001, 5).

Health and Medical Issues

A number of issues relating to health and medical needs affect the situation of women in prison. Again, the tendency of correctional administrators has been to treat women as if they had the same needs as men and to apply traditional gender stereotypes to those incarcerated.

Medicalizing Women

In prison, medical examinations and checks may be imposed on women who are unable to resist or reject them due to their status as incarcerated women. This treatment may occur on occasions when women returning from court appearances may be subjected to a strip search and a check of their bodily orifices, or after a woman prisoner gives birth in the hospital, where she might be subjected to vaginal searches for contraband. Women prisoners often experience these security measures as a form of humiliation and they can be painful and dangerous, resulting in bleeding and infection. Ironically, although these searches are often routine, the administration of pap tests for cervical cancer is not often conducted despite the fact this is a standard medical practice for nonimprisoned women. Concern has also been expressed about the practice of prescribing tranquilizers and psychotropic drugs to women in prison. It has been suggested that the underlying rationale is to control female prisoners as opposed to administering to medical problems (Velimesis 1981). A recent report of the government found that 17 percent of women in jails and 23 percent of women in state prisons in the United States receive drug medication for emotional disorders, and there is a good deal of evidence that prescribing psychotropic drugs is far more common in women's prisons than men's (Greenfeld and Snell 1999). This greater allocation of tranquilizing and psychotropic drugs to women prisoners might be attributable to women suffering more severe reactions to imprisonment than men, to women experiencing trauma due to a forced separation from their children, or perhaps to prison staff seeing women as in greater need of the control that drugs can impose than male prisoners (Belknap 2001).

The issue of using chemical restraints in prisons has been considered judicially in recent years. In *Harper v. State* (1988), the Washington Supreme Court ruled that inmates had the right to refuse to take antipsychotic drugs prescribed by prison authorities and that this right could be overridden only when the state proved a compelling state interest to administer these drugs and that the administration of drugs was necessary and effective to further that interest (Auerhahn and Dermody Leonard 2000, 2). However, the U.S. Supreme Court reversed this ruling, holding that inmates could be medicated against their will if the state could show that medicating is "reasonably related to legitimate penological interests," which the court found to include "the maintenance of order in the prison environment" (2). The Court was of the opinion that because a psychiatrist must prescribe this medication, that prerequisite ensures the protection of the prisoner's medical interest. In the case of *Riggins v. Nevada* (1992) the Court ruled that administering antipsychotic drugs to jail detainees is a violation of due process because it introduces a strong possibility of prejudice into the trial process having regard to the possible impact of such drugs on a person's appearance, testimony, ability to follow the proceedings, and ability to communicate with a lawyer. According to Auerhahn and Dermody (2000, 3), it is common practice to chemically restrain healthy inmates, and jail and prison inmates are often medicated without prior diagnosis or adequate psychiatric and physical assessments.

In 1976 several women in a New York state prison were transported to a state mental hospital following a determination that they were a disciplinary problem (Auerhahn and Dermody Leonard 2000, 3). On arrival at the mental hospital, they were medicated with an antidepressant and a few days later given thorazine, an antipsychotic drug. During the period of their confinement in the hospital, other drugs were administered of an antipsychotic, antidepressant, and sedative nature as well as tranquilizers. No clinical diagnosis of mental disability was made, although staff psychiatrists did conduct brief interviews and physical examinations of each of the women that lasted ten to fifteen minutes each. After the women brought a suit against the hospital staff, the staff psychiatrist admitted that the drugs were not administered for treatment but "to maintain peace and tranquility on the ward" (3). Also, it was admitted that the drugs were sometimes administered forcibly through injections because the women did not like taking certain drugs because of their effects.

Auerhahn and Dermody Leonard (2000, 8) argue that responding to female criminality by medicalizing women has its origins in the nineteenth-century view that the cause for all women's behavior was to be found in their reproductive capacity. Thus, the nature of a woman was conceptualized as "sickly" and this, together with the rise of the medical profession, resulted in curative strategies that emphasized the reproductive function. Medical cures, therefore, focused on treating these organs and treatment contained four stages: a manual investigation, leeching, ejections, and cauterization. During the reformatory movement, this emphasis on treatment and disease of criminal women was continued, as female criminals were seen as perversions of the feminine ideal (9). Allen argues that focusing explanations for women's criminality on women's bodies and physiology serves to neutralize the threat presented by deviant women (Auerhahn and Dermody Leonard 2000, 7). The idea that a female offender is sick is seen as more appealing than the notion of a deviant woman willfully committing crimes.

In Leonard's study, drawing on interviews with forty-two women serving prison terms for the death of their abusive partners, one recurrent criticism was the use of prescription drugs while these women were committed to county jail facilities pending trial (in Auerhahn and Dermody Leonard 2000, 11). One woman reported that at the time of her arrest, she was put on drugs and told by jail administrators that she needed them. She felt that she needed something that would make her sleep to avoid thinking about what was happening to her and she noted that everyone in the jail slept all the time. Another woman, a former high school English teacher serving a sentence of twenty-five years to life, reported that she was put on both a tranquilizer and an antidepressant while in jail and during her trial. As a result, she did not testify convincingly and was told that she was perceived as cold and remorseless. She felt that the drugs made her inarticulate (12). Other women explained that they were administered drugs that were frequently ordered by nurses, psychologists, and even by correctional officers. One Native American woman repeatedly rejected psychotropic drugs and reported that jail staff attempted to force her to accept this medication in exchange for releasing her mail.

Reproductive Freedom

Studies indicate that women prisoners as well as girls in juvenile institutions are encouraged, and perhaps even forced, to give up their newborns for adoption even if they became pregnant while incarcerated (Belknap 2001). Most prisons have no facilities for giving birth, and so pregnant women inmates are transferred to nearby hospitals when they go into labor. Most states remove children from their incarcerated mothers within forty-eight hours after birth. Despite the success of a prison nursery program in New York, both California and Florida have repealed legislation allowing women to keep newborn infants in prison with them for a time (Schoenbauer 1986 in Wright 1997, 89). Only three women's prisons have a program where babies and nursing mothers can remain together for up to eighteen months (Watterson 1996, 211). These are located in Nebraska, New York, and Washington. South Dakota allows infants to remain with their mothers for up to one month after birth. The Bedford Hills Prison for Women in New York remains the only prison nursery in the country where babies are permitted to stay until they are one year old, with extensions possible if the mother's release date is within the upcoming six months (Kauffman 2001). In a study conducted in June 1992, Gabel and Girard (1995, 237) documented the New York prison nurseries that have been running for some ninety years. Expectant mothers receive prenatal care, but the living quarters for mothers and their babies are, according to the women, dilapidated and overcrowded. However, the mothers perceive the program to be valuable and important, noting especially benefits such as bonding with their children and learning acceptable parenting skills.

In Nebraska, the Correctional Center for Women, which opened its nursery in 1994, emphasizes bonding with the mother and continuity in the relationship between the child and its primary caregiver. In Nebraska, mothers who give birth may keep their children in prison only if they are due for release before the child is eighteen months old, and the prison has space for up to eight mothers on a designated floor of one building (Kauffman 2001, 63).

The newest of the prison nurseries for women opened in August 1999 at the Washington Corrections Center for Women. Here, a mother may keep her baby if she has less than three years to serve after the baby is born. The nursery is open to any mother who has custody of her child and will be the primary caregiver when released. This contrasts with other prison programs that restrict participation in prison nurseries to nonviolent offenders. The center allows up to twenty mothers and their children to occupy one wing of a ninety-bed residential unit; intensive parenting classes are provided by the Department of Correction. In an attempt to simulate real world conditions, mothers return to work at the prison, or outside the prison if they are granted work release, six weeks after birth. Other prison inmates who are trained and take part in parenting classes may also serve as caregivers.

It is also known that many women have had abortions against their will while incarcerated, and those who want abortions may not be given access to them. There are no consistent policies in women's prisons regarding contraception, abortion, and general reproductive education, and even if such services are available, it is often in a noncomprehensive or inconsistent form (Belknap 2001).

Women's Medical Needs

There is often hostility, resentment, and discrimination within the prison system toward pregnant women who have special medical needs. Studies indicate that about 5 percent of women are pregnant at the time of their intake to jails and prisons (Greenfeld and Snell 1999); a few suggest that up to one quarter of women in prison were either pregnant on intake or gave birth during the previous year. Obviously, pregnant women need prenatal care including special diets, vitamins, and medical examinations. In fact, some suggest that special nutritional needs are not limited to pregnant women and that incarcerated women in general have greater health and dietary needs than nonincarcerated women (Belknap 2001). To a far greater extent than men, women inmates seem to incur substantial weight gains and have inadequate diets. Some suggest that co-corrections, that is, incarcerating women and men in the same institution, is the answer to meeting the medical needs of women prisoners. They argue that through co-corrections, costs can be saved and the range of services offered to women increased. However, good arguments counter this view. For example, it is likely that based on gender roles outside the prison, men will capture most, if not all, leadership roles in the prison, obtain the best jobs, and dominate all education and training programs and resources. One study of a co-correctional facility found that women were routinely denied access to almost all programs conducted there (Chesney-Lind and Rodriquez 1983), and another found that co-corrections women prisoners are more likely than co-corrections men to be disciplined (Anderson

1978). As well, there is evidence in such facilities of pregnancies occurring during incarceration and of prostitution where women are coerced, or of women agreeing to perform sexual favors in return for cigarettes or contraband (Belknap 2001, 193). Thus, it is quite likely that the coeducational prison would offer no more opportunities for women than do separate women's prisons.

In one study of women's prisons in Ohio, researchers examined the structure of the health care delivery system in those prisons and the medical staff's perception of that structure (Ammar and Erez 2000). In the Ohio Reformatory for Women, which opened in 1916 and now houses about 1,700 inmates, twenty-nine of the approximately 400 staff members are part of the medical or paramedical staff. The reformatory contains a hospital with seven infirmary rooms, but the rooms are archaic and old. The state also maintains a prerelease center in Columbus housing minimum- and medium-security female inmates; it opened in 1988 and in June 1998 housed about 460 inmates. In contrast to the reformatory, this prerelease center is modern, with 135 staff, of which twelve are medical or paramedical staff. A further prerelease center opened in 1988 as a minimum- and medium-security facility; in 1998 it housed 624 inmates and employed 173 staff, thirteen of whom are nurses. The three physicians operating at the center are hired under private contract. According to one of the medical directors, the prison population has increased in recent years without an equal increase in the staff of women's prisons; the usual staffing is three nurses for every three hundred inmates, following the male model. However, women's medical needs in prison are two and a half times the rate of men's (3). According to one of the nurses interviewed in the study, most of the women were "physically a mess," and at the reformatory, one third of the inmates were said to be mentally ill and 20 percent seriously mentally ill (3). The study concluded that health care delivery in the three institutions for women is managed in a state of crisis, the institutions are overcrowded, and the health workers overworked.

The staff reported that in all three institutions there were no routine activities for medical staff and no typical day. This was because the medical staff in the institutions were responsible not only for treating medical problems but also for evaluating the medical condition of inmates who were not ill. For example, during one interview session, the medical staff were called away as one inmate in segregation had acted out emotionally and had to be restrained in a posture that placed pressure on her wrists.

According to policy, medical staff were required to assess her physical condition and report their findings.

A major complaint at all three institutions was the shortage of nurses, and lack of space was a concern in the two prerelease centers. The reformatory's infirmary was dilapidated and lacked basic amenities. It was apparent that hiring qualified candidates for correctional health care was also an issue because such staff need not only medical skills but also the skill to assess truth-telling and manipulation among the prison population, who, staff said, would use any excuse to gain medical attention and get away from the boredom of daily routine (Ammar and Erez 2000, 6). The medical staff at all three institutions agreed that female inmates preferred to be cared for inside the prisons, giving the reason that the women do not like to be treated outside because they have to be shackled and they find it demeaning (7).

Medical staff saw a need to educate women inmates about basic health practices, as most of the women had preexisting conditions that included high blood pressure, diabetes, and HIV (Ammar and Erez 2000, 9). One health administrator thought that the prisoners did not comprehend simple things such as washing their hands after using the bathroom, how to prevent and treat colds, and what was meant by immunization. He found the prisoners to be very poorly educated about health issues. One nurse observed that 75 percent of the women at one of the prisons smoked but no smoking cessation classes were available (10). Medical staff also saw a tension between the concern other staff had for correctional security and the prisoner's medical needs. For the correctional officers, safety was more important than medical needs, and in one case, an appointment with a cardiologist outside the prison for one prisoner did not take place because a correctional officer had cancelled the visit due to weather conditions and understaffing (11).

The medical staff also pointed out that the women often entered prison without having seen a physician in years and emphasized that they showed prolonged neglect and abuse of their bodies and minds (Ammar and Erez 2000, 11). One nurse found the female prison unique compared to a male facility in that

> you get them here, you dry them out, you get them off the drugs, the alcohol, get them on their mental health meds. When you walk out there, it's like a college campus. These people say "hi" and "bye." A lot of the time

they won't make eye contact because they are told not to but these people are very respectful by and large. You'd be surprised how nice they are. (12)

Also, medical staff found women to be less violent than men inside the prison. As one nurse put it, "men lash out, while women lash in. They abuse themselves; they cut themselves" (12).

Female inmates have been successful in claiming that the refusal of a prison to provide them with all medical care relating to pregnancy, including abortion, amounts to "deliberate indifference" to those needs and a violation of the Eighth Amendment since giving birth in prison is not a routine part of punishment (Farrell 2000). High miscarriage rates have been documented in correctional facilities across the country, and one study concluded that high miscarriage rates in the California correctional system were related to problems in perinatal care including difficulties in identifying women with high-risk pregnancies, problems in transporting pregnant women to outside medical facilities, and low levels of competence among correctional medical staff (McCall, Castell, and Shawl 1985). Other issues connected with pregnancy include using shackles and restraints in the delivery room, methods of transportation, and the management of perinatal drug addiction by a pregnant woman inmate.

In relation to the use of shackles during childbirth, one such experience was documented by Amnesty International (1999). The woman reported that she was handcuffed while being taken to the hospital with intense labor pains and was unable to hold her stomach or gain some ease from the pain because of the handcuffs. At the hospital, her right ankle was shackled to a metal bedpost during seven hours of labor and the shackles were not removed until thirty minutes before delivery—despite the fact that a correctional officer was present in the room with her at all times. She described the shackling as painful, traumatizing, and stressful. In another report, following a visit in 1998 to a county hospital in California, Amnesty International delegates were taken through a ward where women were held when seriously ill or in labor and for a short time after birth. The ward was locked and four armed guards stationed inside it. Despite this, each woman's leg was shackled to her bed. Prison officials explained that the shackles were only removed if a doctor certified that it was interfering with medical treatment or was injurious to the woman's health. These reports and other investigations led Amnesty International to conclude that jails and prisons use restraints on women routinely and regardless of whether a woman has a history of violence or has ever attempted an escape.

In a survey of states who allow the practice of shackling pregnant women, Amnesty International was informed that in Ohio, pregnant inmates have one arm or leg secured to the bed during labor; that in Massachusetts, pregnant inmates are transported to the hospital in handcuffs but that restraints are not used on women in active labor unless they are disruptive; that in Kentucky, pregnant inmates may not be restrained from the moment they enter labor until they leave the recovery room, but after that time one leg may be restrained; and that in Michigan, women are transported to the hospital with belly chains and handcuffs and kept in restraints while there. One woman reported that her legs were chained together until shortly before she gave birth and that she was cuffed to her bed soon after giving birth. In Illinois, all pregnant prisoners were restrained while being transported to the hospital and were kept in restraints even when in labor, unless a doctor asked for them to be removed and a correctional officer approved. In January 1999, the Department of Corrections of Illinois informed the organization that it was preparing to cease using restraints on pregnant women.

Pregnant women in prison may undergo emotional problems associated with denial of the right to choose to give birth or to terminate their pregnancy (Bloom 1995, 24). Two case studies provide examples of the issues faced by pregnant women. In *Harris v. McCarthy* (1985) the woman inmate was incarcerated for one year for a violation of probation. When five and a half months' pregnant, she began to experience cramping and vaginal bleeding and sought medical attention throughout the following weeks but was never seen by an obstetrician. After nearly three weeks, she was finally seen by the head physician, an orthopedist, who did not physically examine her yet prescribed a drug usually contraindicated during pregnancy. The following day she went into premature labor and delivered the baby in an ambulance on the way to the hospital; the baby died two hours later. In *Yeager v. Smith* (1987), the woman was incarcerated for one year on a charge of welfare fraud beginning when she was about five months' pregnant. She was obliged to sleep on a thin mattress on the floor for almost two weeks and confined twenty-four hours a day for several months in overcrowded cells. She never saw an obstetrician during her pregnancy and was exposed to several contagious diseases. Going into labor on a Friday night, she reported her condition to the guards but was told to wait until the next morning for medical assistance, as no medical staff were on duty at the time. She gave birth early the next morning on a thin mat outside the door of the clinic with the assistance of an untrained guard.

Harris v. McCarthy was the first of five suits filed on behalf of pregnant and postpartum prisoners at the California Institution for Women. The prisoners alleged that the California Department of Corrections had failed to provide adequate pre- and postnatal care or proper diets and exercise. At the time there was no obstetrician on the prison medical staff. In a comprehensive settlement agreement, the prison was required to hire an obstetrician/gynecologist, adopt protocols covering high-risk pregnancies and emergencies, increase medical staffing, and assess all pregnant women. In the second lawsuit, *Jones v. Dyer* (1986), filed on behalf of women incarcerated at a county jail in California, the plaintiffs made similar claims as well as charging that there was a lack of contact visits for incarcerated mothers and children. Again there was a settlement agreement.

Another medical issue for female inmates is that of mental illness. According to the Department of Justice in a survey report of July 1999, female inmates suffer higher rates of mental illness than do males (Bureau of Justice Statistics 1999a). The report indicates that about 13 percent of female prisoners in federal prisons and about 24 percent of female inmates in state prisons were identified as being mentally ill, compared with 7 percent of male inmates in federal prisons and about 16 percent of male inmates in state prisons. Also noted was the fact that about 64 percent of mentally ill female inmates in federal prisons and 78 percent of mentally ill female prisoners in state prisons reported prior physical or sexual abuse.

HIV/AIDS

At the end of 1995, 2.3 percent of all state and federal prisoners were reported to be HIV infected (Bureau of Justice Statistics 1997). It is commonly believed, however, that the actual number of HIV and AIDS cases is much higher than the official record due to the high concentration of intravenous drug users, and many cases are not revealed due to the long incubation period of the disease, sometimes lasting several years. Compounding the situation are prisoners who are infected with both HIV and tuberculosis. In relation to confirmed cases of AIDS, the rate in U.S. prisons is more than six times the rate in the general population, and in the period 1991–1995, about one in three inmate deaths was attributable to AIDS-related causes (Bureau of Justice Statistics 1997). At the end of 1995, 4 percent of all female state prison inmates were HIV-positive, compared to 2.3 percent of males during the same period. The number of women inmates in state prisons infected with HIV increased 88 percent, a much faster rate than that experienced by males, where the increase was 28 percent. Like their male counterparts, female inmates infected with HIV and AIDS are disproportionately minorities, poor, and have a history of intravenous drug use.

Clearly, these diseases generate special medical and psychological needs, and in prisons such needs are rendered more complex by the fact of incarceration itself. Essentially, imprisonment adds to the suffering by exacerbating feelings of depression, helplessness, and grief. Both inmates and staff devalue those inmates with HIV/AIDS to the extent that they become institutional outcasts, and the degree of fear and hostility expressed against them is often magnified in the prison environment. Misinformation about AIDS can inflame fear and cause hysteria that can result in discriminatory management practices. For example, in 1992, a female prisoner in a county jail was awarded damages for what the court termed humiliating and improper treatment when she was placed in a forensic unit within the jail that was usually reserved for suicidal and mentally disturbed inmates, was required to wear plastic gloves when she used a typewriter in the library of the jail, and was denied the right to attend Christian services (Sullivan 1992). As well, staff attached red stickers to her belongings, indicating she had AIDS, an act in violation of state law. Currently, each state, the District of Columbia, and the Federal Bureau of Prisons test their inmates for HIV on the basis of certain criteria, and most prison jurisdictions will test inmates if they have HIV-related symptoms or if an inmate requests a test. Sixteen states test all inmates, and three states and the Federal Bureau test all inmates on release from confinement. Three states test all inmates in custody, and two states as well as the Federal Bureau conduct random testing.

Prisons were never designed to provide the best of medical care, and with the onset of HIV/AIDS, the situation has deteriorated, resulting in prison litigation that has revealed cases alleging denial of proper medical care. Although this litigation has resulted in some improvements, the courts have ruled that prisoners do not have a right to every potential beneficial medical procedure and that reasonable care is constitutionally sufficient. However, questions persist as to whether inmates actually receive even basic care, and it is significant that prisoners with AIDS live about half as long following diagnosis as persons in the free community. It is commonly agreed that the lack of medical care is the outcome of deliberate indifference to the fate of prisoners or is a form of retaliation for prisoners contesting charges brought against prison administrations.

Many women sentenced to imprisonment for drug offenses as a result of the "war on drugs" are also infected with HIV or have been diagnosed with AIDS. HIV-infected women are typically minorities with low socioeconomic status, and the majority are mothers. Separation from one's family is a severe hardship for these women even under normal circumstances, and this situation is exacerbated in cases where the woman is infected with HIV/AIDS. When their children are also infected, the emotional toll for these women is still higher.

As an outcome of the "war on drugs," therefore, prisons are increasingly forced to function as providers of medical care for prisoners with HIV/AIDS. Without sufficient funding, in addition to being faced with political and public indifference, they are only in a position to aggravate the suffering caused by the disease. As well as treatment, education on HIV/AIDS is required for inmates and can be quite effective. Increasing knowledge about HIV alone might, however, be insufficient in decreasing the risk for women contracting HIV. Instead, interventions that are aimed at women offenders should also aim to increase women's ability to make decisions that might prevent HIV infection, such as condom use. Programs also need to stress the critical nature of HIV as a disease, since upon release many women inmates are more immediately concerned about financial resources, shelter, and food.

Legal Challenges—Equal Protection

The federal government is under no constitutional obligation to provide any benefits to prisoners beyond basic requirements for survival. However, this rule does not allow discrimination among the recipients of benefits, and case law has shown that benefits granted to some cannot be denied to others based on race or sex alone. In equal protection challenges, the issue is whether the separate classification is reasonable or arbitrary and if it bears "a fair and substantial relation to the object of the legislation or practice" (*Reed v. Reed* [1971]), so for example, sex classifications that have been established to suit the convenience of the correctional administrators have been held to be irrational. Most legal challenges to prison conditions have been initiated by male prisoners, largely due to the relative lack of numbers of incarcerated women. However, over time, this situation has changed and women prisoners have brought actions arguing for parity with male prisoners using equal protection and due process clauses. Women have been successful in challenging disparate treatment in the case of a parole system, where male prisoners in the District of Columbia were placed under the control of the D.C. Board of Parole whereas women were subjected to the stricter standards for women applied by the U.S. Board of Parole (*Williams v. Levi* [1976]). In another case, the court held that there must be substantial equivalence in male and female prisoner opportunities to take part in work-furlough programs (*Dawson v. Carberry* [1973]).

Women have brought suit to ensure their access to a prison law library when the court found they had limited access to it compared to male prisoners (*Bounds v. Smith* [1977]); in addition, a strip search policy requiring women to be subjected to a full strip search whereas men were not stripped without substantial reason (based on possession of a weapon or contraband) was ruled to be a violation of the Constitution (*Mary Beth G. v. City of Chicago* [1983]). The practice in North Dakota of routinely transferring women prisoners to serve their sentence in another state prison because of alleged lack of facilities was ruled to be a denial of equal protection. When this matter was brought before the court, it held that such transfers outside the state must not take place without a prior hearing (*State ex rel Olson v. Maxwell* [1977]). The courts have also ruled that discriminatory selection for work release, if based on race, religion, sex, or mental impairment, is not a lawful practice. Such arbitrary or capricious selection for work programs has since been prohibited.

A landmark case on women's prison issues is *Glover v. Johnson* (1979), where a comprehensive challenge was mounted to a system that permitted disparate treatment in educational, vocational, and minimum security programs in the Michigan prisons.

The court held that women prisoners must be provided with programming of parity with that given male prisoners, and the court further ordered the state to provide specific programs, stating that the size of the institution was no justification for disparate treatment for women inmates.

The Prison Litigation Reform Act, enacted in 1996, stated its two purposes as curbing the filing of frivolous lawsuits by prisoners and ending what was thought to be judicial micro-management of correctional facilities through suits brought by prisoners in federal and state courts (Branham 2001, 3). In relation to frivolous lawsuits, the act requires that prisoners must first seek redress for wrongs through a grievance process operated by the correctional authority and that any such process must be exhausted before a lawsuit can be filed. Further, prisoners must pay the full court-filing fee when bringing a lawsuit or appeal in federal court. In addition, the Act directs courts to dismiss claims that are considered frivolous, malicious, or fail to state a claim for which relief can be granted, or seek damages against a defendant with immunity from such claims. Under the act, prisoners may not obtain relief for mental or emotional injuries suffered in custody unless those injuries are associated with some form of physical injury. Indigent prisoners who have already filed three or more civil actions or appeals that were dismissed for being frivolous, malicious, or for failure to state a claim are required to prepay the full filing fee before a court will adjudicate their claims. Further, the act also placed limits and restrictions on the kinds of relief that can be granted and severely limits prospective relief, which must be narrowly drawn and must be the least intrusive means of rectifying any violation. There are further restrictions on the recovery of attorney's fees by prisoners involving limits to the kinds of work for which such fees can be awarded (Branham 2001, 4).

Possible Solutions

What do women in prison need provided for them in order to avoid the kinds of behavior after release that put them in prison in the first place? What can be done both inside prisons and outside in the community to assist in this goal? Should women be put in prison at all? Are there alternatives to imprisonment for women that, while sanctioning their criminal conduct, could more appropriately take account of the many factors, specific to women, that make imprisonment such a severe experience for many of them? These and other questions are concerned with women's criminality in the broad sense and with seeking solutions for the benefit of women and society generally. Many solutions have been proposed; the following discussion represents the range of possibilities.

Decriminalize Offenses for Which Women Are Imprisoned

At one end of the continuum, some argue that the imprisonment of women is directly related to their status under patriarchy, and that imprisoning women is another means of social control and a manifestation of male dominance over women in society generally. Women's crimes, it is argued, have often been based on a sexual definition, and the nature of their imprisonment simply reflects their position in society. It is also argued that the rising numbers of incarcerated women result from society's failure to properly provide for the needs of women and children who live marginalized lives through poverty, lack of education, and lack of economic self-sufficiency. Social and economic factors operate to make the commission of crime a reasonable choice for some women in light of the lack of any viable alternative that will enable them to support themselves and their children. This view blames women's incarceration on policy makers and insists that proper social and economic arrangements for women would result in a huge decrease in women's criminality. Therefore, the argument goes, most women's "criminality" is not in fact criminal, and these women should not be treated as a criminal class, with all that that implies for them and their children. At the other end of the continuum, the case is made that women should be treated equally with men and that they must suffer the consequences of the choices they make, including equally lengthy imprisonment in appropriate cases.

The notion that acts now judged as criminal should be reevaluated is exemplified in the proposal that the offense of possessing crack cocaine should be decriminalized. Some argue that drug possession as opposed to trafficking in drugs is not a criminal but rather a social issue and that possession of such a drug should be seen as a health issue rather than as criminality. Questioning assumptions about criminality in this way could lead us to the conclusion that women, in particular, should not be labeled as criminals for simple drug possession. Instead of being incarcerated for drug possession, they would be provided treatment for drug abuse. Similar suggestions have been made about prostitution, but it is obvious that decriminalization requires that society ask itself difficult questions and challenge long held assumptions. Consequently, there is little likelihood that the accepted criminal models will be totally abrogated.

Also associated with decriminalization is the argument that women's prisons exist today to deal with the failures of other social institutions rather than with "real criminality" (Owen 1998). The proponents of this view argue that institutions such as the family, the school, and the labor market fail to provide women with the economic and educational opportunities they require for survival for both themselves and their children. For women, the family can be a place, not of comfort and security, but of sexual and physical violence. When a woman who has been battered physically and psychologically can see no way out of her pain but to assault or even kill her spouse or partner, those same justice agencies that were unwilling or unable to protect her now label her a criminal that requires punishment through incarceration. Similarly, for many women school is a place of failure rather than learning and accomplishment, handicapping their ability to survive in a society that has little sympathy for those who cannot keep up. It is argued that problems of this nature are best addressed outside the punitive custodial environment; however, in present-day society, complex problems of this nature are still the province of the criminal justice system. Many argue that attacking the root causes of these institutional failures is the only way to resolve them. In the main, prison is an institution designed for men and one that seems confused about the issue of women in prison. It has been adapted in order to incarcerate women but the institution itself does not seem comfortable in this role. Therefore, decriminalization would be an important first step in recognizing the failure of society to properly define the complex problems that go with being a woman in contemporary society.

Develop Community Interventions for Female Offenders

We have seen that most female crime is not of a serious nature, and in light of this conclusion it has been argued that appropriate community sanctions should be developed that can offer treatment for female offenders. Community-based programs of this kind could include vocational training and substance abuse treatment, and in general, programs designed to facilitate and promote self-sufficient and productive lives. Programs of this nature would also be economically sensible compared to the high cost of imprisonment, and would promote the notion that early intervention is a more appropriate policy approach to women's crime than after-the-fact sanctions.

Avoid Confinement by Increased Use of Probation and Parole

Both probation and parole are forms of conditional release; failure to comply with one of the rules or conditions of probation or parole constitutes grounds for incarcerating or reincarcerating the person released. Although there is a continuing movement toward developing a determinate structure of sentencing with fixed terms of imprisonment, about 78 percent of all persons released from prisons continue to be released into parole field supervision. In many states, including those that have abolished or curtailed discretionary release on parole, inmates are released to parole supervision at the expiration of their maximum sentence less time off for good behavior. Though it is consistent with "get tough on crime" policies to keep people in prison for long prison terms, eventually this becomes a very expensive exercise. For example, it has been estimated that if the state of Texas were to abolish parole for all nonviolent offenders for the next fifty years, the Texas government would need to construct almost 61,000 new prison beds, costing $1.9 billion (Austin 1996).

Large numbers of convicted men and women already are on probation or parole throughout the United States. At the end of 1996, almost 3.8 million adults were on probation or parole, with the majority of them under the supervision of probation and about 18 percent on parole (Bureau of Justice Statistics 1999b). Of those on probation, approximately 21 percent were female, and women comprised 10 percent of all parolees. Quite apart from the expense of imprisoning large numbers of women and separating them from their children with all the hardship that provokes, it can be argued that the vast majority of women in prison continue to be incarcerated for nonviolent crimes and ought properly to be released on probation or placed on parole to serve their sentences in the community. It can hardly be said that such women would

constitute a danger to society. Unfortunately, law-and-order policies and the rhetoric associated with criminality tend to obscure
this reality.

Make More Use of Local Jails in the Women's Community

This idea envisages that rather than sending women long dis-
tances to prisons located away from their families, they would do
their time in local jails and so would have access to their families
and be able to maintain cohesion within the family rather than the
dislocation and disruption that imprisonment in a regular
women's prison would cause. Those opposed to this view point
to the general lack of capacity in jails, which are often overcrowded in urban areas, and to the lack of facilities for larger
numbers of women prisoners. Admittedly, treatment and training
programs are often nonexistent in jails because these institutions
are only intended to keep persons in custody for relatively short
periods. Opponents of keeping women prisoners in local jails
therefore stress that women prisoners would be denied even the
limited benefits in terms of training and education currently
available in women's prisons.

Design Treatment Programs Specifically for Women's Problems

The enormous population growth in women's prisons has exacerbated the issue of treatment and training programs for women
inmates. Since 1980 the number of women prisoners has grown
more than 500 percent. Within the prison, women are often provided with treatment programs or work assignments that do not
promote economic self-sufficiency; this lack of financial stability
is very often the reason a woman commits a crime. Most women
in prison lack employment skills and education, yet they still
must support themselves and their children after release. It
makes sense, therefore, to devote resources in prison to the promotion of economic self-sufficiency so that women can emerge
from confinement with skills and assets that will furnish them
with stable employment. Economic self-sufficiency is central to
women's success following imprisonment and in keeping out of
prison in future.

Similarly, substance abuse treatment is critical for women in prison if they are to have any success after their release. The message is clear from the data: Drug-related crime is the single most significant cause of women's imprisonment, and substance abuse acts as a multiplier for other high-risk behavior, as women may turn to petty theft, prostitution, and other criminal acts to support a drug habit. This means it is essential for substance abuse programs, specifically designed for women, to be conducted within prisons. Historically, such programs have been designed by men for men because of the preponderance of male prisoners in the criminal justice system in need of such treatment. Generally, male-oriented drug programs are inappropriate and ineffective for women inmates and have been characterized as hierarchical, punitive, and psychologically destructive for women, who tend to have self-esteem issues of a more serious nature than male prisoners. As a result, programs designed specifically for women tend to be less confrontational and provide more nurturing experiences for those participating. Experience has shown that drug abuse may recur after release from prison for both men and women unless there is adequate aftercare upon release into the community. Thus, community support is essential to complement in-prison substance abuse programs. A treatment approach to substance abuse is also cost-effective. For example, one recent study conducted in California found that every dollar invested in substance abuse treatment generated seven dollars in savings, mainly through reductions in crime and reduced hospitalizations.

Many women sent to prison have experienced trauma in the form of violence within the family, lack adequate parenting skills, or have been incarcerated because of personal issues that have affected their lives in ways that have led to criminal conduct. For this reason, prison programs should address issues that concern women and the family. Surveys have shown that programs that help women learn better parenting skills or that increase and make more effective use of their visitation with their children are in high demand by women inmates. Individual and group counseling should address a wide range of personal and emotional issues. Sexual and physical abuse need to be tackled in a context where women can express their involvement with such issues and attempt to resolve the way they have affected their lives. If this opportunity for treatment is lost, there is every likelihood women will recidivate, and prison will become a revolving door for these women.

There is considerable variance between treatment programs for women in state prisons and those offered in federal prisons. In the latter, programs, especially those that are vocational in nature, tend to be more varied and to provide a higher level of compensation. Often the most tangible gain from employment during incarceration is that women are able to save money that can be used for expenses on release. In one example of an appropriate federal program, one woman was able to qualify as a pipe fitter. Another woman incarcerated in that system was able to secure a real estate license and a nurse's aid certificate during her confinement of almost five years. Despite these examples, neither system offers very much in the way of programs intended to prepare women for release from prison.

Devote More Resources to the Prevention of Crimes that Result in Women's Incarceration

Under this proposal, greater attention would be paid to crimes such as domestic violence and to improving the economic and support systems for women generally so they are able to maintain their families without recourse to criminality. The argument here is that women's crimes are largely confined to minor property crimes and drug abuse, and attacking the root causes of such crimes is a far more effective way of dealing with women than incarcerating them. Of course, many would argue that women should not be given a "free pass" for their crimes, and this proposal would give them disparate treatment not afforded to male criminals.

Employ Restorative Justice Options in Place of Imprisonment

This relatively new field offers a new vision for dealing with criminality that takes the form of interpersonal conflict. Through its mechanisms such as victim-offender mediation programs, family group conferencing, and community-based sentencing boards, responsibility for dealing with interpersonal conflict is taken on by the communities affected by such problems. Restorative justice emphasizes dialogue, negotiation, and the reestablishment of a positive relationship between the offender, the community, and the victim. In practical terms, this means that the offender may have to pay financial compensation to the victim, perform community service, or undergo mediation in the form of a face-to-face acknowledgment of guilt. The overall goal of such programs is to build and maintain a healthy community with positive social relations. Interest in restorative justice has grown worldwide; programs have spread throughout Europe and are especially significant in Australia and New Zealand. In the United States, victim-offender mediation currently is being practiced in more than 290 communities. As of 1998, fifteen states had drafted or proposed legislation promoting restorative justice programs within their juvenile justice systems. At this early stage, there is some evidence to indicate that restorative justice programs have the potential to provide an attractive alternative to custodial sentencing and would assist in reducing the size of the prison population (Beckett 2000, 202).

Allow Women Prisoners to Keep Their Children in Prison

This is a controversial topic, with some arguing that women inmates should be permitted to keep infants and young children with them during their period of incarceration and others maintaining that innocent children should not be exposed to the environment of the prison. It can be argued that it is unfair and a hardship for the mother to be deprived of the custody of her child, especially when the result is that children are often moved from one caretaker to another, from one school to another, and generally suffer major disruptions and dislocations during the formative period in their lives. Prisons and jails have different policies concerning visitation with children and the placement of babies born to women inmates. As we have seen, in the early years of women's prisons and reformatories, administrators often permitted women to keep their children with them until they were two years old, and some provided nurseries and encouraged women to make use of them. In recent times the decision about the placement of babies born to pregnant women in prison has been made by social workers who have elected either to place the infant with relatives or to put the infant up for adoption. According to the American Correctional Association, only two U.S. prisons allow extended visits between mothers and children; however, there are a few prisons that allow women to keep custody of their children up to the age of two years (Baunach 1982, 1992; Schupak 1986). By contrast, in Canada, women prisoners may keep their children with them up to the age of five or six years (Vachon 1994). In a recent study, over half of the mothers in prison surveyed reported that their children had never visited them in prison and that distance between the child's home and the prison was the most-cited reason (Bloom 1993). By its very nature, imprisonment imposes serious constraints to the maintenance of mother-child relations. Child welfare laws commonly allow termination of parental rights if a parent fails to maintain an adequate relationship with a child placed in foster care. In some cases, the mere existence of a prison sentence has been regarded as adequate justification to negate women's parental rights. Clearly, it is difficult for women to respond to custody rights hearings in court, and often there is no available legal assistance or no person present to represent the woman prisoner. Overall, the development of a consistent and comprehensive policy on women prisoners and their children that would recognize the hardship caused to both the parent and the child resulting from incarceration would ultimately benefit mother, child, and society.

Sources

American Correctional Association. 1990. *The Female Offender: What Does the Future Hold?* Arlington, VA: Kirby Lithographic Company.

Ammar, Nawal, and Edna Erez. 2000. "Health Delivery Systems in Women's Prisons: The Case of Ohio." *Federal Probation* 64 (1): 19–26.

Amnesty International. 1999. *"Not Part of My Sentence"—Violations of the Human Rights of Women in Custody.* AI Index AMR 51/19/99, New York, NY. Available online: http://www.amnestyusa.org/rightsforall/women/report/women-27.html. Accessed June 28, 2002.

Anderson, David. 1978. "Co-Corrections." *Corrections Magazine* 4: 33–41.

Atwood, Jane Evelyn. 2000. *Too Much Time: Women in Prison.* London: Phaidon Press.

Auerhahn, Kathleen, and Elizabeth Dermody Leonard. 2000. "Docile Bodies? Chemical Restraints and the Female Inmate." *Journal of Criminal Law and Criminology* 90 (2): 599–634.

Austin, James. 1996. "The Effect of 'Three Strikes and You're Out' on Corrections." In *Three Strikes and You're Out: Vengeance as Public Policy,* edited by D. Shichor and D. Sechrest. Thousand Oaks, CA: Sage.

Austin, James, and John Irwin. 2001. *It's about Time: America's Imprisonment Binge.* 3d ed. Belmont, CA: Wadsworth.

Balogh, T. 1964. "Conjugal Visiting in Prisons: A Sociological Perspective." *Federal Probation* 28 (September): 52–58.

Banks, Cyndi. 2002. "Doing Time in Alaska: Women, Culture, and Crime." In *It's a Crime: Women and Justice*, 3d ed., edited by R. Muraskin. Upper Saddle River, NJ: Prentice-Hall.

Baunach, Phyllis. 1982. "You Can't Be a Mother and Be in Prison . . . Can You? Impacts of the Mother-Child Separation." In *The Criminal Justice System and Women*, edited by B. Price and N. Sokoloff. New York: Clark and Boardman.

Bazzetta v. Mcginnis, Director of Michigan Department of Corrections. 2001. 148 F. Supp. 2d 813, 2001 U.S. Dist. Lexis 8819 (E.D. Mich. 2001): United States Court of Appeals For the Sixth Circuit, 2001.

Beckett, Katherine, and Theodore Sasson. 2000. *The Politics of Injustice: Crime and Punishment in America*. Thousand Oaks, CA: Pine Forge Press.

Belknap, Joanne. 2000. "Programming and Health Care Accessibility for Incarcerated Women." In *States of Confinement: Policing, Detention, and Prisons*, edited by Joy James. New York: Palgrave.

———. 2001. *The Invisible Woman: Gender, Crime, and Justice*. 2d ed. Belmont, CA: Wadsworth.

Bloom, Barbara. 1993. "Incarcerated Mothers and Their Children: Maintaining Family Ties." In *Female Offenders: Meeting the Needs of a Neglected Population*, edited by A. C. Association. Laurel, MD: American Correctional Association.

———. 1995. "Imprisoned Mothers." In *Children of Incarcerated Parents*, edited by Katherine Gabel and Denise Johnston. New York: Lexington Books.

Bloom, Barbara, and D. Steinhart. 1993. *Why Punish the Children? A Reappraisal of the Children of Incarcerated Mothers in America*. San Francisco: National Council on Crime and Delinquency.

Bloom, Barbara, and Meda Chesney-Lind. 2000. "Women in Prison: Vengeful Equity." In *It's a Crime: Women and Justice*, edited by R. Muraskin. Upper Saddle River, NJ: Prentice-Hall.

Boston Globe. "Women Get $10m for Strip Searches at Mass. Jail." Available online: http://www.corrections.com/news/justin/todayoncc. html. Accessed May 30, 2002.

Branham, Lynn. 2001. "Toothless in Truth? The Ethereal Rational Basis Test and the Prison Litigation Reform Act's Disparate Restrictions on Attorney's Fees." *California Law Review* 89: 999–1,053.

Brennan, T. 1998. "Institutional Classification of Females: Problems and Some Proposals for Reform." In *Female Offenders: Critical Perspectives and Effective Interventions*, edited by R. Zaplin. Gaithersburg, MD: Aspen Publishers.

Bureau of Justice Statistics. 1995. *National Crime Victimization Survey.* Washington, DC: U.S. Department of Justice.

―――. 1997. *HIV in Prisons and Jails, 1995.* Washington, DC: U.S. Department of Justice.

―――. 1999a. *Mental Health and Treatment of Inmates and Probationers.* Washington, DC: Bureau of Justice Statistics Special Report (July).

―――. 1999b. *Correctional Populations in the United States, 1996.* Washington, DC: U.S. Department of Justice.

―――. 2001. *Prisoners in 2000.* Washington, DC: U.S. Department of Justice.

Bush-Baskette, Stephanie. 1999. "The 'War on Drugs': A War against Women?" In *Harsh Punishment: International Experiences of Women's Imprisonment,* edited by S. Cook and S. Davies. Boston: Northeastern University Press.

Butterfield, Fox. 1999. "As Inmate Populations Grow, So Does a Focus on Children." *New York Times,* 7 April.

Carlson, Bonnie, and Neil Cervera. 1992. *Inmates and Their Wives: Incarceration and Family Life.* Westport, CT: Greenwood Press.

Casey, Karen, and Michael Wiatrowski. 1996. "Women Offenders and 'Three Strikes and You're Out.'" In *Three Strikes and You're Out: Vengeance as Public Policy,* edited by D. Shichor and D. Sechrest. Thousand Oaks, CA: Sage.

Chesney-Lind, Meda. 1995. "Rethinking Women's Imprisonment: A Critical Examination of Trends in Female Incarceration." In *The Criminal Justice System and Women: Offenders, Victims, and Workers,* edited by B. Price and N. Sokoloff. New York: McGraw-Hill.

Chesney-Lind, Meda, and Noelie Rodriguez. 1983. "Women under Lock and Key." *Prison Journal* 63: 47–65.

Clark, Cheryl, and Leslie Kellam. 2001. "These Boots Are Made for Women." *Corrections Today* 63 (February): 50–54.

Dobash, Russell, Emerson Dobash, and Sue Gutteridge. 1986. *The Imprisonment of Women.* Oxford: Basil Blackwell.

Faith, Karlene. 1993. *Unruly Women: The Politics of Confinement and Resistance.* Vancouver: Press Gang Publishers.

Farrell, Amy. 2000. "Prisoner Rights." In *Encyclopedia of Women and Crime,* edited by N. Rafter. Phoenix, AZ: Oryx Press.

Fishman, L. 1990. *Women at the Wall: A Study of Prisoners' Wives Doing Time on the Outside.* Albany: State University of New York Press.

Fishman, S. 1983. "The Impact of Incarceration on Children of Offenders." *Journal of Children in Contemporary Society* 15: 89–99.

Fleming, Gary, and Gerald Winkler. 1999. "Sending Them to Prison: Washington State Learns to Accommodate Female Youthful Offenders in Prison." *Corrections Today* 61 (2): 132–135.

Fowler, Lorraine. 1993. "What Classification for Women?" In *Classification: A Tool for Managing Today's Offenders*, edited by A. C. Association. Lanham, MD: American Correctional Association.

Freedman, Estelle. 2000. *Their Sister's Keepers: Women's Prison Reform in America, 1830–1930*. Ann Arbor: University of Michigan Press.

Gabel, Katherine, and Kathryn Girard. 1995. "Long-Term Care Nurseries in Prisons: A Descriptive Study." In *Children of Incarcerated Parents*, edited by Katherine Gabel and Denise Johnston. New York: Lexington Books.

Gaudin, J. 1984. "Social Work Role and Tasks with Incarcerated Mothers." *Social Casework* 65: 279–286.

Gerber v. Hickman 103 F. Supp. 2d 1214, 2000 U.S. Dist. Lexis 13124 (E.D. Cal. 2000).

Giallombardo, Rose. 1966. *Society of Women: A Study of a Women's Prison*. New York: John Wiley & Sons.

Glick, Ruth, and Virginia Neto. 1977. *National Study of Women's Correctional Programs*. Washington, DC: National Institute of Law Enforcement and Criminal Justice.

Goetting, A. 1982. "Conjugal Association in Prison: The Debate and Its Resolutions." *New England Journal on Prison Law* 8: 141–154.

Gover, Angela, Gaylene Styve, and Doris McKenzie. 1999. "Evaluating Correctional Boot Camp Programs." In *The Dilemmas of Corrections: Contemporary Readings*, 4th ed., edited by Kenneth Haas and Geoffrey Alpert. Prospect Heights, IL: Waveland Press.

Greenfeld, Lawrence, and Tracy Snell. 1999. *Women Offenders*. Washington, DC: Bureau of Justice Statistics, U.S. Department of Justice.

Greer, Kimberly. 2000. "The Changing Nature of Interpersonal Relationships in a Women's Prison." *The Prison Journal* 80 (4): 442–468.

Grobsmith, Elizabeth. 1994. *Indians in Prison: Incarcerated Native Americans in Nebraska*. Lincoln: University of Nebraska Press.

Harris v. McCarthy. No. 85-6002 JGD (C.D. Cal, filed September 11, 1985).

Hawkins, Richard. 1999. "Inmate Adjustments in Women's Prisons." In *The Dilemmas of Corrections: Contemporary Readings*, 4th ed., edited by Kenneth Haas and Geoffrey Alpert. Prospect Heights, IL: Waveland Press.

Heffernan, Esther. 1972. *Making It in Prison: The Square, the Cool, and the Life*. New York: John Wiley & Sons.

Heney, Jan. 1990. *Report on Self-Injurious Behaviour in the Kingston Prison for Women*. Ottawa: Ministry of the Solicitor General, Corrections Branch.

Henriques, Zelma, and Evelyn Gilbert. 2000. "Sexual Abuse and Sexual Assault of Women in Prison." In *It's a Crime: Women and Justice*, edited by R. Muraskin. Upper Saddle River, NJ: Prentice-Hall.

Holmes, S. A. 1996. "With More Women in Prison, Sexual Abuse by Guards Becomes Greater Concern." *New York Times*, December 27, 9.

Howser, J., and D. MacDonald. 1982. "Maintaining Family Ties." *Corrections Today* 44: 96–98.

Howser, J., J. Grossman, and D. MacDonald. 1983. "Impact of Family Reunion Program on Institutional Discipline." *Journal of Offender Counseling, Services and Rehabilitation* 8: 27–36.

Hughes, J. E. 1982. "My Daddy's Number Is C–92760." *Journal of Children in Contemporary Society* 15: 79–87.

Kauffman, Kelsey. 2001. "Mothers in Prison." *Corrections Today* (February): 62–65.

Koban, Linda. 1983. "Parent in Prison: A Comparative Analysis of the Effects of Incarceration on the Families of Men and Women." *Research in Law, Deviance and Social Control* 5: 171–183.

MacKenzie, D., and H. Donaldson. 1996. "Boot Camp for Women Offenders." *Criminal Justice Review* 21: 21–43.

Mahan, Sue. 1984. "Imposition of Despair: An Ethnography of Women in Prison." *Justice Quarterly* 1: 357–384.

McCall, C., J. Casteel, and N. Shaw. 1985. *Pregnancy in Prison: A Needs Assessment of Perinatal Outcome in Three California Penal Institutions.* Sacramento, CA: Department of Health.

McClellan, D. S. 1994. "Disparity in the Discipline of Male and Female Inmates in Texas Prisons." *Women & Criminal Justice* 5 (2): 71–97.

Morris, Allison. 1987. *Women, Crime, and Criminal Justice.* Oxford: Basil Blackwell.

Nelson, Lane. 2000. "Women on Death Row." In *Death Watch: A Death Penalty Anthology*, edited by L. Nelson and B. Foster. Upper Saddle River, NJ: Prentice-Hall.

Owen, Barbara. 1998. *"In the Mix": Struggle and Survival in a Women's Prison.* Albany: State University of New York Press.

Pollock-Byrne, Joycelyn M. 1986. *Sex and Supervision: Guarding Male and Female Inmates.* New York: Greenwood Press.

———. 1990. *Women, Prison, and Crime.* Belmont, CA: Wadsworth Publishing.

Raeder, M. S. 1993. "Gender and Sentencing: Single Moms, Battered Women, and Other Sex-Based Anomalies in the Gender-Free World of the Federal Sentencing Guidelines." *Pepperdine Law Review* 20: 905–990.

Rosenfeld, J., M. Rosenstein, and M. Raab. 1973. "Sailor Families: The Nature and Effects of One Kind of Father Absence." *Child Welfare* 52: 33–44.

Ross, Luana. 2000. "Imprisoned Native Women and the Importance of Native Traditions." In *States of Confinement: Policing, Detention, and Prisons*, edited by J. James. New York: St. Martin's Press.

Sabol, W. J., and J. McGready. 1999. *Time Served in Prison by Federal Offenders, 1986–97*. Washington, DC: U.S. Government Printing Office.

Sack, W. H. 1977. "Children of Imprisoned Fathers." *Psychiatry* 40: 163–174.

Sack, W., J. Seidler, and S. Thomas. 1976. "The Children of Imprisoned Parents: A Psychosocial Exploration." *American Journal of Orthopsychiatry* 46: 618–628.

Schupak, Terri. 1986. "Comments: Women and Children First: An Examination of the Unique Needs of Women in Prison." *Golden Gate University Law Review* 16: 455–474.

Sherman, L., D. Gottfredson, D. MacKenzie, J. Eck, P. Reuter, and S. Bushway. 1997. *Preventing Crime: What Works, What Doesn't, What's Promising: A Report to the U.S. Congress*. Vol. NCJ 165366. Washington, DC: National Institute of Justice.

Streib, Victor. 1995. "Capital Punishment of Female Offenders." Unpublished manuscript. Cleveland-Marshal College of Law, Cleveland State University.

Sullivan, R. 1992. "Ex-inmate Wins Award in Bias Case." *New York Times*, August 26, 4.

Swan, A. 1981. *Families of Black Prisoners*. Boston: G. K. Hall & Co.

Turner v. Safley. 1987. 482 U.S. 78, 107 S. Ct. 2254, 96 L. Ed. 2d 64.

U.S. General Accounting Office. 1999a. *Women in Prison: Issues and Challenges Confronting U.S. Correctional Systems: Report to the Honorable Eleanor Holmes Norton, House of Representatives*. Washington, DC: General Accounting Office.

———. 1999b. *Women in Prison: Sexual Misconduct by Correctional Staff: Report to the Honorable Eleanor Holmes Norton, House of Representatives*. Washington, DC: General Accounting Office.

Vachon, Maria. 1994. "It's about Time: The Legal Context of Policy Changes for Female Offenders." *Forum on Corrections* 6: 3–6.

Vazquez v. New Jersey Department of Corrections. 2002. 348 N.J. Super. 70, 791 A. 2d 281; 2002 N.J. Super. LEXIS 88.

Velimesis, M. I. 1981. "Sex Roles and Mental Health of Women in Prison." *Professional Psychology* 12 (1): 128–135.

Ward, David, and Gene Kassebaum. 1965. *Women's Prison: Sex and Social Structure*. Chicago: Aldine-Atherton.

Watterson, Kathryn, and Meda Chesney-Lind. 1996. *Women in Prison: Inside the Concrete Womb*. Boston: Northeastern University Press.

Williams, M. 1996. "Bill Seeks to Protect Inmates from Guards who Seek Sex." *New York Times*, April 23, A1, B4.

Winifred, Mary. 1996. "Vocational and Technical Training Programs for Women in Prison." *Corrections Today* 58 (August): 168–170.

Wright, Richard. 1997. "Should Prisons Exist?" In *Corrections: An Issues Approach*, 4th ed., edited by M. Schwartz and L. Travis. Cincinnati, OH: Anderson.

Yager v. Smith. 1987. No. CN-F-87-493-R.E.C. (E.D. Cal., filed September 2, 1987).

3

Voices of Women behind Bars

Having considered many of the issues surrounding the imprisonment of women, it is helpful to now gain an understanding of the actual experience of women in prison and of the circumstances that led to their incarceration. A recent development in researching prisons has been the publication of studies that allow prisoners, including women prisoners, to express their experience of imprisonment and reveal the circumstances of their lives before prison. This kind of research has been promoted by feminists who see women's voices as an essential component of such studies, believing that only the authentic everyday experience of women can accurately communicate the feeling of being an incarcerated woman. Research studies have provided a means for women to articulate the experience of incarceration, and these projects add another dimension to the facts and figures of women's imprisonment (Owen 1998; Bosworth 1999; Banks 2002; Atwood 2000; Watterson 1996; Wojda and Rowse 1997).

Victims of Domestic Violence

Janet is serving the first year of a sentence of seven to twenty-five years. She is a maximum-security inmate who killed her husband during an argument. She is in her late thirties. She explains that her husband made her keep her hair short and forbid her using makeup because he did not want her to be attractive to other men.

He was very manipulative. I was very much in a prison. I was under watch all the time. I have more freedom here than I had in my own marriage. (Wojda and Rowse 1997, 7)

She recounts the details of her abusive marriage. Her husband checked on her all the time at work, and she was constantly made aware of how to act and how to dress. She tried to leave but always went back; when she did leave he would seek her out and bring her back. In the prison she is a member of a battered women's group, and she explains that there are women in the prison who have suffered her kind of experience in marriage and so they understand her situation.

I never thought I'd end up in prison. I never did anything wrong before. But something happened. I'm still trying to understand why. (ibid.)

Lori Girshick reports that of the forty women she interviewed in a medium-security prison in western North Carolina, 90 percent had been abused as adults, with 85 percent having been physically battered by an intimate; 83 percent were emotionally abused; and 43 percent had been raped (1999, 57). One woman described her battering:

The first time he beat me, he nearly killed me. He had struck me so hard I had six concussions. I had a broke nose, he knocked out my tooth. I had stitches all the way across my body on the inside of my body. I looked like something from the monster's club 'cause my face was all swelled. He beat me and I took a warrant out on him and he came and broke in my house the next night. They didn't even keep him in jail. And when he raped me and left, I felt so nasty. I felt so dirty. And now, I have no choice but to go back to him. They weren't keeping him in jail. I was scared to death. I would either commit murder or live with it. And so, I live with it for about another four months. (59)

Crack Cocaine Users

Lois is serving three to ten years for burglary and one year for violation of probation. She has used marijuana since the age of thirteen. Her father was a drug dealer, and drugs, she explains, were always available for free to her. When she was arrested in 1986, she had been "shooting up speed" for six years. She also had been introduced to crack cocaine, and for about two months before her imprisonment she lived for nothing else.

I didn't care about my kids. I didn't care about nothing but smoking crack. I was breaking in houses to get more crack. I turned to prostitution. I turned to the streets, lying, stealing. And it took me down real quick. (Wojda and Rowse 1997, 12)

She says her husband is an alcoholic and she persuaded him to smoke crack with her. She notes an absence of discipline in her life, never being told what to do or where to go and being put out of the house at the age of fifteen because she was considered old enough to manage on her own.

Girshick (1999) reveals how drug addiction rules the life of a thirty-year-old woman who has prostituted herself and been in trouble since she was a juvenile:

I've used alcohol everyday for the past 15 years. I've had frequent blackouts. I say and do things I can't remember the next day. . . . I was a heroin addict for about 3 years. I used every day, otherwise I'd be sick. . . . I was a heavy, heavy addict; once I start smoking cocaine I can't stop. I could smoke a thousand dollars a day, I was bad. . . . I like anything that feels good and makes me not have to deal with anything. (69)

Victims of Child Sexual, Physical, and Emotional Abuse

Leora is now forty-one years old and into her third prison sentence. Here is her story:

I was an abused child. I was raped when I was a kid. I couldn't perform with my husband because of what had happened as a kid. (Wojda and Rowse 1997, 14)

She explains that she met a man on the street who made her feel good about herself and she started to write bad checks to buy his love and affection and ended up in prison.

More than half of the women Girshick interviewed reported being emotionally abused as children or adolescents, such as in the following narrative:

[My dad] would make us stand and strip, literally, strip naked. Then he would whup us with switches, I mean, until blood would run out of our legs, or wherever, on us. He did it until I was sixteen years old and then I finally told him "no." He started beating me with fists, and I started hitting him back, which left no respect for neither one of us. I take that as it was sort of not right in the head. Because a normal person wouldn't stand and make a child that's not a child anymore, that's already been turned into a woman, stand naked and gloat and whup 'em and stuff. (Girshick 1999, 35–36)

Another woman relates that her parent's drug abuse influenced her own drug and alcohol problem:

I think [my childhood emotional abuse is] where my drug and alcohol problem comes from. And it really bothers me. I figure that if I was loved more and paid more attention to, instead of my parents running around doing their own thing. Of course, they were hooked on drugs, too. My parents were hippies and stuff, and they were just, they ran crazy, I guess. Not so much my dad, but after my mother left him he did find a girlfriend. But he was always there. [My mother] drug-overdosed when I was eight years old . . . but I can remember her. She'd be under the table, eating pills. I remember her being on the telephone, lying on the floor. (38–39).

Prison Life

Nancy became a realtor at the age of twenty-two and had a flourishing career by the age of thirty. She purchased a downtown block, and after a fire broke out, destroying the entire block, Nancy was convicted of arson. For her, prison is an alienating experience as she feels she comes from a different culture and class background than other women in prison. She feels that she will gain nothing in prison and compares herself to other women who acquire a GED or learn parenting skills and can leave prison knowing they have gained something from the experience.

It's just incarceration. It's just a lifeless and spiritless existence. But it's a very lonely existence for me, because for the most part, the things I see and the things I witness around here, I want no part of. (Wojda and Rowse 1997, 10)

Nancy complains that male officers have access to the women's rooms in the prison. They can walk in any time, but the women are responsible for ensuring that they are dressed appropriately when the men enter. She is bothered by having no privacy and asks her roommate to leave the room when she has to take a shower or perform normal bodily functions.

Claudia works in the prison garage and is a certified welder. She thinks the correctional officers are a "mixed bag." She mentions one guy who "if you just look at him you get a ticket for sexual advances" (26). She complains about male officers in her room and mentions a time when one walked in and she had her blouse off. She says he didn't announce himself or call attention to his presence in any way.

Anne is in maximum security serving eight to twenty-five years, and she accepts that the male officers are going to look if they see women undressed (27). She thinks that if an officer pays attention to one of the women, she will think he likes her. She knows that the men like to look.

Leora has no close friends in the prison and "does her time" by herself. She has learned not to trust people because she has always trusted the wrong people. She works in admissions, receiving incoming prisoners.

The women are so scared. They're sweet and they're innocent. And three weeks later, you can't recognize them. It's a mixture of all kinds of people in here. Some want to change. Some get an attitude. Some just want to do their time. (37)

She says there are sometimes fights in the prison but that tension isn't that high and no weapons are used.

Darlene is a middle-class woman of twenty-one serving fifteen years to life for assisting her lover in the murder of his wife. She believes it is best not to confide in people in prison. It is too easy to have confrontations with other people when they violate your trust.

There is a kind of pecking order in here. The inmates are especially hard on people who committed crimes involving children. They're not physically abusive toward them but they'll abuse them verbally. "Child killer, child molester." They do it to me. "Murderer." Just to make you miserable. I'm still catching on. I don't know all the games but I'm catching on. But I didn't come down here to be liked. I pretty much stay to myself. (39)

Laverne is sixty-two years old and has been in prison for eight years. She is happy with the prison surroundings and has made good friends. She sometimes thinks it's harder for people on the outside but she does miss the finer things in life.

The food packages and the clothes packages mean a lot. It picks your spirits up. (39–40)

Twenty-two-year-old Marie is serving three years for forgery. She complains about the "crazy" prison rules and gives the example that prisoners are not allowed to be in front of another prisoner's door. One time she stopped at the door of a friend to tell her to get up and got into trouble for it. She lives in a cottage that is just a dorm, just rows of bunk beds. She complains that things get stolen easily and that you need money to ease the prison life. She thinks it's hard to keep out of fights and mentions trouble over choosing which television programs to watch.

She thinks she will not come back and will stay with her father, who is an alcoholic. She too is an alcoholic (40).

Denise, *age thirty-five, has been in prison for over two years and thinks the only place where you can have privacy is the shower stall. She thinks there isn't much violence in the prison, just "cat fights" with no weapons. She believes women fight over stupid things and that there is a big difference with the younger women in prison for crack cocaine. She finds them rude and disruptive with a bad attitude. She contrasts these women with those serving longer sentences. The short-termers are usually right back in prison in no time. The advice she would give to a new prisoner is to get the feel of the place and not to form any close relationships with one person right away to combat the strangeness of prison. If you do that there will be rumors that you're lovers. She herself sat back for six months and watched and didn't let anyone know her until she was ready (41).*

Joyce, *age fifty-one, shot her husband during an argument and is serving ten to twenty-five years for manslaughter. She describes her typical day:*

I get up about 7:30, get dressed, go out in the common area and have a cup of coffee. When there are classes, I go to school in the morning. Then, after lunch I'll go back to my cottage and do some reading or crocheting. After dinner, I'll go to recreation or just relax. It's normally just like living out there, only you just don't get on the phone and you just don't go out the door anytime you want to. (45)

Nancy, *in contrast to Joyce, says,*

It's generally monotonous. You get up, get dressed, go to work, work all day. You don't deviate any day. Same thing day after day after day. You can feel good or you can go in when everyone's PMS-ing. (45)

Concerning visitors, she reports:

Before we go into the visiting room, we have to squat and we have to cough. They look under your arm pits and they lift your breasts up. They lift up your hair, look in your mouth, have you squat frontwards, squat back. Then you go in to visit your family. And when you leave, you go through the same strip, squat, and cough procedure again. (46)

Anne *is a maximum-security inmate serving twenty-five years for manslaughter. Speaking of prison programs, she says:*

I've taken parenting. I don't have children. But there's only so many programs I can get into because I'm a max. And there is only certain jobs I can have because I have to be escorted. So I try to get all the certificates I can get so it looks good before the board. (54)

Linda is serving a life sentence and is still six years away from her first parole hearing. Her four children were taken away from her when she was sentenced. She has not had any contact with them since then and does not know where they are. She says, "The loss of children hurts worse than anything" and that most of the time she doesn't think about them because she "can't handle it."

I see a lot of people sit and cry and can't concentrate on their work after they've had a visit. They'll just be out of it because little Susie at home has gotten in some trouble or when the kids are sick. That's a big thing but you have to shut that off because you can't do anything. You just can't do anything. (61–62)

Interviewing the women in the Central California Women's Facility (CCWF), Barbara Owen (1998) gives a voice to women who describe their pathway to imprisonment. Drug and alcohol problems shape the lives of many women.

Zoom speaks about her alcoholic parents and says she grew up with her mother's drinking and remembers feeding her, undressing her, putting her to bed, and becoming the parent of her small brothers or sisters from the age of thirteen or fourteen. Her stepfather was abusive toward her when he started drinking heavily and then he would become very violent. She explains that being raised in a home with alcoholic parents is "like walking on eggshells" (Owen 1998, 51). She would always think, "If I do this, is it going to tick him off? Her off? Or, is it going to make them fight?"

One time I came home and he was beating my mother. I will never forget this. I went to the kitchen and got a steak knife and it seems like I must have stabbed that man fifty thousand times. But I guess I was not doing any damage because he didn't stop. So the police came and handcuffed him and took him away and took my mother to the hospital. (51)

Owen writes of "the mix" as part of prison culture found at CCWF. The mix represents "continuing the behavior that got you here in the first place" (179) and is something to be aware of and avoided because new-comers are advised to "stay out of the mix" (179). The mix is any behav-ior that can bring trouble and conflict with staff and other inmates and can result in reducing "good time" credits and other sanctions.

Tabby says "the mix" is the way you support yourself.

The mix here is the loud types selling drugs, but the mix is really in you, you are like that on the streets. The homegirls know how things are and [tell you] I have to sell this. Some people don't have people on the streets to take care of them, or send them anything. You have to do something in here to survive [whether it's] to sell dope or steal. . . . Me, I get the impression that people in the mix don't want to go home. That they have nothing to look forward to on the streets. They like being here with their buddies. Clowning and talking about people. (181)

Girshick discovered that many women at the minimum-security facility in North Carolina found the prison rules and regulations too strict and lacking in certainty.

The rules will change from day to day, like one officer will say do it this way and another officer will say, "No, you can't do that" and write you up, and so-and-so said you could but that don't matter. You gonna take a write-up. We just go through a lot of mental anguish every day. We don't know what kind of mood the officer may be in or sergeant or even another inmate. You might just say something in joking and they might take it serious and it creates a problem there. . . . Some of the rules here you wouldn't believe. . . . it's just petty. I mean, you can't sit down, you can't comb a lady's hair outside; one person in the bathroom at a time [after 10 P.M.]. (Girshick 1999, 79–80)

Owen investigated the "play family" as a feature of women's prison culture and found that the prison family may be large or small and may be temporary or last for some time (Owen 1998, 134). Typically an older woman will play the role of the mother, and a younger woman, the role of the kid. In creating families, women reproduce gender relations on the outside. One woman said she was Mom to many people in the prison, like she was on the streets:

There are about 5 women here who called me Moms on the streets. I would say this is my play family. Almost everybody is involved in them one way or another. It could be just 2 people or a bunch. It is just like the family on the streets—you start depending on them. You treat them like family. You can tell them anything. Then there is the loose-knit family. That is just what you call each other, but you don't really care that much about each other. All families do not have women who play the male role—some based on couples, others on friendships. I think it is about half and half. (136)

Girshick also observed pseudo families in her study:

I had one girl that kinda attached herself to me and used to call me Momma, which was okay. If I would influence her in the right way then that's fine. But I've seen them daddies, they call each other daddy and brother all the stuff like that. . . . I don't partake in that because we are women.

I think it's something needed 'cause it's kept a lot of girls in line, out of trouble, because especially the parent figure will get on that child if that child's doing things against the rules or doin' things to hurt themselves or somethin'. That parent figure will discipline and it's kept things in control. (Girshick 1999, 91–92)

Guards and Inmates

Respect and being respected are major issues for women in prison, and the expectation is that if a prisoner respects her guards, they will in turn respect her.

There's a few here that I do respect, and will always respect, and I show them respect. The other ones I just kind of stay away from because the way I see it, respect is something that's mutual. If you want it, you give it. And I don't care if I'm an inmate or not, I'm still a human being. I'm a woman just like they are. Yeah, I may have committed a crime, but I'm paying for it. I've been paying for it almost a decade of my life. You don't have to talk to me like I'm a dog, 'cause I'm not. If I do something wrong, you write me up for it. Don't you stand there and you talk to me like I'm dirt on your shoe just because you get off on it. (94)

Alice has been in prison for seven months and is serving a one-year sentence for aggravated trafficking and failure to comply with the police. She speaks about the rules and the guards:

Some of the rules make no sense at all. It should be common sense, but it's not. Some officers go strictly by the book. Disrespect for another inmate . . . how can you go to the hole for that?

The male officers hit on the women all the time. Sometimes it's the women starting it, sometimes the men stop. I think it's mostly the women who start it.

You come in here as a woman, 100 percent. But the minute you step in here, you get into these games because people want to belong rather than be individuals. (Wojda and Rowse 1997, 42)

Betty, age twenty-five, has been classified as maximum security after a series of violations in her first two years in prison.

It seems like the unit is not moving me like I want to be moved [out of maximum custody]. Because I've been good. I haven't laid down in a year. But you got to beg and plead just to get your status dropped and I don't think that's fair. Because if you work hard and don't get tickets, I think they should make you what you should be, but they don't.

In July, I'm going to re-class, and I don't know if I'll get it . . . but I don't understand why [not] if I've worked hard. They say I don't get in enough programs or it is the drug abuse. That has nothing to do with it. I think it should be based on your attitude and how you accomplish things for yourself.

I went to re-class in January, and they left me the same. They said I was doing good, but still they're not moving me. I have no knowledge of why. It's because they want you to suffer. I don't think nobody should suffer. (71)

Visiting Husbands in Prison

When wives visit their husbands in prison, as Fishman (1990) puts it, they are "doing time on the outside"; this is reflected in their experiences with guards during visits.

I didn't like going to Newport [prison]. The guards treat you like you're an inmate. They're so snotty to you and they give out smart remarks. If you bring stuff in, they go through the stuff. When they look at you, they look like they think we're beneath them.

At Londonderry [prison] they make you feel like you are dirt. We have to go through this detector. Sometimes they like to ridicule you by making the buzzer ring for any object so that you have to go back and forth through the detector. They think it is funny. (Fishman 1990, 145)

Strip searches take place routinely when wives visit their husbands in one prison. Strip searches are considered by the wives as indignities performed on them as innocent persons (145).

I felt degraded. It was especially degrading when I had my period because you have to remove your Tampax in front of them. One time when I was being strip searched, a man looked into the window. Now they assured us that no men could witness the searches. . . . It's degrading. When I was strip searched I signed the paper under protest. . . . [One lieutenant] has made some nasty comments to me like, "women like you should be strip searched." (145–146)

For the wives of men in prison, visiting their husbands accompanied by their children is not an easy event.

I don't feel very comfortable. The guards breathe down your neck. It's hard to talk there because there are all these people yelling around you. And you can't do nothing when you're there. You can't get close to one another. If you do, the guards break it up immediately. . . . When the kids are there, they can't do anything but sit quietly. You can't expect the kids to sit for hours in one place. But if they don't the guards come over and tell the kids to sit. . . . Sometimes when I visit [my husband], we just sit there and look at each other for one or two hours without having a thing to say. (161)

The "Free World"

When women make the transition from incarceration to the "free world," they reflect on their prison experience and on the future.

Janet speaks about treatment for drug abuse during her time in prison and how she thinks it has changed her.

What I do now is I have goals. Part of it was in that drug program. It's not that they said that, it's just somethin' I figured out on my own when I was in there. When I got out, that if you set a goal, then you know what you're workin' for. Instead of just doin' it everyday. So, if you reach a milestone, then it's like, "Oh I've done this. This is the next thing I need to do." I want to achieve more, because this is the first time I've ever not done drugs, and I have a little streak of ambition runnin' through me that I never knew. (O'Brien 2001, 70)

In a similar fashion, Ashley believed that her time in prison had made her a stronger and more positive person.

I've seen a hell of a lot. An awful lot. To be real honest and not meaning to sound silly, I wouldn't change what's happened. I think that it's made me a hell of a stronger person. I don't think that there will be anything on this earth that I cannot deal with. I think that I have a lot of potential to help others, and I see things in ways that other people may not. (71)

Some women expressed their belief that their faith in God was a mainstay in coping with a period of incarceration. Nan, after almost five years of imprisonment, testifies to her faith.

I know that there is a God, and I believe in Him. The Lord didn't send me to prison. The Lord allowed man to sentence me, because durin' my sentence, I was originally up for ten years. Now, I do believe the Lord stepped in and intervened in that and seen to it I only got five. . . . I look at the Lord knowin' that He's here with you and I today. Without him, I could have been dumped in the road. (84–85)

Family circumstances change while the wife and mother is in prison, and when she reenters the free world, she may find herself in a struggle to regain her role as mother and wife. **Suzy** *describes her experience:*

The whole time I was gone, David, my husband, was stayin' with my parents, and my Mom had taken over the role of mother, and she did not and to this day does not want to relinquish the role. That infuriates the hell out of me. So, that was a lot of adjustment. My Mom was tryin' to control every aspect of my life, like when I could shower and when I could feed my husband and when I could do my laundry. It was worse than bein' in prison. So, I told David, "you've got to quit this job and get us a good job, so we can get the heck out of here," so he did. We saved every penny we had. We moved into a run-down little dump, but it was out of my Mom's house. (98)

Sources

Banks, Cyndi. 2002. "Doing Time in Alaska: Women, Culture and Crime." In *It's a Crime: Women and Justice*, 3d. ed., edited by R. Muraskin. Upper Saddle River, NJ: Prentice-Hall.

Bosworth, Mary. 1999. *Engendering Resistance: Agency and Power in Women's Prisons*. Aldershot, England: Dartmouth Publishing Company.

Enos, Sandra. 2001. *Mothering from the Inside: Parenting in a Women's Prison*. Albany: State University of New York Press.

Fishman, L. 1990. *Women at the Wall: A Study of Prisoners' Wives Doing Time on the Outside*. Albany: State University of New York Press.

Girshick, Lori. 1999. *No Safe Haven: Stories of Women in Prison*. Boston: Northeastern University Press.

O'Brien, Patricia. 2001. *Making It in the "Free World": Women in Transition from Prison*. Albany: State University of New York Press.

Owen, Barbara. 1998. *"In the Mix": Struggle and Survival in a Women's Prison*. Albany: State University of New York Press.

Watterson, Kathryn, and Meda Chesney-Lind. 1996. *Women in Prison: Inside the Concrete Womb*. Boston: Northeastern University Press.

Wojda, Raymond, and Judy Rowse. 1997. *Women behind Bars*. Lanham, MD: American Correctional Association.

4

Chronology

The following chronological listing of events in the history of women in prisons encompasses both historical occurrences that were important in the development of prisons for women and issues of public policy that have affected women's incarceration.

1764   The publication in Europe of *On Crimes and Punishments* by Cesare Beccaria, a leading early criminologist. He advocates the use of imprisonment as a punishment, submitting that the harsh punishments in use did not deter criminal acts. This work, and others like it, are extremely influential in changing the focus in the United States from capital and other forms of physical punishment to imprisonment as the principal sanction for criminal activity.

1815   A period of great social change in the United States begins, marked by the movement from rural to urban areas, immigration, and the growth of a market economy. Women begin to experience social and economic problems resulting from their limited ability to earn income and the lower salaries paid to them; this prompts an increase in the rate of women's imprisonment as they begin to be incarcerated for property offenses such as theft and prostitution, often committed for economic survival.

1823   The Quakers of Philadelphia, Pennsylvania, begin to visit women in prison, offering instruction, a library,

1823
(cont.)

and sewing and writing classes to female inmates. This marks the beginning of the influence of the Quakers on women's prison reform because, for the first time, women begin to show concern about the conditions in which women prisoners are kept.

1827

Elizabeth Fry, the great English prison and social reformer, publishes *Observations in Visiting, Superintendence and Government of Female Prisoners,* a work that lays down the principles that will greatly influence the reform of women's prisons in the United States. Contrary to the thinking of the time, Fry believes that women criminals can be reformed. She also stresses the responsibility of women to assist their "fallen" sisters in prison.

1832

Auburn Prison in New York hires a matron to supervise female inmates.

1835

The Mount Pleasant Female Prison at Ossing, New York, is established as the first women's prison in the United States.

1845

Margaret Fuller, an early feminist and editor of the *New York Tribune,* publishes a series of articles exposing women's prison conditions and questions the prevailing notion that such women cannot be redeemed. She later campaigns to raise funds for a home for discharged women and visits the women's department at Sing Sing Prison in New York herself. She is among the first of the reformists to see women in prison as victims rather than sinners.

1864

Mary Carpenter, an English prison reformer, publishes *Our Convicts,* arguing that women prisoners should be placed together in one prison where a merit system would regulate treatment, privileges, and punishments and where female rather than male guards would be employed. These ideas influence American women reformers such as Elizabeth Buffom Chance, who meets with Carpenter in London in 1872.

1868   Following the passing of legislation allowing for inde-
        terminate sentences (and hence, parole) in Michigan,
        Zebulon Brockway, the superintendent of the Detroit
        House of Corrections, establishes a House of Shelter
        for women, adjacent to the House of Corrections but
        separate from it, where he is able to hold prostitutes
        for up to three years with the aim of reforming them.
        Brockway engages a matron, Emma Hall, who sets up
        a merit system in the House of Shelter for a group of
        thirty female prisoners who live in well-furnished
        surroundings intended to replicate the home and the
        family. The House of Shelter closes in 1874 after
        Brockway's resignation from the Detroit House of
        Corrections.

1870   A new penal philosophy is presented to a meeting of
        prison administrators and reformers in Cincinnati,
        Ohio, following increasing disillusionment by these
        officials about prison conditions and prison reform for
        both men and women. Importantly, the meeting
        acknowledges the need for a new penal philosophy of
        reformation in place of a policy that emphasizes retri-
        bution. Their development of the notion of classifica-
        tion of prisoners leads to the recognition that separate
        prisons ought to be established for women prisoners.

        Abby Hopper Gibbons joins with Josephine Shaw
        Lowell to campaign for setting up separate prisons for
        women in New York that would be run by women.
        Gibbons, a leading member of the Female Department
        of the Prison Association, supports the idea of
        halfway houses for women discharged from prison
        that would provide them with shelter and a pious
        environment.

        Due largely to the efforts of Elizabeth Buffum Chance,
        a Quaker from Rhode Island, her native state passes
        legislation for a Board of Lady Visitors to inspect pris-
        ons housing women.

1873   In Indiana, Rhoda Coffin opens the Indiana Refor-
        matory for Women and Girls, the first completely

1873
(cont.)

independent women's prison. It is also the first to be administered and operated by a totally female staff. Women prisoners are permitted to wear dresses rather than prison garb, and refinement and decoration are emphasized.

1879

Eliza Mosher, a doctor, becomes the superintendent of the Women's Reformatory in New York and attempts to introduce reforms and improve conditions, bringing in a merit system, calling the prisoners women rather than girls, and hiring staff to provide training and teaching. The standards set by reformers like Mosher during this period survive into the next century, so that differential treatment for women remains a cornerstone of penal policy until the 1970s and the advent of the women's movement.

1887

Due mainly to the efforts of Josephine Lowell, the Hudson House of Refuge for women opens in 1887 in New York as the first cottage-based adult female reformatory, staffed almost completely by women. The model of the cottage is followed for other reformatories, which, like the earlier Detroit House of Shelter, emphasize a family and home environment rather than a custodial model.

1900

In Texas, female convicts are sent away from the main state prison to a private farm, which provides food and clothing to the women prisoners in exchange for their labor, for which the state is paid. This form of contract labor proves to be popular in the southern states. Indeed, it bears many similarities to slavery, including the fact that African American women prisoners often are assigned to work in the fields under contract while white women prisoners are assigned work as domestics.

1901

Bedford Hills Reformatory for Women opens in New York, pioneering a new anti-institutional approach to incarceration. Located in rural Westchester County, Bedford Hills is located on a 200-acre site, uses the cottage system, and attempts to expand the kinds of training programs offered to women. This approach reduces the traditional emphasis on domestic skills. Gradually this prison gains use for the most difficult cases, such as those suffering from mental illness, with the effect that it becomes overcrowded. By 1919 the prison houses mainly recidivists—a situation quite the opposite from that originally envisioned.

1927   The first federal prison for women opens in West Virginia.

1930   The beginning of the end for the reformatory system. Following the Great Depression, states can no longer afford the cost of holding petty offenders for substantial periods of time to permit their reformation. In response, they begin to relocate felons to reformatories, which quickly revert to conventional prisons.

1940   By this date, twenty-three states have established separate prisons for women.

1971   Texas establishes the first coeducational corrections prison, housing both men and women prisoners who share programs and services provided to the prison population. This cost-cutting sharing of facilities and assets is intended to improve the training possibilities for women prisoners.

1980   The number of women incarcerated in the United States triples, due mostly to drug offenses and an increase in minor property crime.

1993   In *Jordan v. Gardner* [986, F.2d. 1521], women prisoners at the Correctional Center for Women in Gig Harbor, Washington, argue that their constitutional rights are being violated by the prison policy that allows random body pat-searches by male guards. The court decides that the policy violates the Eighth Amendment prohibiting unnecessary and wanton infliction of pain, noting that women who had been previously sexually or physically abused would suffer psychological pain during such searches by male

1993 *(cont.)*	guards. Thus, the court recognizes that women inmates have different histories and treatment needs than male prisoners.
1994	Legislation providing for "Three Strikes and You're Out" is passed in California and adopted in other states. Originally intended to incapacitate only violent repeat offenders, the legislation is also applied to other crimes where there is no element of violence. This legislation has a significant effect on the rate of incarceration for women.
1996	Human Rights Watch draws attention to the issue of sexual abuse of women inmates by male guards with the publication of a report called *All Too Familiar: Sexual Abuse of Women in U.S. State Prisons.* In a climate where women are more likely to be guarded by male guards, the report documents incidents of rape, sexual assault, and sexual misconduct, as well as random but mandatory pat-searches and male guards viewing female inmates while dressing or showering.
1998	Karla Faye Tucker is executed by lethal injection in Texas, becoming the first female to be executed since 1863. She and her boyfriend were convicted of murder after killing two people and plunging a pick-axe at least twenty times into the victims' bodies. Tucker never claims to be innocent but believes she should be spared the death penalty because she had embraced Christianity. Supporters around the world join appeals for clemency from the United Nations and the European Parliament. However, the Texas Parole Board votes 16 to 0 against commutation.

5

Guarding Women in Prison

Women in Corrections

In 1793 Mary Weed became the first woman correctional administrator, having been appointed the principal keeper at the Walnut Street Jail in Philadelphia (Morton 1992). The first woman to hold the position of a "corrections officer" was Rachel Perijo, who was appointed to the post of matron in charge of female offenders at the Baltimore Men's Penitentiary in 1822 (Britton 2000, 33). Women entered correctional services initially as volunteers, visiting women prisoners between 1860 and 1900. Gradually, through the efforts of women reformers, women came to be employed as wardens, assistant wardens, and staff in women's reformatories and in men's penitentiaries, where women were housed in custodial conditions. Female staff were typically single, working-class women and often had to resign if they got married. In reformatories, they worked twelve-hour shifts and lived and took their meals in inmate cottages (Britton 2000, 33). Accordingly, their work conditions differed dramatically from those of male correctional officers in men's prisons, who usually lived off the prison grounds.

During the period 1930 to 1970, women who worked as security officers, counselors, and probation and parole officers were rarely allowed to guard male prisoners; indeed, it is only since the 1980s that women have been admitted to all areas of correctional service (Feiman 1994). In the late 1970s, following legal pressure, women first worked as correctional officers in men's prisons. This came about through the 1972 amendments to Title VII of the 1964

Civil Rights Act, which extended protection against discrimination based on sex to public sector employees (Britton 2000, 33). However, there was resistance to this movement. For example, in 1977 the Supreme Court in the case of *Dothard v. Rawlinson* allowed Alabama to exclude women from correctional officer positions in men's prisons, reasoning that they were vulnerable to sexual assault from "predatory male sex offenders" (Britton 2000).

The prison system went through a period of instability during the 1960s and 1970s, with riots occurring in some prisons, and court interventions requiring the formalization of rules and regulation, due process requirements to be followed in disciplinary action, and a general professionalization of the role of correctional officers (Irwin 1980). Prior to the 1970s, white men constituted the majority of correctional officers in men's prisons; this changed in the early 1970s, when African Americans were recruited in significant numbers (Jacobs 1977). Nowadays, all states and the Bureau of Prisons employ women as correctional officers at every security level in both men's and women's prisons (Britton 2000, 34). However, though the Bureau of Prisons allows women to work as correctional officers in all positions in the twenty-four medium-security federal institutions, they may not work as guards in the six maximum-security prisons, where they are employed in nonsecurity positions. This policy was adopted after an attack and murder on a part-time female dietician by a prisoner in the Atlanta penitentiary in 1979 (Potter 1980).

The move toward the recruitment of women as correctional officers fit with notions of rehabilitation that argued that women would bring "feminine" qualities to prisons, display greater sensitivity to inmates, have greater communication skills than male officers, and be able to defuse conflict better than men (Jurik and Halemba 1984). In addition, in prisons located in isolated rural areas, there was a shortage of male workers, which meant there was more incentive to recruit women (Crouch 1980). Studies reveal that women officers tend to favor a treatment approach over a custody approach and to supervise inmates using a more personal style than male officers typically exhibit (Crouch 1985; Jurik and Halemba 1984; Pollock 1986). For example, rather than tell inmates to perform tasks, women will ask them to do so, and they will talk to inmates about children and family matters.

Despite these advances, women make up only 13 percent of the correctional officer force in men's prisons, although overall

(Morton 1991a), they comprise about 31 percent of the total correctional workforce (ACA Vital Statistics in Corrections in Schmalleger and Smykla 2000, 228). There are considerable variations between states; for example, a 1988 survey of federal and state prisons revealed that in Mississippi, 36 percent of correctional officers in men's prisons were female, as compared with only 3.1 percent in North Carolina. A total of 10 percent of corrections positions are supervisory, that is, sergeant or above, and women occupy 22.5 percent of those in adult male and female institutions but only 18 percent of those at the level of warden or superintendent. African Americans fill approximately 21 percent of positions at the level of warden or superintendent (229). A survey of the principal administrators of women's prisons revealed that three quarters of women's prison administrators are women, and half have held their positions less than five years (Morash, Bynum, and Koons 1995).

Women Guarding Men

Studies have shown that women correctional officers employed in state prisons are more highly educated than their male counterparts, more likely to come from professional urban families, and are less likely to be married than male officers (Zupan 1992). African Americans make up a large proportion of women correctional officers. For example, in New York City in 1991, 24.7 percent of the Department of Corrections officers were women, and of those, 84 percent were African American (Maghan and McLeish-Blackwell 1991).

Women give a number of reasons for joining the corrections profession, including an interest in working with people and in rehabilitation, but they also consider salary and conditions and lack of other employment opportunities as significant incentives. Sometimes women come from rural areas where a nearby correctional facility is the largest employer, and sometimes their husband or father may be employed by the institution (Merlo and Pollock 1995, 98). Typically, women want to work in a prison for men because the prisons are closer to their home or they have a chance of getting preferred assignments or shifts. Additionally, some women report a preference for working with men, believing male prisoners to be more compliant and easier to handle (Zimmer 1986; Pollock 1986). Male officers tend to emphasize salary, job security, and lack of other employment. In a study of women correctional officers in a county jail, Belknap (1991) found that most women employed there chose the occupation for its salary, benefits, and experience, but many wanted to find employment as police officers; that African American women were more interested in a career in corrections than in a move into police work; and that African Americans were more likely to be single heads of households (Maghan and McLeish-Blackwell 1991).

Generally, correctional officers feel unappreciated because their occupation carries low prestige (Martin and Jurik 1996, 171). The constraints of their employment include their being dependent on each other for support, having to work shift hours, and the isolated location of many prisons. Correctional officers must follow administrative rules in their employment and are subject to punishment for rule violations. This becomes a tension in their work because there is a tendency among officers to ignore rules in situations where they are perceived to be a barrier to effective action (172).

Formerly, and perhaps now, correctional service is seen as a working-class occupation with strong connections to maleness and masculinity because of its social control and risk aspects (Crouch 1985; Horne 1985). The occupational culture of corrections tends to stress physical and verbal aggression, and because women correctional officers do not ordinarily exhibit those qualities, the male officers may see their presence as threatening those values. To this occupational culture must be added a feeling of alienation and isolation among officers at having to enforce rules formulated by the courts and by administrators, about which they are not consulted, but for which they are accountable if issues arise in their enforcement. For this reason, many correctional officers perceive themselves as subject to unfair treatment as compared to the due process rights granted to inmates (Hawkins and Alpert 1989, 352–353).

Masculinity in prisons tends to be identified with demonstrating competence. Male officers perceive feminine competence by constructing women officers as "little sisters" who accept the protection of the male officers, or as "seductresses" who accept the sexual advances of their male counterparts (Jurik 1985; Owen 1985; Peterson 1982; Zimmer 1986). It is through such constructions that most men rationalize the presence of women as coworkers in a correctional environment. For many male correctional officers, projecting a masculine identity in prison means showing a superiority to what are perceived as feminine qualities. Women who refuse the protection of their male coworkers or reject their sexual advances risk being labeled by the men as "too manly" or as "man haters," or as "bitches" or "lesbians" (Martin and Jurik 1996, 1,974). Tensions arising from gender differences within corrections center on the old-style work culture associating competence with physical strength and emotional toughness. Opposed to this is the modern philosophy of corrections that is managerial in style and calls for educated, rational, and rule-oriented officers able to use conflict management and communication techniques. It is easier for women to overcome gender difference by becoming managerial because in this role they can be seen to be competent in their work since the managerial style is gender-neutral.

The relationship between male inmates and women correctional officers is quite complex. Initially, studies have shown that inmates whistle, flirt, stare, and in other ways display their masculinity for new female correctional officers. However, this initial display becomes muted once the women have demonstrated competence. Among African American male and female officers there is some discomfort in exercising authority over African American inmates; these inmates may display special resentment toward African American women officers, perceiving them to be violating racial unity and participating in the oppression of African American men by whites (Martin and Jurik 1996, 175). However, most surveys suggest that inmates are positive about the presence of women correctional officers despite points of conflict and tension, especially in relation to privacy issues for male inmates. For example, a number of lawsuits have been filed challenging the inspection of male inmates by women officers as a violation of their right to privacy. A number of suits have challenged the assignment of opposite-sex officers in shower, toilet, and dressing areas (for example, *Forts v. Ward* [1980], *Bowling v. Enomoto* [1981], *Avery v. Perrin* [1979], and *Gunther v. Iowa* [1980]). Other suits have contested the practice of opposite-sex pat-searches (for example, *Smith v. Fairman* [1982] and *Bagley v. Watson* [1983]). The approach followed by the courts in such cases has been to try to balance women's employment rights with inmates' rights to privacy by directing changes in institutional policies or in the physical organization of the prison. An example is *Forts v. Ward* (1980), where the court ordered that inmates be permitted to cover the windows on their cell doors for fifteen minutes each day.

A recent decision of the U.S. Court of Appeals found there was no constitutional violation where female guards were permitted to monitor male inmates in bathrooms and showers whereas male guards were not used to monitor female inmates under similar circumstances (*Oliver v. Scott* [2002]). The case concerned a correctional facility operated by the Corrections Corporation of America in Texas under a management contract. During the period in question, the prison housed about 250 females on the ninth floor of a ten-story facility with about 1,750 male inmates on the other floors. A few female guards were assigned to monitor male housing areas. The plaintiff claimed that female prison employees conducted strip searches of male inmates and observed male inmates showering and using the bathroom, but that male officers did not carry out similar duties in respect to female inmates. Female prisoners' showers and toilet facilities contained partitions that shielded them from view while in use, but the same structures were not available for male inmates. The district court ruled that the prison's interest in preserving security and equal employment opportunities justified any privacy invasion. The court of appeals affirmed that decision, holding that some courts have held cross-sex searches and monitoring to be capable of violating the prohibition against cruel and unusual punishment and that Supreme Court precedent establishes that any minimal invasion of privacy is justified by the interest of the state in promoting security. Further, a right of privacy under the Fourth Amendment is incompatible with the close and continual surveillance of inmates and their cells, which is required to maintain security and order. The court mentioned two previous cases in which it had found that security concerns can justify the strip search of a male inmate in front of female guards; that is, the strip search of an inmate during a lock-down after a fight about food and an increased incidence of prison murders, stabbings, and suicides as justifying a shake-down that included mass strip searches in front of female employees. Referring to earlier cases, the Court pointed out that if only men can monitor showers this means that female guards become less useful to the prison, and if female guards are not able to perform this task then the prison must have more guards on hand to cover for them. In one case, it was pointed out that restricting female guards from occasionally viewing male inmates would necessitate a complete rearrangement of work schedules, which might itself introduce a risk not only to security but also to equal employment opportunities. Further, many courts have previously identified the protection of female prison guards' right to equal employment opportunities as a legitimate penological objective.

Male and Female Officers

Women officers have identified their male supervisors and coworkers and not male inmates as their major opposition in men's prisons. Male correctional officers continue to argue that women are too weak physically and emotionally for correctional work, cannot perform in violent encounters, will become too fearful or depressed to perform the work, or will be taken in by the machinations of inmates (Jurik 1985). Male officers believe they have to step in and protect women in conflict situations, and they then complain that women fail to reciprocate. In one study, 72 percent of male officers reported that they believed they were occasionally obliged to protect a female correctional officer (Kissel and Seidel 1980). In the same study, 92 percent of male staff felt that women made a special contribution to the facility, and 96 percent believed that women increased its livability. In contrast, women officers believe they can defend themselves and that the fears of their male coworkers are unwarranted. In addition, it has been found that women resent male offers of protection (Bowersox 1981). In one study that looked at differences in the frequency and outcome of assaults against male and female officers, little was found to confirm these male fears because the study found that women officers were assaulted significantly less often than male officers and that when women were assaulted they were as likely as male officers to be injured or suffer a major injury (Shawver and Dickover 1986). One study, however, found that there was more reluctance to accept women as coworkers among older male correctional officers with substantial years of correctional experience than among younger male officers with less experience (Lawrence and Mahon 1998, 82). Also, more of the male officers assigned to maximum-security facilities believe that women could not work effectively without endangering themselves or others. This contrasted with men working in minimum- and medium-security prisons, who did not share this concern to the same degree.

Male officers also worry about women becoming intimate with inmates, and some will watch for situations where they perceive the women as getting too close to the male inmates. In response, women officers complain that their male counterparts are not monitored in the same way they are (Martin and Jurik 1996, 176).

Sexual harassment of women officers by their male counterparts is seen as an issue by women officers. Belknap's 1991 jail survey found that about 31 percent of women correctional officers complained of sexual harassment, including offensive sexual comments and behavior (Belknap 1991). Complaints of sexual harassment are often handled internally, and women officers have until recently been poorly informed about procedures for lodging complaints. For many women officers, the correctional workplace is a hostile environment because of overt and covert sexual harassment, with most complaints involving harassment by their male coworkers or supervisors (Martin and Jurik 1996, 177).

Constraints Faced by Women Correctional Officers

Apart from sexual harassment and the privacy issue for male inmates, there are organizational constraints that women guards face and men do not. For example, taking leave for pregnancy becomes an issue because of the demand for shift work in corrections; this means that matters connected with the family, always seen to be the responsibility of women, produce tensions between work and home. Initially, some correctional authorities required that pregnant women take a leave of absence or resign, but an American Correctional Association survey of 1991 revealed that over three quarters of correctional agencies responding stated they had pregnancy or maternity leave policies. Nevertheless, 22 percent had no written policy, which left women officers subject to the discretion of supervisors in pregnancy or family matters (Morton 1991b).

Work assignments for women officers have been an issue first because of the privacy issue for male inmates, and second, because of the perception that women have a reduced role within the correctional workplace. Morton (1991a) reported a decrease in the number of correctional agencies restricting work assignments for women officers between 1978 and 1988, but some thirty-four agencies nonetheless disclosed limitations on female assignments in men's prisons. The limitations were all concerned with privacy; for example, in Delaware, women were prohibited from entering the housing area of the prison, and in other states they were prevented from undertaking strip searches or collecting urine samples.

These issues point to the ambivalence shown by administrators as to the "proper" role of women in men's prisons. Different agencies apply different approaches. For example, the policy of one department assigned women officers to all areas of the prison unless such assignment would violate privacy rights in relation to strip searches and viewing inmates when nude (Morton 1991a). As a practical matter, policy varies from prison to prison and supervisor to supervisor, and in some institutions women officers are restricted to clerical duties or prohibited from working in yards and housing even when there are no privacy issues at stake. One outcome of these limitations placed on women officers is that they are unable to gain complete experience in working with inmates, which has an adverse effect on their opportunity for promotion. In the end, they may be left only with the "women's slots" (Morton 1991a).

A number of studies have looked at evaluating the performance of women officers; Zimmer (1997) found that women officers who use unique work strategies may receive adverse evaluations because their approach is different to that of their male counterparts. An analysis of one performance evaluation report (Jurik 1985) showed that of the eighteen categories of performance listed, "security" was emphasized throughout, and only one category dealt with communication skills and service. Conflict diffusion was not addressed at all. Jurik also noted that supervisors scrutinize and take note of the interactions between women officers and male inmates more carefully than such encounters between their male counterparts and male inmates. In terms of actual performance, studies show that women can perform in corrections as well as men but tend to experience higher levels of stress in the work (Cullen et al. 1985) and have to adapt to the masculine culture prevailing in prisons (Merlo and Pollock 1995, 101). As one woman officer put it, "I work here all day, talk loud, act tough. I go home at night and find myself talking in a deep loud voice to my kids" (Jurik 1988, 303).

Gender differences in guarding inmates tend to arise in relation to the level of discretion that officers may exercise. Male officers see a need to be granted more discretion, whereas women officers have a preference for a structured environment, which reduces discretion (Jurik and Halemba 1984). Both men and women officers rated administrators and supervisors as causing them the most problems, but women rated coworkers as their next major source of problems whereas men listed inmates second and coworkers last. Similarities exist in their approach, despite gender, in that both perceived many working conditions and the needs of inmates in the same way. Studies indicate that women officers have a more calming effect on male inmates than male officers, including diffusing potentially violent situations through nonviolent interventions (Kissel and Katsamples 1980; Graham 1981); that women help to humanize and normalize the male prison environment; and that women officers challenge "old guard" images and are more likely to attempt innovative strategies (Zimmer 1986; Peterson 1982). Peterson (1982) found that a majority of male inmates sampled believed that the presence of women officers helped reduce tension and hostility within the institution. Crouch and Alpert (1982) found that women officers in women's prisons held less tough-minded views than male correctional officers working in men's prisons.

In terms of the role followed by women officers, Zimmer (1986) identified three roles: the institutional, the modified, and the innovative. In the institutional role women adhere closely to prison rules to maintain professionalism and may be viewed by other staff as rigid and inflexible. In the modified role, women rely on the men to protect them from the inmates, believing they are unable to perform the work as well as men. In the innovative role, the women officers rely on inmate guidance to do their job (Zimmer 1986). A contrary view is taken by Jurik (1988) suggesting that women use a variety of strategies and do not fall into easily classified role types. Such strategies include adopting a professional demeanor, requiring adherence to rules but not requiring that rules be enforced at all times, emphasizing consistency and fairness but also showing flexibility, and replacing "old guard" approaches with conflict management techniques. Another strategy is for women to identify unique talents they might possess, such as writing, counseling, or public speaking.

A recent study reports a number of disadvantages women identify in correctional work. These include not being taken seriously and having to work harder to get respect, being seen as affirmative action appointees in supervisory roles, and failing to gain the respect that their male counterparts enjoy automatically.

In addition, they felt that being visible as a woman tended to magnify their errors; that a woman's voice may lack power or not be audible; that male coworkers might be less willing to share information with women colleagues; that women were sometimes asked to type, take notes, or check grammar; and that women were pressured to attend social functions to an extent that sometimes amounted to sexual harassment. Also identified in the study were widespread sexual harassment, male coworkers using premenstrual syndrome (PMS) as an explanation for any woman's action of which they did not approve, and differing communications styles between the genders, with women's styles being perceived as less professional (Withrow, Courtnay, and Peterson 1992 in Merlo and Pollock 1995, 102–103).

The experience of being a woman correctional officer has been documented in a number of studies; reading the words of these women adds another perspective to an understanding of what it means to be a woman guarding women in prison.

Officer Carol Lutes has been a prison guard for more than ten years at a women's prison and sums up her experience:

> I've never had a problem. I go by the rules. I believe that if you talk to them decently and humanely you get that back, not all the time, of course, but most of the times that works. (Wojda and Rowse 1997, 24)

> I find it less stressful now, even with more inmates here. All we had for programs back then was cosmetology, OPI [prison industries], and the laundry. Today, we have all kinds of programs. But if they want to be rehabilitated, it's up to them. Some of them have [got] two or three degrees, and they still come back. I've seen some of them come back four and five times. (67–68)

Claire Adams is a senior administrator at a women's prison. She is in her mid-thirties with a no-nonsense approach and a reputation for results:

> The women who are in here for killing their husbands tend to make ideal inmates. They never get a ticket [citation for misconduct]. They go to church services, visit their families, and go to school. You see, they had a problem, and they eliminated their problem. Now they're getting on with their lives. . . . One of the biggest complaints among the inmates is that they are treated

like children. That's true. There's so much structure
here . . . they're told where to go and when. But our job
is to teach them the rules. They want to blame everyone
else. But until you assume responsibility for your
actions, you can't see anything wrong in what you did.

It's definitely a bigger stigma for a woman to have
been in prison than it is for a man. The public attitude
is much harsher. . . . Personally, I think that 30 to 35 percent of these women don't belong here. A lot of them
are just kids coming in for drugs. They need treatment,
and they could be rehabilitated on the outside. (23)

Officer Inez Stark, age twenty-six, has worked in several
areas inside a woman's prison, and her father, sister, husband,
and brother-in-law also work in corrections:

The majority of them want to do their time and go
home. Although they're here, they want to be with
their friends. They don't want to go in the hole. They
don't want to lose their visiting privileges. . . . I don't
trust any of them. If I was in here, I would do anything
and everything that would help me. There's always a
motive for what they do. It's not that you don't like
some of them. It's just that you don't trust them. (22)

Officer Pauline Lightner has worked at a women's prison for
twelve years and speaks about the stress of being a woman
guarding women:

I think there's a lot of stress for officers: I think officers
have a lot of responsibility. There's stress that goes
along with that. You have to account for their every
move, and there's lots of stress connected with how
the women are getting along, if there's arguments or
someone is stealing.

We have to be understanding of the inmates' problems, but they have to abide by the rules. (21)

When women guard women of another culture, this adds to
their stress because indigenous women may, for cultural reasons,
adopt different behaviors and respond toward guards differently
than members of the dominant culture. In a women's prison
housing Alaskan Native women, one of the white women guarding them expressed some concern about cultural difference:

Natives act like they don't understand when they do, they act stupid when they're not, and act confused as though they don't understand. This helps get staff off their back; they can accuse you of prejudice, usually by telling someone else what they think of you and it gets back to you. It's a form of control because staff don't want to be accused.

They won't look you in the eye, don't show emotions, won't cry, some will laugh but look away. They keep to themselves. You don't even know they are there unless you go to them.

We don't have time to seek them out. If they come to us we'll talk to them; they are really hard to deal with because you don't know what's going on with them. (Banks 2002, 244)

Sources

Avery v. Perrin. 1979. 473 F. Supp. 90.

Bagley v. Watson. 1983. 579 F. Supp. 1099 (D.C. Ore.).

Banks, Cyndi. 2002. "Doing Time in Alaska: Women, Culture, and Crime." In *It's a Crime: Women and Justice*, 3d ed., edited by R. Muraskin. Upper Saddle River, NJ: Prentice-Hall.

Belknap, Joanne. 1991. "Women in Conflict: An Analysis of Women Correctional Officers." *Women & Criminal Justice* 2: 89–116.

Bowersox, Michael. 1981. "Women in Corrections: Competence, Competition, and the Social Responsibility Norm." *Criminal Justice and Behavior* 8: 491–499.

Bowling v. Enomoto. 1981. 514 F. Supp. 201.

Britton, Dana. 2000. "History of Corrections Officers." In *Encyclopedia of Women and Crime*, edited by Nicole Rafter. Phoenix, AZ: Oryx Press.

Crouch, B. 1980. *The Keepers: Prison Guards and Contemporary Corrections.* Springfield, IL: Charles C. Thomas.

———. 1985. "Pandora's Box: Women Guards in Men's Prisons." *Journal of Criminal Justice* 13: 535–548.

Crouch, B., and G. Alpert. 1982. "Sex and Occupational Socialization among Prison Guards: A Longitudinal Study." *Criminal Justice and Behavior* 9: 159–176.

Cullen, Francis, Bruce Link, Nancy Wolfe, and James Frank. 1985. "The Social Dimensions of Correctional Officer Stress." *Justice Quarterly* 2: 505–533.

Dothard v. Rawlinson. 433 U.S. 321 1977.

Feinman, Clarice. 1994. *Women in the Criminal Justice System.* Westport, CT: Praeger.

Forts v. Ward. 1980. 621 F.2d. 1210 (2d Cir.).

Graham, C. 1981. "Women Are Succeeding in Male Institutions." *American Correctional Association Monographs* 1: 27–36.

Gunther v. Iowa. 1980. 612 F.2d. 1079, cert. Denied 446 U.S. 996 (8th Cir.).

Hawkins, Richard, and Geoffrey Alpert. 1989. *American Prison Systems: Punishment and Justice.* Englewood Cliffs, NJ: Prentice-Hall.

Horne, Peter. 1985. "Female Corrections Officers: A Status Report." *Federal Probation* 49: 46–54.

Irwin, John. 1980. *Prisons in Turmoil.* Boston: Little, Brown.

Jacobs, James. 1977. *Statesville: The Penitentiary in Mass Society.* Chicago: University of Chicago Press.

Jurik, Nancy. 1985. "An Officer and a Lady: Organizational Barriers to Women Working as Correctional Officers in Men's Prisons." *Social Problems* 32: 375–388.

———. 1988. "Striking a Balance: Female Correctional Officers, Gender Role Stereotypes, and Male Prisons." *Sociological Inquiry* 58: 291–305.

Jurik, Nancy, and Gregory Halemba. 1984. "Gender, Working Conditions, and the Job Satisfaction of Women in a Non-Traditional Occupation: Female Correctional Officers in Men's Prisons." *The Sociological Quarterly* 25: 551–566.

Kissel, P., and P. Katsamples. 1980. "The Impact of Women Corrections Officers in the Functioning of Institutions Housing Male Inmates." *Journal of Offender Counseling, Services and Rehabilitation* 4: 213–231.

Kissel, P., and J. Seidel. 1980. *The Management and Impact of Female Corrections Officers at Jail Facilities Housing Male Inmates.* Boulder, CO: National Institute of Corrections.

Lawrence, Richard, and Sue Mahon. 1998. "Women Corrections Officers in Men's Prisons: Acceptance and Perceived Job Performance." *Women & Criminal Justice* 9 (3): 63–86.

Maghan, Jess, and Leasa McLeish-Blackwell. 1991. "Black Women in Correctional Employment." In *Change, Challenge, and Choices: Women's Role in Modern Corrections,* edited by J. B. Morton. Laurel, MD: American Correctional Association.

Martin, Susan Ehrlich, and Nancy C. Jurik. 1996. *Doing Justice, Doing Gender.* Thousand Oaks, CA: Sage Publications.

Merlo, Alida, and Joycelyn Pollock. 1995. *Women, Law, and Social Control.* Boston: Allyn & Bacon.

Morash, M., T. S. Bynum, and B. A. Koons. 1995. *Findings from the National Study of Innovative and Promising Programs for Women Offenders.* Rockville, MD: National Criminal Justice Reference Service.

Morton, Joann. 1991a. "Women Correctional Officers: A Ten-Year Update." In *Change, Challenge, and Choices: Women's Role in Modern Corrections,* edited by J. B. Morton. Laurel, MD: American Correctional Association.

———. 1991b. "Pregnancy and Correctional Employment." In *Change, Challenge, and Choices: Women's Role in Modern Corrections,* edited by J. B. Morong. Laurel, MD: American Correctional Association.

———. 1992. "Women in Corrections: Looking Back on 200 Years of Valuable Contributions." *Corrections Today* (August): 76–77.

Oliver v. Scott. 2002. United States Court of Appeals for the Fifth Circuit. 276 F.3d. 736; 2002 U.S. App. LEXIS 278.

Owen, Barbara. 1985. "Race and Gender Relations among Prison Workers." *Crime and Delinquency* 31: 147–159.

Petersen, Cheryl. 1982. "Doing Time with the Boys: An Analysis of Women Correctional Officers in All-Male Facilities." In *The Criminal Justice System and Women,* edited by B. Raffel Price and N. Sokoloff. New York: Clark Boardman.

Pollock, Joycelyn. 1986. *Sex and Supervision: Guarding Male and Female Inmates.* New York: Greenwood Press.

Potter, Joan. 1980. "Should Women Guards Work in Prisons for Men?" *Corrections Magazine* 6 (5): 30–38.

Schmalleger, Frank, and John Ortiz Smykla. 2000. *Corrections in the 21st Century.* New York: Glenco, McGraw-Hill.

Shawver, Lois, and Robert Dickover. 1986. "Research Perspectives: Exploding a Myth." *Corrections Today* (August): 30–34.

Smith v. Fairman. 1982. 678 F.2d. 52, cert. Denied 461 U.S. 907 (7th Cir.).

Zimmer, Lynn. 1986. *Women Guarding Men.* Chicago: University of Chicago Press.

———. 1997. "How Women Reshape the Prison Guard Role." In *Workplace/Women's Place: An Anthology,* edited by Dana Dunn. Los Angeles, CA: Roxbury Publishing Company.

Zupan, Linda. 1992. "The Progress of Women Correctional Officers in All-Male Prisons." In *The Changing Roles of Women in the Criminal Justice System: Offenders, Victims, and Professionals,* edited by Imogene Moyer. Prospect Heights, IL: Waveland Press.

6

People and Events

People

Clara Barton (1821–1912)

Barton is best known as the first president of the American National Red Cross, and she served the Red Cross in that capacity for twenty-two years, beginning in 1882. In 1883 she reluctantly succeeded Eliza Mosher as superintendent of Framingham Women's Reformatory, serving for only nine months. She was an enthusiastic superintendent, maintaining on open-door policy for the women inmates, and was able to deal with state officials who were skeptical about the existence of the reformatory. She contributed to the professionalism of women's prison reform by assuming the financial management of the prison as well as its overall administration. Barton was a believer in a nonpunitive approach toward women prisoners, arguing that reformation would only come through good influence, self respect, and trust, and that punishment simply degraded and disgraced the women and contributed nothing to the process of reformation.

Maud Booth (1865–1948)

Born in England, Booth was the leader of the Salvation Army, cofounder of the Volunteers of America, and a prison reformer. Booth and her husband were charged with establishing the United States arm of the Salvation Army in 1887; soon after, she and her husband began expanding the social work aspects of the Army, the philosophy of which combined religion with practical work and assistance to others. In 1896 she was invited to speak to prisoners at Sing Sing Prison; appalled by what she saw there, she dedicated herself to improving prison administration and the rehabilitation of prisoners through religion. She formed the Volunteer Prison League, at first composed of Sing Sing prisoners, which was subsequently adopted within other prisons. Members followed strict standards of conduct, including obeying prison rules, untiring prayer, and emphasizing the need for them to change their ways. In 1913 she served as president of the American Prison Association's auxiliary Association of Women Members.

Zebulon Brockway (1827–1920)

A leading penologist in the history of the prison in the United States, Brockway is best known for trying to introduce the indeterminate sentence for first offenders during his time as superintendent of the House of Correction in Detroit, Michigan. Following a visit to the Lancaster, Massachusetts, Girls Reform School in 1867, Brockway was inspired to try an experiment in reformatory treatment for women under his custody in the Detroit House of Correction. He aided Emma Hall in establishing a Women's House of Shelter in Detroit (Hall served as its first matron). In 1869 Michigan enacted the country's first indeterminate sentencing law, allowing Brockway to hold women convicted of prostitution for up to three years. This was a longer period of confinement than previously authorized based on the theory that there would now be sufficient time to reform these women. The possibility of parole was also present under this legislation. Brockway was therefore able to parole women and send them to the shelter, which held them until their sentences expired. Brockway believed that "fallen women" stood a better chance at reformation if they were placed under the sisterly care, counsel, and sympathy of other women. In New York, he organized the first state reformatory for male prisoners at Elmira and was its first superintendent from 1876 to 1900.

Elizabeth Buffum Chance (1806–1899)

A Quaker, Chance began her career as an abolitionist and after the Civil War campaigned for the appointment of prison matrons and for women to be appointed to state prison boards.

Visiting prisons in Rhode Island, she learned that classes were available for men but not women, and that female prisoners received neither exercise nor any intellectual occupation. She advocated reformatories for women and questioned the usefulness of providing only domestic training for female prisoners, arguing that male prisoners were taught profitable and useful trades. In 1870 she was named by the governor of Rhode Island to the Board of Lady Visitors of Prisons. This was the first time a woman had been appointed to a state board of control. Finding that the board lacked power to enforce its recommendations, she resigned in 1876 but was reappointed when adequate powers were later granted to the board. She addressed the first National Prison Congress on the subject of reforming women in prison, contending that most people accepted the notion that male prisoners could be redeemed but viewed "fallen women" as beyond redemption.

Rhoda Coffin (1826–1909)

Having initially learned about the practice of visiting prisons on a trip East in 1858, Coffin, a Quaker from Richmond, Indiana, began visiting soldiers' families and prisoners during the Civil War. Inspired by **Sarah Smith** and others, she and her husband launched a prison reform committee in Indiana in the 1860s. With Smith, she established a Home for the Friendless in Richmond in 1870. The home attempted to reform women prisoners through prayer, music, Bible study, and work. She visited state prisons, undertook a campaign for a separate prison for women in the state, and campaigned against the sexual abuse of women in prison. She assisted in setting up the first reformatory for women in Indiana, which commenced operations in 1874 in Indianapolis as the first totally separate state women's prison in the United States. In 1875, she delivered the first paper by a female member to the American Prison Association (formed in 1870), arguing that a prison for women should be entirely under the control of women, a proposal that met with some unease among male members, one of whom expressed his belief that while a prison should be "homelike," a home that did not contain men was not a true home at all. By 1876, she was arguing that the instruction of women prisoners should not be limited to domestic proficiency but should also encompass trade skills.

Katherine Bement Davis (1860–1935)

Davis was a schoolteacher initially and earned sufficient income from that occupation to attend Vassar, where she graduated at the top of her class in 1892. Later she earned a Ph.D. from the University of Chicago. Davis was active in many social fields, including penology, women's rights, and higher education. When she was appointed New York City's correction commissioner in New York in 1914, she became the first woman to head a major New York City agency. She held the office of commissioner for two years and then became the chair of the City Parole Commission, which she had helped establish. As superintendent of the State Reformatory for Women in Bedford Hills, Westchester, New York, she helped found the Bureau of Social Hygiene as a center for evaluating inmates to determine suitable sentencing for women offenders. Her penal philosophy included the notion that women prisoners should be taught to be self-sufficient; all would receive instruction in cooking, sewing, plain and fancy laundry, and general household work. As well, she stressed outdoor life in the form of working in a prison greenhouse, vegetable and fruit growing, and recreational games. She intended that her prison matrons be women of culture and character who would interact closely with the prisoners at their work, eat with them, and sit with them in the evening. She emphasized that each prisoner would be assessed on her performance in the reformatory rather than on her past record. She sought college graduates as the reformatory's instructors. Though she believed in the influence of hereditary factors in women's criminality, especially the existence of a history of mental disorder, she also adhered to a progressive view that saw society as having contributed to women's criminality through its failure to provide them with education and jobs. Davis rejected the argument of the eugenicists, who asserted that criminality existed as an inherited genetic trait among immigrants and African Americans.

Sarah Doremus (1802–1877)

Doremus was a wealthy New York philanthropist and a founding member of the Female Department of the Prison Association in New York. In the 1840s she visited women incarcerated in the New York City Tombs and assisted in establishing a house of industry for poor women, a women's hospital, a missionary society, and a home for older women. Together with **Abby Hopper Gibbons, Catherine Sedgwick,** and **Caroline Kirkland** she worked with the Prison Association of New York. She became the second directress of the Home for Discharged Female Convicts and was promoted to be the first directress of the same house in 1863 following the resignation of Catherine Sedgwick.

Eliza Wood Farnham (1815–1864)

In 1844, Farnham, a Quaker, became the matron of the Mt. Pleasant Prison for Women, a division of Sing Sing Prison at Ossining, New York. She had previously worked as a teacher and had edited a book concerned with phrenology and crime. (Phrenology was a "science" of the time that attributed criminal traits to the state of certain sections of the brain.) On being appointed matron, Farnham appointed four assistant matrons and introduced a series of reforms, including a relaxation of the strict rule of silence in the institution. During Farnham's appointment, prisoners were allowed to converse for a half hour each day. She also allowed the prison library to acquire novels, which might be read to the inmates instead of the customary readings from scripture. Generally, she tried to brighten the prison atmosphere, introducing flowers, curtains, and a piano. However, her innovations shocked the members of the board, which administered Sing Sing and Mt. Pleasant, and she was particularly criticized for relaxing the silence rule. She was forced to resign in 1848.

Ellen Foster (1840–1910)

Foster was admitted to the Iowa bar in 1872 and became an active campaigner in the Women's Christian Temperance Union and a board member of the Red Cross. She moved to Washington, D.C., in 1888 and was assigned to survey labor conditions affecting women and children in the South. In 1907 she was appointed to the Department of Justice as an examiner, the position later to be called Superintendent of Prisons. In this capacity she was required to travel throughout the country inspecting prisons where federal prisoners were located. She showed a special concern for the conditions of women prisoners and proposed a separate cellblock at Leavenworth Prison for locating all federal women prisoners, who were then scattered throughout the federal prison system in men's prisons. This proposal was implemented in 1910, foreshadowing the first separate federal prison for women, established in 1927.

Elizabeth Fry (1780–1845)

Born into a prominent Quaker family in England, Fry was eighteen years old when she heard American Quaker William Savery preach; afterward, she determined to devote her life to aiding those in need. Initially she collected clothes for the poor and visited the sick. When a family friend who had visited Newgate prison in London told her he had been refused admission to the women's yard of the prison because the women were too unruly and his safety could not be assured, Fry decided to visit the women. She found 300 women and children confined to two wards and two cells. The women and children slept on the floor without bedding or blankets and occupied their time swearing, gaming, and fighting. She began a program of prison visits and in 1818, together with a group of Quakers, formed a group called the Association for the Improvement of Female Prisoners in Newgate. In 1827 she published a treatise called *Observations in Visiting, Superintendence, and Government of Female Prisoners* that laid down principles that would greatly influence the women's prison reform movement in the United States.

Margaret Fuller (1810–1850)

Fuller was one of the leading intellectuals and feminists of her day. After having received an education equal to males of the time, she became a teacher and then an education administrator. She was a member of the Transcendentalists and a leading writer and literary critic. In 1844 she visited the women's department at Sing Sing Prison, New York, later defending the women prisoners in public statements and reaching the public with her views in a series of articles for the *New York Tribune* in 1845. She also advocated for the establishment of a home for discharged women prisoners, exposing the shocking sights of women and children to be found in the almshouses and prisons, and stressing the scrutiny of male visitors and the dreary routines the women had to endure. She noted the lack of matrons and the appalling conditions in which the women were forced to live and questioned the view that such women were "fallen" and incapable of being redeemed. She argued in favor of classifying women prisoners, of providing them with training, and installing adequate sanitary systems. Following the opening of the Home for Discharged Prisoners she made a public appeal for funds for the home and called upon "people of leisure" to inspect the sick and ruined women in the penitentiary and hospitals and to accept that society should have some responsibility for them.

Abby Hopper Gibbons (1801–1893)

At the urging of Isaac Hopper, a founding member of the New York Prison Association, the association established a Female Department to supervise former women prisoners who needed a place to live after their sentences were completed. Abby Hopper Gibbons, the wife of Isaac Gibbons, was a member of the executive committee of the Female Department. Gibbons and her committee first visited women in prisons in the state, observing their unsanitary living conditions, poor food, and severe discipline. Next, Gibbons and her colleagues rented a three-story house where they could locate discharged women prisoners while they prepared to reenter life on the outside. They opened the Home for Discharged Female Convicts in 1845, having engaged two women as matrons, thus establishing the world's first halfway house. Residents at the home were free to leave, but they had to comply with the house rules, which prescribed a strict daily schedule that included rising at 5:30 A.M. and classes on sewing, reading, writing, and arithmetic. Religious education included daily readings of the Bible and sermons by local missionaries. Appointed to the first committee responsible for the oversight of the home, Gibbons continued to be involved in its operations until she reached the age of ninety-two, attending board meetings and also visiting women's prisons in the state. Gibbons was able to attract middle-class women with reformist views (including **Caroline Kirkland**) to serve with her on the board, which supervised the home. Over the years Gibbons and her women colleagues of the Women's Prison Association in New York maintained an interest in reformatories for women and considered whether such an institution might be established in New York, especially in a location within commuting distance of the city of New York. This idea met with resistance from legislators who wanted to locate women's institutions in more remote locations. Using the Hudson House of Refuge as a model, Gibbons had legislation drawn up and presented to the state legislature, and she lobbied hard for it to be passed. However, despite gaining the support of the state assembly and senate, the plan was vetoed by the governor. Gibbons decided to shelve the project until after a new governor was elected and by 1891, with a new governor in place, Gibbons was ready for another attempt. After much lobbying and delays, the bill was finally passed and signed by the governor in May 1891; by the end of that year the board of the new institution had taken an option on land in Bedford, Westchester County, for its construction. The reformatory was finally opened in 1901 and the cottage for inmates under the age of twenty-one was named Gibbons in honor of her efforts.

Emma Hall (1837–1884)

Formerly a Detroit public school teacher, Hall served as teacher and, later, matron of the House of Shelter in Detroit from 1869 to 1874. About thirty women lived in the shelter as a family in well-furnished surroundings. Hall introduced a system based on merit and offered training for employment. She fostered the development of strong bonds between the women residents, emphasizing also religious uplift and domesticity. Under her leadership, education became a most important part of the regime at the house; inmates prepared lessons during their work break and attended school four evenings each week. By 1871 Hall had trained seven inmates who assisted with schooling. Along with education, Hall stressed the need for the women to lead the "true" womanly life and accomplished this through training them in the practices and manners of genteel society as well as in the middle-class roles expected of women at that time. The House of Shelter closed in 1874 following Hall's resignation from the Detroit House of Corrections (the reason, according to **Zebulon Brockway**, was overcrowding).

Mary Belle Harris (1874–1957)

Harris earned a Ph.D. in Sanskrit from the University of Chicago in 1900 and taught Latin at Bryn Mawr. In 1914 **Katherine Bement Davis**, a former classmate and the Commissioner of Corrections for New York City, persuaded her to become superintendent of the Women's Workhouse on Blackwell's Island, a short-term women's prison. The daily inmate population at the workhouse averaged 700 women living in 150 cells, where they spent most of their time as there were no recreational facilities. Harris remained there for three and a half years. Beginning in 1918 she spent five years as superintendent of the New Jersey State Home for Girls, known as Clinton Farms, an antiinstitutional facility where inmates lived in cottages, each with its own form of government. At the age of fifty-one she became the first warden of the first federal women's prison at Alderson, West Virginia. Harris was determined to treat the women inmates as ladies, believing that reform would come through a regime of kindness, and she endured a degree of conflict with the Federal Bureau of Prisons, which she thought did not appreciate her special position within the federal prison system as a woman custodian of women prisoners. She felt little in common with other wardens. The Alderson prison was unique in having an advisory board authorized and defined by legislation that included some nationally known members. Harris typically had to contest issues such as the relative importance of inmates working at industrial or maintenance tasks as opposed to cultural and educational projects, which she favored. She insisted that staffing be reserved for women, and staff positions for men were few and kept at low levels. She felt that each prisoner should be given individual treatment and devised a classification system, which operated in conjunction with a classification committee composed of the resident physician, a psychologist, the head teacher, and the wardens of the cottages. Harris retired from the position of warden in 1941 and returned to Pennsylvania, where she served on the state parole board until 1943.

Jessie Donaldson Hodder (1867–1931)

Along with **Katharine Bement Davis,** Hodder shared the outlook that prisons for women should be less institutional and more concerned with preparing inmates for life on the outside. Working in Massachusetts, she attempted to change the prison system by stressing the need for a cottage-type environment, for parole, and for outdoor work and recreation. She also advocated less domestic training for women and a greater emphasis on training for employment, including employment in occupations not traditional for women.

Hodder served as matron at the Lancaster State Industrial School for Girls and in 1910 became the superintendent of the

Framingham, Massachusetts, Prison for Women. In her first annual report she urged dropping the word "prison" from the name of the institution and replacing the term "prisoners" with "women"; the following year she secured a change of name of the institution to the Massachusetts Reformatory for Women. She was concerned about the structure and design of the institution, calling it a "big shut-in house," and asked for a special grant from the state to transform it. As an alternative, she suggested it be shut down. Hodder believed the facility itself and its standards of care and training generally were far below those offered in men's prisons and reformatories. She wanted to enlarge the area of the reformatory, create a gymnasium out of an old cellblock, and establish several cottages with no enclosing walls. Eventually she intended that the institution become an industrial training institute for women. Believing in a psychological and scientific approach to treatment, she tried to segregate women who needed psychological treatment, hired a resident physician, and invited students from Harvard to use the institution for a course on the psychology of delinquency. By 1915, she had expanded the reformatory programs to include physical fitness and training in farming. However, despite her efforts the old regime of domestic training still survived. Though her success at changing this institution was limited, Hodder was able to influence events at new institutions in states such as Connecticut, and her influence appears in the thirteen women's reformatories established between 1900 and 1920, all of which avoided the use of the word "prison" and over half of which utilized the cottage plan.

Ellen Johnson (1829–1899)

Johnson was an advocate of temperance who taught domestic skills to women in the city slums. While searching for the dependants of veterans and survivors after the Civil War, she found many women receiving no attention in local jails and workhouses. In 1864 she helped establish the Dedham Asylum for Discharged Female Prisoners. With others, she led a statewide campaign in Massachusetts for a separate women's prison; she later became the superintendent of the Massachusetts Reformatory Prison for Women following the resignation of **Clara Barton** in 1884. She believed that women's criminality was caused through social and economic conditions, regarding these women as downcast but not forsaken. She was a firm believer of

differential treatment for male and female prisoners and advocated "softening influences" for women such as flowers, animals,
and music. At the same time, however, she saw the rehabilitation
of women prisoners as coming about through a process of control, first through the prison routine, and then through self-control by the women inmates themselves. She combined a merit
system with strict discipline and an appeal to the women's emotions, disapproving of unsupervised conversation among the
inmates. She applied her notions of discipline not only to the prisoners but also to the reformatory staff, which helped her win the
support of the Massachusetts legislature. During her term as
superintendent, Johnson promoted outdoor labor, as she believed
this would make women more content if they had to live away
from the city. This meant that women prisoners were to be found
whitewashing walls and painting buildings in the reformatory. In
1896, she became the first woman to serve on a standing committee of the American Prison Association.

Caroline Kirkland (1801–1864)

Kirkland served with **Abby Hopper Gibbons** on the board that
supervised the Home for Discharged Female Convicts in New
York. In 1853 she published *The Helping Hand*, a book that
described the early years of the home. She wrote that it was the
duty of women to see themselves as a community committed to
the proper care of every woman who had encountered misfor-
tune or disgrace.

Josephine Shaw Lowell (1843–1905)

The daughter of a wealthy retired merchant, Lowell was linked
through her large family to prominent New England families and
attended schools in Paris and Rome as well as private schools in
New York City and Boston. During the Civil War she worked with
women's relief organizations and then served on the Staten Island
visiting committee of the Prison Association of New York. Lowell
helped gain passage of the law that established the New York City
Department of Corrections as a separate city agency. As a member
of the state Board of Charities, she campaigned for the establishment of a house of refuge for women and girls in New York; due
to her efforts, legislation establishing such a house was enacted in
1881. However, the institution itself was not constructed until 1887

in Hudson, New York. Women were housed in cottages instead of a single building, and women made up the staff at all levels. The refuge stressed family responsibilities and domesticity. By 1889 the refuge was fully occupied, and Lowell lobbied for the construction of two further refuges. She was supported in this effort by the Women's Prison Association. In 1890, the state legislature approved plans for a Western House of Refuge in Albion to be constructed following the same cottage plan as at Hudson. Throughout her life as a social reformer, Lowell showed support for workers, not only through advocating the removal of women and children from poorhouses to reformatories staffed by women but also in founding a Consumers League of New York, organizing relief work for the unemployed, and assisting in the formation of women's trade unions.

Edna Mahan (1900–1968)

After earning a degree from the University of California at Berkeley in 1922, Mahan did postgraduate work at the California Bureau of Juvenile Research. In 1923 she joined the Los Angeles County Probation Department; the following year she joined Juvenile Hall. Miriam Van Walters, also an outstanding reformatory superintendent of the time, trained Mahan as superintendent of a small school for juvenile girls who were wards of the juvenile court. In 1928, largely through the urging of Van Walters, Mahan accepted the position of superintendent of the Reformatory for Women in Clinton, New Jersey, and there she was to remain as superintendent until her death in 1968. During her period of forty years as superintendent, Mahan gained a national and international reputation as an enlightened superintendent who believed that allowing inmates the greatest amount of freedom and self-government was the most effective means of achieving their reformation. She dispensed with locks and bars on windows during most of her tenure, and it was only in the period from the late 1950s onwards that she came to believe that she needed to increase security after she began to receive inmates who were violent and had committed drug offenses. Very early in her tenure Mahan worked to integrate African American inmates and children with the prison population; in this she was far in advance of her time. She ensured that a full-time physician and psychologist were added to the staff and insisted on an honor system for the inmates, believing that reformation is encouraged in an atmosphere of freedom and trust, where persons must assume responsibility for their own progress. Her main means of enforcing discipline was through the withdrawal of privileges earned through the honor system. Mahan's philosophy centered on knowing the women intimately, on not making rules that could not be enforced, in removing causes of friction between staff and inmates, and in a willingness to keep trying measures to find those most effective.

Eliza Mosher (1846–1928)

Mosher, a Quaker, studied medicine in Boston and at the University of Michigan and later practiced medicine in New York. She was invited to serve as physician at the Reformatory for Women at Framingham, Massachusetts, which opened in 1877. She had the care of some 350 inmates and organized the dispensary and hospital within the prison as well as performing the functions of prison surgeon, obstetrician, and dentist. She found a high incidence of venereal disease, insanity, and drug addiction among the prisoners and encountered a high birth rate of illegitimate children. The superintendent of the reformatory tried to interfere with her work and, in the view of Mosher, inflicted excessively severe punishments on the women, with a daily average of ten cases of solitary confinement. Mosher believed in a reforming rather than a punitive approach and took the opportunity to meet with prisoners and read to them from the Bible and to pray with them. She resigned in 1879 but returned within a year to the reformatory when the state governor threatened to appoint a male superintendent if she would not accept the position. She served as superintendent only from 1880 to 1882 but was able to reform the institution to the satisfaction of the prison commissioners. As superintendent she improved the conditions that earlier had caused her great concern as prison physician. She showed prisoners respect by referring to them as "women" and "ladies" rather than "girls," as had been the common practice, brought in a merit system, attracted new staff members, and stressed the need for individual teaching and training of women.

Catherine Sedgwick (1789–1867)

Sedgwick worked with **Abby Hopper Gibbons**, **Sarah Doremus**, and **Caroline Kirkland** within the Prison Association of New York to improve the situation of women imprisoned in New York.

Sedgwick became the first directress of the Home for Discharged Female Convicts in New York and remained there until ill health forced her to resign in 1863. She wrote many articles on the needs of discharged prisoners.

Sarah Smith (1814–1885)

A Quaker minister from Indiana, Smith inspired **Rhoda Coffin** to turn her social activist efforts toward prison reform and the visiting of prisoners. She visited soldiers and prisoners during the Civil War and together with Rhoda Coffin established the Home for the Friendless in Richmond, Indiana. She campaigned with Coffin for the establishment of a women's prison in the state, a proposal finally realized in 1874 in Indianapolis, where the first completely separate state women's prison was established in the United States. A male board of managers controlled the finances of the women's prison in its earliest years, and as its first superintendent, Sarah Smith believed they interfered with the internal running of the prison. In 1877 an all-female board was installed for the women's prison. When she received Sallie Hubbard as the first inmate of the new exclusive women's prison, Sarah Smith ordered that Hubbard be set free from the shackles in which she was confined, embraced her as a "fallen woman," prayed for her, and allocated her a room in the prison complete with curtains, a bedspread, and a Bible and hymn book. Smith believed that love was the first principle of correction, followed by the strength to resist temptation and by caring for oneself. She explained that her management strategy was to offer constant personal interest and oversight, special care in case of sickness, and kindness tempered by prompt punishment and firm training. She banned the vice of smoking tobacco and permitted only religious newspapers within the prison.

Mary Surratt (1823–1865)

On July 7, 1865, Mary Surratt became the first woman to be executed in the United States. At the time of her execution by hanging she was forty-two years old. She was found guilty of conspiracy in the murder of Abraham Lincoln by virtue of her association with John Wilkes Booth, with whom she became infatuated. Her husband and Booth had assembled a group of eight individuals who plotted to kidnap Lincoln; in 1865 the group attempted an abduction but failed when Lincoln changed his plans at the last minute. Mary Surratt was arrested two days after Lincoln's later assassination by Booth and charged with conspiracy. Although the nine-member military commission that found her guilty voted for the death penalty, five of the members signed a plea for clemency, asking for her to be given life imprisonment due to her "sex and age." President Andrew Johnson claimed he never saw this recommendation and signed the order of execution. She was hanged in the courtyard of the Old Penitentiary, now Fort McNair, in Washington, D.C., and buried on the prison grounds.

Julia Strudwick Tutwiler (1841–1916)

Born in Alabama, Julia Tutwiler grew up in a home that stressed the importance of education and studied the same subjects as boys of that time. She and her father taught reading to slaves and poor white children. After spending some time in Europe, where she was exposed to vocational education in prisons and visited several women's reformatories in Germany, she enrolled in Vassar College in 1866. Upon her return to Alabama she taught and campaigned for women's education. When her maid was arrested in 1879 she visited her in jail and was shocked by the conditions she found there and appalled to find that children were incarcerated with adults and women with men. She criticized the convict leasing system operating in the state, taught prisoners to read and write, and implemented training programs for prison guards. The first state prison for women in Alabama at Wetumpka was named after her.

Mary Waln Wistar (1765–1843)

Inspired by the work of **Elizabeth Fry** in England, Wistar led a group of Quaker women in Philadelphia in visiting women prisoners in the Arch Street Jail in 1823, reading scripture with them and supplying them with clothing. That same year she organized the Female Prison Association of Friends in Philadelphia. Their efforts met with discouragement from members of the Pennsylvania Prison Society who believed the women imprisoned there were beyond redemption. Yet this did not dissuade the women, who later offered them classes in reading and sewing.

Nevertheless, Wistar and others persisted, established a House of Refuge in 1828, and arranged for a matron to supervise the female prisoners at Arch Street Jail.

Caroline Bayard Wittpenn (1859–1932)

Born into a family in New Jersey with a tradition of philanthropy, Wittpenn was educated privately and later became the manager of the New Jersey State Home for Feeble-Minded Girls and Women in 1897. In 1903 she was appointed by the governor to a commission to study the possibility of a separate prison for women, and she urged the creation of a separate institution for women offenders. In 1910 her son introduced a bill in the state legislature providing for a separate prison for women; in 1913 the Clinton Farms reformatory for women was opened.

Events

1835   **The Mount Pleasant Female Prison at Ossining, New York, is established as the first prison for women in the United States.** The founding of this prison constituted a milestone in the history of women in prison. It was the first deliberative act of a legislature to establish a women's prison, in contrast to the previously random creation of units within prisons in which women could be incarcerated. This prison was still not completely independent since it relied on the men's prison at Sing Sing for administrative support, but it was a vast departure from prior practice since, for the first time, women were recognized as having different custodial needs than men. During the period of its administration this prison became a place for experimentation in penology affecting women under its matrons, **Eliza Farnham** and Georgiana Bruce. According to a description of the 1860s, the prison was a handsome building, the interior composed of three tiers of twenty-four cells each. In addition to the main building, the prison included a workshop, nursery, and two separate cells for punishment. Final authority for the administration of the prison rested with the board of the men's prison at Sing Sing but daily management was in the hands of a matron and her assistant matrons. The first matron, **Eliza Farnham,** was a strict disciplinarian who nevertheless relaxed the rule of strict silence that had been copied from men's penitentiaries; the second, Georgiana Bruce, referred to the prison as "our reformatory." The inmates worked long hours making buttons and sewing clothes for the male prisoners. Mount Pleasant seems to have been the first prison to include a nursery within its establishment. Here, for the first time, women were confined apart from men and supervised by other women, and the inmates were encouraged to reform, thus marking the beginning of the reformatory movement in women's prisons. Overcrowding led to the end of the prison, which by 1865 had almost 200 prisoners, close to double its planned capacity.

1854   **Formation of Women's Prison Association of New York.** The first prison association devoted to the care and conditions of female prisoners was created in response to disagreement with the Prison Association of New York, formed in 1840 under male tutelage. When visiting members of the latter organization became concerned at the presence of female prisoners alongside male inmates, they formed a Female Department of the Prison Association. **Abby Hopper Gibbons** became a leading member of the Female Department, working with **Sarah Doremus, Catherine Sedgwick, Caroline Kirkland,** and other women from prominent families. The Female Department decided to open a home for discharged women prisoners, which, as a halfway house, would provide shelter, a place for prayer, and training to prevent the women from committing other offenses on their release. Their campaign for this house had the support of **Margaret Fuller,** who raised money for the cause and wrote articles in support of prison reform in the *New York Tribune.* The home was opened in 1845 and named the Isaac Hopper Home after Abby Hopper's husband. By 1852 Abby Hopper Gibbons and her committee were experiencing problems with

1854
(cont.)
the all-male Prison Association of New York, especially in relation to the Home for Discharged Female Convicts. Some of the issues included the men's disinterest in fundraising for the home and the men's insistence that all women residents of the home must have been convicted of a crime, thus preventing access to, for example, women arrested for drunkenness in public or vagrancy and then released. In response, Abby Gibbons and her colleagues formed a separate and independent association called the Women's Prison Association and Home in 1854. The Women's Prison Association functioned as an organization for the propagation of the middle-class values and images reflected in its members. The new association promoted a model of reformation for women that relied on religion and domesticity and through which the "true woman" would be reclaimed.

1868
Zebulon Brockway establishes a House of Shelter for Women in Detroit. The superintendent of the Detroit House of Correction and a noted penologist, Brockway established a House of Shelter for Women in Chicago as an adjunct to the Detroit House of Correction. Aiming to "save" his women prisoners in the Detroit House, he utilized recent legislation that allowed for indeterminate sentencing for women convicted of prostitution to release the women on parole and place them in the House of Shelter, where they would remain until their sentences expired. Other women also resided in the shelter, including well-behaved women from the House of Correction who had earned a transfer to the shelter as a reward for their good behavior, and wayward girls. The custodial regime in the shelter sought to blend a relaxed form of prison discipline with the atmosphere and environment of a home. In this, the shelter mirrored the principal features of the reformatory for women.

1870
The formation of the American Prison Association (APA). Originally called the National Prison Association, the APA was formed as a meeting place for prison reformers, public officials, and prison adminis-

trators. It recommended reforms in penology, including training for inmates, the indeterminate sentence, and the creation of specialized institutions for categories of offenders. Its first president was the future U.S. president Rutherford B. Hayes. The Declaration of Principles adopted at its first meeting in 1870 in Cincinnati set the tone for future debates in penology in both the United States and Europe. A central theme of the declaration was the need to classify prisoners, seen as an essential first step in individualizing the treatment of prisoners as a means of reforming them. The discussion of classification naturally led to the conclusion that women ought to be treated separately from male prisoners and should have their own prisons. The declaration formally announced that "prisons, as well as prisoners, should be classified or graded so that there shall be . . . separate establishments for women." This action by the congress gave significant impetus to the women prison reformers' ideal of having separate institutions for women. In 1954, the APA became the American Correctional Association.

1873   **Sallie Hubbard, known as "the Wabash Murderess," becomes the first inmate of an exclusively female prison in the United States.** Hubbard was the first inmate of the Women's Prison in Indianapolis, Indiana. Together with her husband, she had murdered a pioneering family of seven who had sought refuge in their home. Her husband was executed, and she received a life sentence.

1887   **Opening of the Hudson House of Refuge for Women.** This was the first women's reformatory to adopt the cottage plan as opposed to the custodial style of a central building containing cells for prisoners. The House of Refuge was set on forty acres in northeastern New York and began with four cottages (three more were later added). The cottages at Hudson had a combined capacity of only ninety-six persons, but a central prison building with cells where new intakes were assigned during a probationary

1887
(cont.)

period held up to 150 inmates. The first Hudson cottages did not include living rooms, though those built later did include such rooms. In 1897 the state Board of Charities recommended that the cellblocks at Hudson be removed and the space utilized for dormitories.

1893

Opening of the Western House of Refuge at Albion, New York. Albion was a refinement of the Hudson model of cottages; though it also contained a central building and outlying cottages, its cottages held the majority of its inmates, and each had its own kitchen and adjoining dining room that matrons and inmates used in common and a sitting room where all could assemble in the evening. Original photographs of the cottages show homelike interiors, with flowers, tablecloths, and pictures on the walls promoting the ideal of family life.

1901

The opening of the Bedford Hills Reformatory for Women in New York. As well as a central administration building, the rolling campus of Bedford Hills included a reception hall, four cottages, a laundry building, a powerhouse, a gatehouse, and a stable. In one wing were three tiers of twenty-four cells each, along the lines of a traditional prison design, but in the other wing were individual rooms. The cottages housed groups of twenty-eight women as well as babies up to the age of two years. The various cottages represented different levels of merit and accomplishment among the women so that an inmate might be promoted from one cottage to another based on her conduct and performance in the reformatory. Each cottage had a garden and its own kitchen where inmates cooked their "family" meals under matron supervision. Women at the reformatory were subjected to the least amount of restraint in accordance with the philosophy of superintendent **Katherine Bement Davis**. There were no bars or prison walls, just a fence of wire netting, and women were not required to wear uniforms, to form squads, or be subjected to the discipline of marching and similar activities. In improving facilities at Bedford Hills, Davis herself organized and conducted construction activity there, clearing land for farming and laying roads and sidewalks. She was forced to take this activist role because of erratic funding by the state, which often resulted in the governor vetoing money for improvements. Davis welcomed the opportunity for the women to be engaged in such projects, believing that exercise and fresh air were vital to building the women's confidence and moral fiber. This institution focused on a medical approach to criminal women and was considered a leader in that approach.

1913   **Opening of the Reformatory for Women in Clinton, New Jersey.** Established by law of the state legislature in 1910, the reformatory, known as Clinton Farms, opened with four staff, three old farmhouses, and some barns and outbuildings, with the largest of the two farmhouses renovated to accommodate twenty-four inmates and the staff. Its first superintendent was May Caughey, a graduate of the University of Michigan. With its small inmate population, Clinton Farms began with an informal and flexible regime, and by 1931 the population had expanded to 230, with most of the women committed for morals offenses and property crime. The inmate population reached a peak of 472 in 1948, a state of gross overcrowding given the capacity then of about 200 prisoners. Between 1915 and 1930, six cottages were built as well as a chapel and a sewing room and a storeroom were added while the staff resources grew from five in 1913 to fifty in 1930. Following the resignation of Caughey in 1917, four women were appointed as superintendent from 1917 until the appointment of **Edna Mahan** in 1928.

1927   **The first federal prison for women opens in Alderson, West Virginia.** Erected on a site of 515 acres, the Alderson Prison initially was constructed of two groups of residential buildings that changed the confinement conditions for federal women prisoners dramatically into a standard previously not approached. By the end of 1928 it had more than 200

1927
(*cont.*)
   inmates in an open, campus-like environment. Women were housed in cottages complete with private dining rooms, tablecloths, flowers, and curtains. There was no perimeter fence or other custodial features. During the first thirty years of its existence, Alderson permitted inmate mothers to keep babies born there.

1930
   The beginning of the end of the women's reformatory system. After 1920, women's reformatories had become custodial institutions through overcrowding. The science of eugenics had all but supplanted rehabilitation as the focus of treatment. As well, following the economic blight caused by the Great Depression, states could no longer afford to put resources into confining women for lengthy periods for minor offences. The era of the women's reformatory had come to an end, but aspects of the model continue to be seen in modern-day imprisonment, such as an overreliance on domestic skill training for women inmates and in women's unequal access to training programs.

1980
   During the 1980s, the number of women incarcerated triples. This increase in women's incarceration is seen to have happened without any corresponding increase in women's criminality, and the proportion of women imprisoned for violent crimes has actually decreased. Most of the increase in women's imprisonment is accounted for by minor property crime (largely larceny/theft) and drug and public order offenses. Two thirds of women now in prison are there for offenses such as larceny, prostitution, and disturbing the peace. With this growth in incarceration has come a surge in the building of women's prisons and in adding female units to existing prisons, despite the minor nature of a large proportion of the offenses for which women are imprisoned. Some argue that the War on Drugs became the War on Women in view of conscious and sustained efforts by law enforcement to arrest and imprison women for drug offenses, especially those relating to possession and selling of crack cocaine.

7

Facts and Data

This chapter provides information about women's offending and incarceration, including sentencing, prison populations, and the characteristics of women prisoners. The statistics quoted are taken from L. Greenfeld and T. Snell (1999), *Women Offenders*, Bureau of Justice Statistics, Department of Justice, Washington, D.C.

Women Offenders

Violence: Based on the reports of victims of violence, women account for about 14 percent of violent offenders. Three out of four violent female offenders were convicted of simple assault. Three out of four victims of violent female offenders were women, and nearly two out of three victims had a prior relationship with the female offender. The per capita rate of murder by women in 1998 was the lowest recorded since 1976, and the rate at which women commit murder has been declining since 1980. Even so, arrests of adult females for violence in 1998 were at the highest level ever recorded—about 80 percent higher than the rate ten years earlier. Nearly 90 percent of the increase in the number of violent felons was accounted for by aggravated assault, reflecting perhaps an increase in the number of prosecutions of women for domestic violence.

Arrests: In 1998 there were an estimated 3.2 million arrests of women, accounting for about 22 percent of all arrests made in that year. Women made up about 17 percent of those arrested for violent crimes—murder, rape, robbery, and aggravated assault—and 29 percent of those arrested for property crimes—burglary, larceny, and motor vehicle theft. An estimated 22 percent of all female arrests for both violent and property crimes were of juveniles. The arrest rate translates into one arrest for every forty-two adult women aged eighteen years or older. Larceny was the offense category with the most female arrests.

Drug Offenses: In 1998 there were more than a quarter of a million female drug arrests, accounting for about 18 percent of all arrests for drug law violations. This amounts to one arrest for every 426 adult women. Of women convicted of felonies in state courts in 1996, 37 percent had been charged with a drug offense; between 1990 and 1996, the number of drug trafficking convictions grew by 34 percent, and the number of convictions for drug possession increased 41 percent.

Convictions: Since 1990 the number of female defendants convicted of felonies in state courts has grown more than two times the rate of increase in male defendants. Women made up 8 percent of convicted violent felons, 23 percent of property felons, 17 percent of drug felons, and 41 percent of all felons convicted of forgery, fraud, and embezzlement.

Property Offenses: For every category of major crime in the period 1990–1996 the rate of increase in the number of convicted females had outpaced the changes in the number of convicted males. This is especially significant in the case of property felonies, where the number of males convicted of property felonies dropped by about 0.2 percent while the number of convicted female defendants increased 44 percent.

Offender Backgrounds: Nearly six in ten women in state prisons had experienced physical or sexual abuse in the past; of that amount, just over one third had been abused by an intimate in the past and just under a quarter reported abuse by a family member.

Female Corrections Populations

Population and Increases: In 1998 there were an estimated 951,900 women under the custody, care, and control of the criminal justice system. This amounts to a rate of about one out of every 109 adult women in the United States. Of this total about 85 percent were being supervised in the community through probation and parole and 15 percent were confined in prisons and jails. At year-end 2000, 91,612 women were confined in state or federal prisons, amounting to 6.6 percent of all prison inmates, up from 5.6 percent in 1990.

Since 1990 the number of male prisoners has grown 77 percent, and the number of female prisoners has increased 108 percent.

The annual rate of growth in the female prison population has since 1990 averaged 7.6 percent, as compared to a rate of 5.9 percent for male inmates. In proportion to their number in the resident population, men were about fifteen times more likely than women to be imprisoned in a state or federal prison. At year-end 2000, there were fifty-nine sentenced female inmates per 100,000 women in the United States, compared to 915 sentenced male inmates per 100,000 men.

Jurisdictions Where Women Prisoners Are Held: Over one third of all female prisoners as at year-end 2000 were held in the three largest jurisdictions: Texas, California, and the federal system. The highest female incarceration rates existed in Oklahoma, with 138 female inmates per 100,000 female state residents; Mississippi, with 105; and Texas and Louisiana, with 100. At the other end of the scale, Massachusetts had a rate of seven, Maine ten, and Rhode Island twelve.

Since 1990 the female inmate population has grown at an annual average rate of at least 10 percent in seventeen states, with Texas reporting the highest average annual increase of 18.7 percent, followed by Idaho with 15.2 percent.

Characteristics of Female Prisoners

Race: In 1998 nearly two thirds of women confined in local jails and in state and federal prisons were minorities. In state prisons 48 percent were black, and in federal prisons 35 percent were black; this is compared to 33 percent and 29 percent who were white, respectively. Hispanics made up 15 percent of women in state prisons and 32 percent of those in federal prisons.

Age: The greatest number of female prisoners in state and federal prisons fall in the age range of twenty-five to forty-four. Women inmates aged twenty-four or less make up only 12 percent of women in state prisons and 9 percent of women in federal prisons.

Education: An estimated 56 percent of women inmates in state prisons and 73 percent of those in federal prisons have completed high school. Between 30 and 40 percent of high school graduates have attended some college.

Inmate's Children: An estimated 65 percent of women in state prisons and 59 percent of women in federal prisons have young children, with the average being two children under the age of eighteen years. If women on probation are included in the total, the result is that more than 1.3 million minor children are the children of women held in the criminal justice system. More than a quarter million of these children have mothers in jail or prison.

Economic Background: Generally female inmates had experienced more difficult economic circumstances than males before incarceration. In state prisons about four out of ten women reported that they had been employed full time prior to incarceration. This contrasts with male inmates, where nearly six out of ten had been working full time before incarceration. In terms of income, about 37 percent of women and 28 percent of men had incomes of less than $600 per month prior to arrest, and nearly 30 percent of female inmates reported receiving welfare assistance at the time just before arrest.

Health: In 1997 an estimated 2,200 women in state prisons were HIV positive, making up about 3.5 percent of the female inmate population. This compares to a rate of about 2.2 percent for male inmates. The highest rate for female inmates occurred in 1993 at 4.2 percent.

Alcohol and Drugs: About half of all women offenders in state prisons had been users of drugs or alcohol or both at the time of the offense that resulted in their incarceration. An estimated 29 percent of women in state prisons and 15 percent of women in federal prisons had been consuming alcohol at the time of their offense. Daily drinkers accounted for about 25 percent of female inmates and 29 percent of male inmates. In state prisons about six out of ten women described themselves as using drugs in the month before the offense, and five out of ten reported they were daily drug users. Nearly one out of three women in state prisons reported they had committed the offense that resulted in their incarceration in order to obtain money to support a need for drugs.

Prior Criminal History: About 65 percent of women in state prisons had a prior criminal history, compared to 77 percent of male inmates. Whereas about one third of women inmates had three or more prior convictions, about 43 percent of male inmates had at least three prior convictions.

Death Sentences: At the end of 1997, forty-four inmates, or 1.3 percent of the death row population, were women. During that year two women were sentenced to death and five had their death sentences commuted. Of the forty-four women, thirty were white and fourteen were black. For these women under sentence of death, an average of seventy-eight months had elapsed since sentencing.

Recidivism: In a sample of women inmates discharged from prisons in eleven states in 1983, it was found that 52 percent of the women were rearrested. An estimated 39 percent were reconvicted within three years, and 33 percent were returned to prison. Prior arrest history was a significant predictor of postprison recidivism. For example, among women with two to three prior arrests, 33 percent were rearrested, as compared with a rate of 69 percent for those women with seven to ten prior arrests.

The Prevalence of Imprisonment: The most recent estimate, made in 1999 by the Justice Department, is that about eleven women out of 1,000 will be incarcerated at some time in their lives and that the likely rate varies according to race. For white women the rate is five out of 1,000, for black women it is thirty-six out of 1,000, and for Hispanic women it is fifteen out of 1,000.

Prison Expenditure

For the fiscal year 1996, the fifty states and the District of Columbia reported spending $22 billion for adult prisons, both male and female, including the costs of building, staffing, and maintaining prisons. To this can be added a further $2.5 billion spent by the Federal Bureau of Prisons. The average cost of housing each inmate in 1996 was $20,100 in state prisons and $23,500 in federal prisons.

From 1990 to 1996 state prison expenditure increased 83 percent, or a rate of about 11 percent each year. Medical and dental care for inmates cost an average of $6.54 per day for each inmate, and inmate programs cost about $3.28 per day.

Gender in State Prisons

Data from three states is presented to give a picture of the state female inmate population. The states are Massachusetts, home to the oldest women's prison in the country at Framingham; Indiana, which has the Indiana State Prison for Women, now a maximum-security facility for women; and California, one of the largest jurisdictions for women prisoners, with eight institutions housing women offenders.

Massachusetts

According to the Massachusetts Department of Correction Massachusetts Correctional Institution (MCI), Framingham is a medium-security correctional facility for female offenders and the oldest female correctional facility in operation in the United States. Its inmate population reflects various levels of classification and includes women awaiting trial. There are four housing units within the prison compound and a two-story, 120-bed housing unit. A minimum-security prerelease facility called Hodder House with thirty-five beds is located about one quarter of a mile outside the prison perimeter; its goal is to facilitate community integration of women inmates. The treatment and educational opportunities at the prison include the following:

- Catch the Hope
- City Mission Society
- Domestic Violence Program
- First Step Program
- Fully Alive Program
- Healthy Human
  Relationships

- Overeaters Anonymous
- Parenting Programs
- Computer Technology
- Building Trades
- Manicuring
- Mandatory Literacy Program
- English as a Second
  Language

Inmate statistics for offense categories, prison offenses, sex offenses, property offenses, and drug and other offenses are shown according to gender for the state as follows:

TABLE 7.1
Current Offense Catagories by Gender

	FEMALE		MALE		TOTAL	
	Number	(%)	Number	(%)	Number	(%)
Person	186	34	4,596	48	4,782	47
Sex	15	3	1,800	19	1,815	18
Property	93	17	892	9	985	10
Drug	190	35	1,975	21	2,165	21
Other	60	11	288	3	348	3
Total	544	100	9,551	100	10,095	100

Source: Research and Planning Division, Massachusetts Department of Corrections. "January 1, 2001 Inmate Statistics." December 2001. Available online: http://www.state.ma.us/doc/pdfs/1101.pdf.

TABLE 7.2
Person Offenses by Gender

	FEMALE		MALE		TOTAL	
	Number	(%)	Number	(%)	Number	(%)
Armed Robbery	27	15	1,018	22	1,045	22
Murder 2nd Degree	18	10	734	16	752	16
Murder lst Degree	15	8	704	15	719	15
Assault / A&B with a Dangerous Weapon	22	12	467	10	489	10
Assault with Intent to Rob or Murder, Being Armed	9	5	401	9	410	9
Manslaughter	21	11	353	8	374	8
Unarmed Robbery	6	3	270	6	276	6
Armed Assault in Dwelling Houses	2	1	78	2	80	2
Assault/Assault and Battery	19	10	46	1	65	1
Unarmed Robbery, Victim 60 and Over	4	2	59	1	63	1
Mayhem	6	3	52	1	58	1
Kidnapping	4	2	49	1	53	1
Vehicular Homicide	5	3	42	1	47	1
Carjacking	1	1	43	1	44	1
Assault and Battery upon a Child	8	4	28	1	36	1
Assault with Intent to Commit Murder	2	1	33	1	35	1
Assault with Intent to Commit Felony	2	1	24	1	26	1
Home Invasion	0	0	24	1	24	1
Accessory before the Fact	3	2	19	0	22	0
Accessory after the Fact	4	2	15	0	19	0
Stealing by Confining or Putting in Fear	0	0	19	0	19	0
Conspiracy	2	1	15	0	17	0
Assault to Rob not Being Armed	1	1	15	0	16	0
Stalking	0	0	15	0	15	0
Murder 2nd Degree, Juvenile Offender Law	0	0	15	0	15	0
Attempted Murder	1	1	12	0	13	0
Armed Asst w/Intent to Rob/Murder, Victim 60+	2	1	9	0	11	0
Violation of Civil Rights	0	0	9	0	9	0
Extortion	0	0	8	0	8	0
Murder 1st Degree, Juvenile Offender Law	0	0	8	0	8	0
A&B with a Dangerous Weapon, Victim 60+	1	1	7	0	8	0
A&B Upon an Elderly or Disabled Person	0	0	4	0	4	0
Assault with a Dangerous Weapon, Victim 60+	1	1	1	0	2	0
Total	**186**	**100**	**4,596**	**100**	**4,782**	**100**

Please Note: The offenses are arranged in descending order by offense total

Source: Research and Planning Division, Massachusetts Department of Corrections. "January 1, 2001 Inmate Statistics."
December 2001. Available online: http://www.state.ma.us/doc/pdfs/1101.pdf.

TABLE 7.3
Sex Offenses by Gender

	FEMALE		MALE		TOTAL	
	Number	(%)	Number	(%)	Number	(%)
Rape and Abuse of a Child	8	53	512	28	520	29
Rape of a Child with Force	2	13	379	21	381	21
Rape	1	7	317	18	318	18
Aggravated Rape	0	0	285	16	285	16
Indecent Asslt & Battery on Child under 14	3	20	143	8	146	8
Assault with Intent to Commit Rape	0	0	90	5	90	5
Indecent Asslt & Battery on Victim 14 or Older	0	0	30	2	30	2
Assault with Intent to Rape, Child under 16	0	0	23	1	23	1
Sexual Assault, Out of State/Federal Inmates	1	7	5	0	6	0
Sex Offenses Involving a Minor	0	0	5	0	5	0
Other Sex Offenses	0	0	4	0	4	0
Incest	0	0	3	0	3	0
Indecent A&B on Mentally Retarded Victim	0	0	2	0	2	0
Unnatural Acts with Child under 16	0	0	1	0	1	0
Crimes against Nature	0	0	1	0	1	0
Unnatural Acts	0	0	0	0	0	0
Total	**15**	**100**	**1,800**	**100**	**1,815**	**100**

Please Note: The offenses are arranged in descending order by offense total.

Source: Research and Planning Division, Massachusetts Department of Corrections. "January 1, 2001 Inmate Statistics." December 2001. Available online: http://www.state.ma.us/doc/pdfs/1101.pdf.

TABLE 7.4
Property Offenses by Gender

	FEMALE		MALE		TOTAL	
	Number	(%)	Number	(%)	Number	(%)
Unarmed Burglary/Breaking and Entering	10	11	483	54	493	50
Theft of Motor Vehicle or non-Motor Vehicle	4	4	87	10	91	9
Shoplifting	10	11	1	0	11	1
Receiving Stolen Goods	8	9	14	2	22	2
Possession of Burglary Tools	0	0	14	2	14	1
Larceny/Stealing	32	34	74	8	106	11
Larceny from the Person	4	4	11	1	15	2
Larceny from Elder or Disabled Person	4	4	5	1	9	1
Fraud	0	0	4	0	4	0
Forgery and Uttering	8	9	21	2	29	3
Embezzlement	0	0	2	0	2	0
Destruction of Property	2	2	19	2	21	2
Common and Notorious Thief	0	0	12	1	12	1
Burglary, Armed or an Assault	0	0	69	8	69	7
Arson and Attempted Arson	11	12	76	9	87	9
Total	**93**	**100**	**892**	**100**	**985**	**100**

Please Note: The offenses are arranged in descending order by offense total.

Source: Research and Planning Division, Massachusetts Department of Corrections. "January 1, 2001 Inmate Statistics." December 2001. Available online: http://www.state.ma.us/doc/pdfs/1101.pdf.

TABLE 7.5
Property Offenses by Gender

	FEMALE		MALE		TOTAL	
	Number	(%)	Number	(%)	Number	(%)
Being Present Where Heroin is Kept	1	1	0	0	1	0
Possession of Hypodermic Syringe/Instrument	4	2	0	0	4	0
Conspiracy to Violate Controlled Substance Act	2	1	32	2	34	2
Possession of Controlled Substance - No Class Specified	22	12	13	1	35	2
Possession of Controlled Substance - Class A	1	1	14	1	15	1
Possession of Controlled Substance - Class B	2	1	3	0	5	0
Possession of Controlled Substance - Class D	0	0	0	0	0	0
Fraudulent Prescriptions	0	0	1	0	1	0
Class A Distribution or Possession w/Intent to Distribute	32	17	269	14	301	14
*Class A Distribution or Poss w/Int to Dist, Subsequent	2	1	78	4	80	4
Class B Distribution or Possession w/Int to Distribute	22	12	211	11	233	11
*Class B Distribution or Poss w/Int to Dist, Subsequent	10	5	112	6	122	6
*Specific Class B Distribution or Poss w/Int to Distribute	20	11	125	6	145	7
*Specific Cl B Possession w/Int to Distribute, Subsequent	3	2	68	3	71	3
Class C Distribution or Possession w/Int to Distribute	0	0	1	0	1	0
*Marijuana Trafficking 50–100 Lbs	1	1	1	0	2	0
*Marijuana Trafficking 100–2,000 Lbs	0	0	1	0	1	0
*Specific Class B Trafficking 14–28 Grams	15	8	251	13	266	12
*Specific Class B Trafficking 28–100Grams	10	5	294	15	304	14
*Specific Class B Trafficking 100–200 Grams	9	5	176	9	185	9
*Specific Class B Trafficking 200+ Grams	10	5	141	7	151	7
*Class A Trafficking 14–28 Grams	0	0	10	1	10	0
*Class A Trafficking 28–100 Grams	4	2	18	1	22	1
*Class A Trafficking 100–200 Grams	0	0	11	1	11	1
*Class A Trafficking 200+ Grams	0	0	7	0	7	0
Class D Distribution or Possession w/Int to Distribute	2	1	5	0	7	0
*Drug Violation, School/Park	18	9	127	6	145	7
Induce Minors in Sale and Distribution of Drugs	0	0	6	0	6	0
Total	**190**	**100**	**1,975**	**100**	**2,165**	**100**

* Denotes an offense which carries a mandatory sentence.
Please Note: The offenses are arranged in order by drug violation category.

Source: Research and Planning Division, Massachusetts Department of Corrections. "January 1, 2001 Inmate Statistics." December 2001. Available online: http://www.state.ma.us/doc/pdfs/1101.pdf.

Indiana

Formerly known as the Indiana Reformatory for Women and Girls, the Indiana Women's Prison is now a maximum-security facility with housing in the form of cells. Female offenders in this institution typically have been convicted of violent or weapons-based offenses and require close supervision and tight security to protect the public, prison staff, and other offenders.

The Indiana Department of Correction's 2001 annual report states that the prison provides CAD (computer-aided design) and commercial laundry services. Its educational and other programs include:

- Individualized Prerelease and Standard Prerelease Orientation Programs
- Substance Abuse Treatment
- Substance Abuse Education
- Mental Health Counseling
- Alcoholics Anonymous Services
- Community Transition Program for all felons except murderers with a sentence of at least two years

The department reports that the adult population at the Indiana Women's Prison has increased 480 percent since 1981 and 56 percent since 1996. It identifies a number of factors contributing to this increase, including the fact that a majority of the female offenders are found in an at-risk group, recent harsher criminal sanctions against women, an attitude of "getting tough on crime," more effective law enforcement, and continued substance abuse. In contrast to the 480-percent increase in the female prison population, the increase in the male prison population was 200 percent during the same period.

The following provides a picture of the adult female population according to offense committed and of the growth in the female population from 1992 to 2001:

FIGURE 7.1
Adult Female Female Felon Population by Most Serious Committing Offense Class
(Includes Offenders Held in Jail and Contracted Beds due to Overcrowding)
July 1, 2001

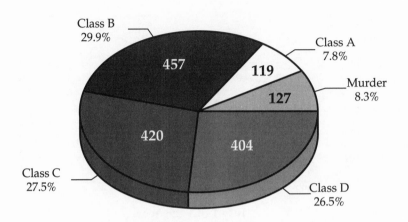

The three most common Class A offenses are: (1) Dealing in Cocaine or Narcotic Drug, (2) Conspiracy, and (3) Voluntary Manslaughter. Forty-four percent of all Class A commitments are for drug offenses

The three most common Class B offenses are: (1) Dealing in Cocaine or Narcotic Drug, (2) Burglary, and (3) Dealing in Schedule I, II, or III Controlled Substance. Sixty-three percent of all Class B commitments are for drug offenses.

The three most common Class C offenses are: (1) Forgery, (2) Robbery, and (3) Battery. Eight percent of all Class C commitments are for drug offenses.

The three most common Class D offenses are: (1) Theft, (2) Prostitution, and (3) Possession of Cocaine or Narcotic Drug. Fifteen percent of all Class D commitments are for drug offenses.

*A person conspires to commit a felony when, with intent to commit the felony, he agrees with another person to commit the felony. A conspiracy to commit a felony is a felony of the same class as the underlying felony. For example, if a person conspires to deal in cocaine and this is determined to be a Class A felony, then the person will be committed for Class A Dealing in Cocaine or Narcotic Drug.

Source: Monthly Statistical Report, Offender Information System, http://www.ai.org/indcorrection/AnnRep.pdf

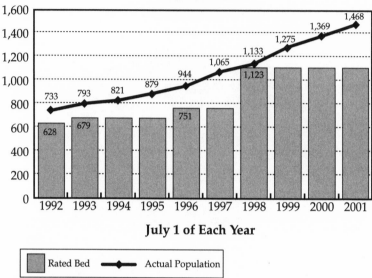

FIGURE 7.2
Adult Female Population
Population and Rated Bed Capacity
1992–2001

July 1 of Each Year

Source: Monthly Statistical Report, Offender Information System,
http://www.ai.org/indcorrection/AnnRep.pdf

California

Along with Texas and the federal prison system, California has a high female inmate population. Among its female facilities is the California Institution for Women (CIW), which opened in 1952 on a 150-acre site and which housed 2,107 female prisoners in June 2000. Until 1987, CIW was California's only prison for female felons, and its campus-like design was in keeping with the then-notions of prisoner rehabilitation. According to the California Department of Corrections, CIW accommodates all custody levels of female inmates and houses female inmates with special needs such as pregnancy, psychiatric care, methadone addiction, and those with HIV infection.

CIW runs inmate programs, which include textile and clothing manufacture, and vocational programs that include computer training, data processing, electronics, graphic arts, printing, plumbing, and upholstery. Inmate programs are stated to include:

- Prerelease
- Adult Basic Education
- Arts in Corrections
- Victim Awareness
- Drug Treatment/Diversion

A picture of the female inmate population by offense, race, and age for the year 1999 follows:

TABLE 7.6
Institution Population by Age Group, Mean Age, and Sex,
December 31, 1999

Age Group	TOTAL		MALE		FEMALE	
	Number	(%)	Number	(%)	Number	(%)
Under 18	115	0.1	111	0.1	4	0.0
18–19	2,417	1.5	2,351	1.6	66	0.6
20–24	22,147	13.8	21,326	14.3	821	7.3
25–29	28,160	17.5	26,591	17.8	1,569	14.0
30–34	30,217	18.8	27,860	18.6	2,357	21.1
35–39	31,162	19.4	28,349	19.0	2,813	25.2
40–44	22,844	14.2	20,861	14.0	1,983	17.7
45–49	12,606	7.8	11,672	7.8	934	8.4
50–54	6,150	3.8	5,762	3.9	388	3.5
55–59	2,692	1.7	2,536	1.7	156	1.4
60 and Over	2,177	1.4	2,094	1.4	83	0.7
Mean Age	34.7		34.6		36.0	
Total	160,687	100.0	149,513	100.0	11,174	100.0

Source: State of California, Department of Corrections, Offender Information Services Branch, Estimates and Statistical Analysis Section, Data Analysis Unit. "California Prisoners and Parolees 2000." Available at http://www.cdc.state.ca.us/pdf/CalPris2000elect2.pdf.

TABLE 7.7
Institution Population by Offense and Sex,
December 31, 1999

	TOTAL		MALE		FEMALE	
	Number	(%)	Number	(%)	Number	(%)
CRIMES AGAINST PERSONS	70,359	43.9	67,777	45.4	2,582	23.3
Homicide	21,273	13.3	20,242	13.6	1,031	9.3
Murder 1st	8,908	5.6	8,552	5.7	356	3.2
Murder 2nd	9,211	5.7	8,761	5.9	450	4.1
Manslaughter	2,728	1.7	2,548	1.7	180	1.6
Vehicular Manslaughter	426	0.3	381	0.3	45	0.4
Robbery	16,881	10.5	16,274	10.9	607	5.5
Assault and Battery	18,390	11.5	17,616	11.8	774	7.0
Assault Deadly Weapon	9,653	6.0	9,260	6.2	393	3.5
Other Assault/Battery	8,737	5.5	8,356	5.6	381	3.4
Sex Offenses	11,512	7.2	11,410	7.6	102	0.9
Rape	2,116	1.3	2,109	1.4	7	0.1
Lewd Act with Child	6,302	3.9	6,248	4.2	54	0.5
Oral Copulation	696	0.4	692	0.5	4	0.0
Sodomy	228	0.1	228	0.2	0	0.0
Penetration with Object	357	0.2	354	0.2	3	0.0
Other Sex Offenses	1,813	1.1	1,779	1.2	34	0.3
Kidnap	2,303	1.4	2,235	1.5	68	0.6
PROPERTY CRIMES	34,076	21.3	30,896	20.7	3,180	28.6
Burglary	14,355	9.0	13,491	9.0	864	7.8
Burglary 1st	7,900	4.9	7,556	5.1	344	3.1
Burglary 2nd	6,455	4.0	5,935	4.0	520	4.7
Theft	12,776	8.0	11,198	7.5	1,578	14.2
Grand Theft	2,666	1.7	2,309	1.5	357	3.2
Petty Theft with Prior	7,204	4.5	6,168	4.1	1,036	9.3
Receiving Stolen Property	2,906	1.8	2,721	1.8	185	1.7
Vehicle Theft	4,494	2.8	4,330	2.9	164	1.5
Forgery/Fraud	1,870	1.2	1,407	0.9	463	4.2
Other Property	581	0.4	470	0.3	111	1.0
DRUG CRIMES	45,328	28.3	40,455	27.1	4,873	43.9
CS Possession	19,753	12.3	17,223	11.5	2,530	22.8
CS Possession for Sale	12,974	8.1	11,753	7.9	1,221	11.0
CS Sale	6,850	4.3	6,175	4.1	675	6.1
CS Manufacturing	2,992	1.9	2,753	1.8	239	2.2
CS Other	948	0.6	822	0.6	126	1.1
Hashish Possession	27	0.0	25	0.0	2	0.0
Marijuana Possession for Sale	936	0.6	900	0.6	36	0.3
Marijuana Sale	714	0.4	676	0.5	38	0.3
Marijuana Other	134	0.1	128	0.1	6	0.1
OTHER CRIMES	10,497	6.5	10,030	6.7	467	4.2
Escape	295	0.2	265	0.2	30	0.3
Driving under the Influence	2,300	1.4	2,201	1.5	99	0.9
Arson	432	0.3	392	0.3	40	0.4
Possession of Weapon	4,362	2.7	4,283	2.9	79	0.7
Other Offenses	3,108	1.9	2,889	1.9	219	2.0
TOTAL	160,687		149,513		11,174	
OFFENSE DATA UNAVAILABLE	427		355		72	
TOTAL KNOWN OFFENSE DATA	160,260	100.0	149,158	100.0	11,102	100.0

NOTE: Components may not add to totals due to independent routing.

Source: State of California, Department of Corrections, Offender Information Services branch, Estimates and Statistical Analysis section, data analysis Unit. "California Prisoners and Parolees 2000." Available at http://www.cdc.state.ca.us/pdf/CalPris2000elect2.pdf.

TABLE 7.8
Institution Population by Racial/Ethnic Group and Sex,
December 31, 1999

Racial/Ethnic Group	TOTAL		MALE		FEMALE	
	Number	(%)	Number	(%)	Number	(%)
White	47,279	29.4	42,993	28.8	4,286	38.4
Hispanic (Mexican)	54,690	34.0	52,070	34.8	2,620	23.4
Black	50,321	31.3	46,570	31.1	3,751	33.6
Other	8,397	5.2	7,880	5.3	517	4.6
Total	160,687	100.0	149,513	100.0	11,174	100.0

Source: State of California, Department of Corrections, Offender Information Services branch, Estimates and Statistical Analysis section, data analysis Unit. "California Prisoners and Parolees 2000." Available at http://www.cdc.state.ca.us/pdf/CalPris2000elect2.pdf.

8

Directory of Organizations, Associations, and Government and International Agencies

Information follows with respect to international, federal, state, and nongovernmental organizations related to women's prisons and issues affecting women in prison.

American Civil Liberties Union National Prison Project
733 15th Street NW, Suite 620
Washington, DC 20005
(202) 393-4930
E-mail: check website for local office
Website: http://www.aclu.org/issues/prisons

The National Prison Project was founded in 1972 by the ACLU and seeks to create constitutional conditions of confinement and to strengthen prisoners' rights though class-action litigation and public education. The focus of the project includes issues relevant to women in prisons, such as reducing prison overcrowding, improving medical care in prisons, and eliminating violence and maltreatment. Project staff publish a quarterly journal and conduct public education through conferences. They also work with a network of private lawyers throughout the country. Among the publications of the project are a guide for prisoners and the *AIDS in Prison Bibliography* (1998), which catalogues resource material on AIDS in prisons.

Amnesty International, Women's Human Rights
Amnesty International USA
322 Eighth Avenue
New York, NY 10001
(212) 627-1451
E-mail: check website for local office
Website: http://www.amnesty-usa.org

This program aims to promote and advocate for observance and enforcement of the human rights of women throughout the world. As well as reporting on concerns affecting women's rights, Amnesty International publishes a quarterly bulletin on women's rights and handbooks on issues relevant to rights. A recent report—*About Women in Custody: Sexual Misconduct and the Shackling of Pregnant Women*—reveals how states have a poor record in providing female inmates with protection against sexual abuse and that many allow the shackling of women prisoners during pregnancy.

Bureau of Justice Statistics, Department of Justice
810 Seventh Street NW
Washington, DC 20531
(202) 307-0765
E-mail: askbjs@ojp.usdoj.gov
Website: http://www.ojp.usdoj.gov/bjs

The Bureau of Justice Statistics is an important source of statistical and other information on the criminal justice system generally, including women offenders and women in prison. Reports from the bureau can be downloaded from its website, and it maintains an e-mail system for advance notification of publications.

California Coalition for Women Prisoners (CCWP)
100 McAllister Street
San Francisco, CA 94102
(415) 255-7036
E-mail: ccwp@igc.org
Website: http://www.womenprisoners.org

The CCWP fights for basic human rights and against the medical neglect of women prisoners in California. It aims to raise public awareness of the cruel and inhumane conditions under which women prisoners live and advocates for changes in those conditions. It promotes the leadership of, and the giving of voice to, women prisoners, including former prisoners and their families. Coalition members visit women in prison, produce a newsletter, make protests, and conduct advocacy, education, outreach, and support for former prisoners. The organization began in 1995 to support a lawsuit filed by women incarcerated at the Central California Women's Facility and the California Institution for Women seeking adequate medical care.

Chicago Legal Advocacy for Incarcerated Mothers (CLAIM)
220 South State Street, Suite 830
Chicago, IL 60604
(312) 332-5537
E-mail: info@c-l-a-i-m.org
Website: http://www.c-l-a-i-m.org

CLAIM was formed in 1985 to address the gap in legal aid and advocacy for women inmates and their families. As it has grown over time, it is now a source of legal aid for female prisoners and their families and includes two volunteer lawyer programs and an active board of directors. CLAIM provides legal advice to assist mothers in taking steps to prevent their incarceration from causing permanent damage to the family structure. This action includes enforcing legal rights such as mother-and-child visits, appropriate placement and guardianship options for children of women in prison, and the gaining of public benefits for these children during their mother's periods of confinement. Using volunteer lawyers and paralegals, the organization assigns appropriate cases and supports its volunteers with malpractice insurance, training in family law, and mentoring. CLAIM's Jail Project teaches classes on the criminal court system and in family law to women at Cook County Jail, and its Advocacy Project includes a women's peer support group working for personal and institutional change. Through this group, former prisoners address issues such as reentering the community after a term in prison and wider issues that affect them and their families.

Correctional Association of New York
135 East 15th Street
New York, NY 10003
(212) 254-5700

E-mail: info@correctionalassociation.org
Website: http://www.corrassoc.org

Founded in 1844, the Correctional Association of New York has a long history of concern about conditions in prison and the lack of support services for former prisoners. The association was granted the right in 1846 by special law to inspect prisons and report its findings to policy makers and the public. It now runs four working projects: the Public Policy Project, the Women in Prison Project, the Prison Visiting Project, and the Juvenile Justice Project. Through advocacy, public education, and the development of workable alternatives the Correctional Association seeks to create a fairer and more humane criminal justice system and a safer and more just society.

The Corrections Connection
159 Burgin Parkway
Quincy, MA 02169
(617) 471-4445
E-mail: contact from website
Website: http://www.corrections.com

The Corrections Connection calls itself "the official home of corrections" and provides a directory of information as well as links to many topics in corrections. It came on line in 1996 as the first weekly news source committed to improving the lives of corrections professionals and their families. Although not directly focusing on the subject of women in prison, it is a good source of daily information on corrections generally and through its chatrooms and bulletin boards provides a useful insight into how correctional professionals see their task and the constraints they believe they face in providing effective correctional services.

The Drug Reform Coordination Network (DRCNet)
2000 P Street NW, #210
Washington, DC 20036
E-mail: drcnet@drcnet.org
Website: http://www.drcnet.org

DRCNet was founded with the objective of stopping the chaos and violence of the illegal drug trade and to end the mass incarceration suffered by hundreds of thousands of nonviolent offenders. It aims to reform drug laws, opposes the building of prisons, and supports reforms that it argues have been compromised by the war on drugs. DRCNet advocates public dialogue on the range of alternatives to current drug policy and the implementation of public health-based approaches to reduce the suffering caused by drug use and the "war on drugs". The organization offers to provide professional information to activists and members of the public interested in becoming involved in its mission.

Families Against Mandatory Minimums Foundation (FAMM)
1612 K Street NW, Suite 1400
Washington, DC 20006
(202) 822-6700
E-mail: contact from website
Website: http://www.famm.org

FAMM is a nonprofit organization founded in 1991 with the objective of challenging inflexible and excessive penalties required under mandatory sentencing laws. The organization promotes sentencing laws that give judges the discretion to distinguish between appropriate sentences for defendants, taking into account factors such as offense seriousness, potential for rehabilitation, and the role played by the defendant in the commission of the crime. FAMM aims to educate people about the unjust nature of mandatory minimum sentences and to mobilize a reform movement through lobbying federal and state lawmakers, building coalitions, and promoting efforts at the grassroots level. FAMM believes that judicial discretion is the appropriate method of arriving at a just sentence and that judges and not lawmakers should determine an appropriate sentence for a crime. It wants to see mandatory penalties replaced with sentencing laws with flexible sentencing guidelines.

Family and Corrections Network (FCN)
32 Oak Grove Road
Palmyra, VA 22963
(434) 589-3036
E-mail: fcn@fcnetwork.org
Website: http://www.fcnetwork.org

Family and Corrections Network is concerned with the families of offenders and offers information, training, and technical assistance relating to the children of prisoners, parenting programs for prisoners, prison visiting, incarcerated fathers and mothers, returning to the community, and prison marriage. It publishes the

FCH Report, which is devoted to issues concerning families of offenders. It has an online reading room with over ninety articles and links to related sites.

Legal Services for Prisoners with Children (LSPC)
1540 Market Street, Suite 490
San Francisco, CA
(415) 255-7036
E-mail: info@prisonerswithchildren.org
Website: http://www.prisonerswithchildren.org

LSPC advocates for the civil rights and for the empowerment of incarcerated parents, children, family members, and people at risk of incarceration. It responds to requests for information, training, technical assistance, litigation, and community activism. Its focus is on women in prison and their families, and it stresses that race is a core issue in any discussion of incarceration.

National Criminal Justice Reference Service, Department of Justice (NCJRS)
P.O. Box 6000
Rockville, MD 20849-6000
(800) 851-3420
E-mail: askncjrs@ncjrs.org
Website: http://www.ojp.usdoj.gov

NCJRS is a resource maintained by the Department of Justice that offers justice information to support research and policy and program development worldwide. Its resources are available to all, and it offers extensive reference and referral services to deal with questions about crime and crime related issues, including corrections. This information includes statistics, publications, and compiling information packages and assistance tailored to particular needs. By registering online with NCJRS, it is possible to receive a bimonthly newsletter and e-mail notifications about new publications and resources. Many reports are available through the NCJRS website, including reports on prison and jail inmates, mental health treatment in state prisons, and HIV in prison and jails.

National Institute of Corrections (NIC), U.S. Department of Justice
320 First Street NW

Washington, DC 20534
(800) 995-6423
E-mail: asknicic@nicic.org
Website: http://www.nicic.org

The NIC Information Center provides research assistance and document delivery for correctional policy makers, practitioners, elected officials, and members of the public interested in corrections issues. Its services are provided free of charge and cover a wide range of policy and program issues concerning prisons and prisoners. The center produces a series of publications such as those concerned with jails, community corrections, and those of general interest.

Parents and Children Together, Inc. (PACT)
2836 Hemphill
Forth Worth, TX 76110
(817) 924-7776
E-mail: dkpact@juno.com
Website: http://www.fcnetwork.org

PACT is a nonprofit organization established in 1984 with the aim of preserving and strengthening the families of those incarcerated in prisons. Its primary objective is to prevent the incarceration of future generations by encouraging stronger and healthier families. PACT provides a community network and referral service to the families of incarcerated prisoners and former offenders, a family support group, a hospitality house for inmate families, parent education and life skill classes to various correctional institutions across the country, a volunteer mentor program designed to provide emotional support to prisoners and their families, and a program called SKIP—Support Groups for Kids with Incarcerated Parents—to elementary schools in the Fort Worth area. PACT also issues a newsletter and runs other kinds of programs concerned with the general issue of prisoners and their families.

The Prison Activist Resource Center (PARC)
P.O. Box 339
Berkeley, CA 94701
(510) 893-4648
E-mail: parc@prisonactivist.org
Website: http://www.prisonactivist.org

PARC states that it is the source for progressive and radical information on prisons and the criminal prosecution system. Among the prison issues in which it is interested are women in prison. It provides news and support to activists and advocacy groups working on prison reform as well as prison support, working with other groups in the Bay area and nationally. It also organizes public forums, film showings, and demonstrations to build public awareness. The main goals of PARC are to expose the myths that sustain widespread injustices in prisons, to inspire and motivate people to take positive action against the mass incarceration system and for prisoners' civil and human rights, and to provide practical support to activists engaged in this advocacy. The PARC website contains many links to other organizations concerned with prison and prison reform, including those involved with women in prison.

Stop Prisoner Rape (SPR)
6303 Wiltshire Boulevard, Suite 205
Los Angeles, CA 90048
(323) 653-7867
E-mail: info@spr.org
Website: http://www.spr.org

SPR seeks to put an end to sexual violence committed against men, women, and youth in confinement. As well as posting relevant news items on its website, SPR has issued a number of publications, press releases, and news items. A number of legal articles concerned with rape and sexual assault laws, and a state-by-state review of custodial sexual misconduct laws, are also published on its website. The organization was founded by survivors of prison rape over twenty years ago.

United Nations Asia and Far East Institute for the Prevention of Crime and the Treatment of Offenders (UNAFEI)
1-26, Harumi-cho, Fuchu-shi
Tokyo 183-0057
Japan
81-42-333-7021
E-mail: unafei@moj.go.jp
Website: http://www.unafei.or.jp

UNAFEI is a United Nations regional institute established in 1962 by agreement between the United Nations and the government of

Japan with the aim of promoting the development of criminal justice systems and cooperation in the Asia and Pacific region. The activities of the institute include training courses and seminars for personnel in crime prevention and research studies of the treatment of offenders. UNAFEI also organizes two international training courses and one international seminar each year and publishes information on the criminal justice systems and treatment of offenders in the Asia and Pacific region.

Vera Institute of Justice
233 Broadway, 12th Floor
New York, NY 10279
(212) 334-1300
E-mail: webmaster@vera.org
Website: http://www.vera.org

The Vera Institute was established forty years ago by an active philanthropist to campaign against the bail system, regarding it as a practice that granted liberty based only on income. Sentencing and corrections is one of the current areas of interest of the institute. Its website provides information about past and current projects, which span the core areas of the criminal justice system, including the diversion of drug abusers from prison, the effect of state sentencing guidelines, and support for drug-abusing offenders and their families. Its research department has just completed an evaluation of New York City's system of alternatives to incarceration for felons.

Women Coping in Prison
Institute for Law, Psychiatry, and Public Policy
P.O. Box 800660
1107 West Main Street
University of Virginia
Charlottesville, VA 22908
E-mail: contact from website
Website: http://curry.edschool.virginia.edu/prisonstudy/

Women Coping in Prison is a joint project of the University of Virginia and the Fluvanna Correctional Center for Women. The project is intended to explore the subjective and objective parameters of the experience of women living in a prison environment, including patterns of victimization that existed prior to incarceration, the extent of violence occurring within a maximum-security prison for women, patterns of adjustment made by women as a result of incarceration, and family stress caused by confinement in prison. Inmates participate in this research through structured interviews and other studies.

Women's Prison Book Project (WPBP)
2441 Lyndale Avenue South
Minneapolis, MN 55405
E-mail: wpbp@prisonactivist.org
Website: http://www.prisonactivist.org/wpbp/

Since 1994, the WPBP has been providing women in prison with free reading materials covering a range of subjects from law and education to politics, history, and health. The project believes that incarcerated women have needs for particular kinds of information such as that on families, children, women's self-help, women's health, and legal aid for women who fight back against those who abuse them. WPBP is an all-volunteer organization composed of an administrative collective and a group of volunteers who assist with weekly book mailings and with fundraising events.

9

Selected Print and Nonprint Resources

Bibliography

This bibliography classifies books into categories: general books by criminologists that include material on women in prison, more detailed criminological works and works with a feminist focus, and popular works. Also included are relevant chapters in books, journal articles, government publications, core periodicals, and nonprint resources.

General Books

Belknap, J. 2001. *The Invisible Woman: Gender, Crime, and Justice,* 2d ed. Belmont, CA: Wadsworth. 446 pages.

A standard textbook on women and crime, this volume covers the field of women in the criminal justice system and has an informed and comprehensive section concerned with incarcerating, punishing, and treating offending women and girls.

Butler, Anne. 1997. *Gendered Justice in the American West: Women Prisoners in Men's Penitentiaries.* Urbana and Chicago: University of Illinois Press. 262 pages.

Focusing on groups of women who lived in the American West during the late nineteenth and early twentieth centuries, the author explores the circumstances of women imprisoned with men in the West, including the circumstances that caused them to be incarcerated, and the life of the male prison world and the violence women encountered inside men's prisons. The nature of work performed by women and women's health issues are also examined. The book reveals how gender shaped the experience of women incarcerated in the West.

Chesney-Lind, M. 1997. *The Female Offender: Girls, Women, and Crime.* Thousand Oaks, CA: Sage Publications. 219 pages.

Beginning with the subject of female delinquency, this book brings a focus on trends in women's crime, discusses the place of drugs and violence in women's criminality, and addresses the issue of sentencing women to prison, arguing that effective community-based strategies and programs would be more appropriate than building more prisons for women.

Cook, S., and S. Davies. 1999. *Harsh Punishment: International Experiences of Women's Imprisonment.* Boston: Northeastern University Press. 326 pages.

This comparative volume examines women's imprisonment in a number of countries including the United States, Canada, England, New Zealand, and Thailand and discusses issues such as the "war on drugs" and African American women in U.S. prisons. It also provides personal accounts from women of their experience of incarceration.

Fishman, L. 1990. *Women at the Wall: A Study of Prisoners' Wives Doing Time on the Outside.* Albany: State University of New York Press. 337 pages.

The author presents women's accounts of the issues they face as wives of prisoners and describes their experience as "doing time on the outside." She explores the women's knowledge about their criminal husbands before incarceration and their domestic lives and fast living and traces events from before their husbands' arrest, through the court process and sentencing, ending in their incarceration. She presents accounts of how the wives are stigmatized as prisoners' wives and their experiences in prison visiting, living alone, and coping with their husbands' reentry into society after release.

Fletcher, B. R., L. D. Shaver, and D. G. Moon. 1993. *Women Prisoners: A Forgotten Population.* Westport, CT: Praeger. 212 pages.

An examination of prison subculture that presents an in-depth study of incarcerated women and the attitudes, beliefs, and values of the women and correctional staff.

Heidensohn, F. 1995. *Women and Crime.* Washington Square: New York University Press. 242 pages.

The author presents the experiences of women and crime and addresses the issue of women and the penal system as well as providing a discussion of female criminality through various criminological theories. The author shows how feminist analysis of family life has a bearing on the social constraints faced by women and brings a comparative approach to the subject using material from England, Australia, Canada, and the United States.

Muraskin, R., ed. 2000. *It's a Crime: Women and Justice,* 3d ed. Upper Saddle River, NJ: Prentice-Hall. 488 pages.

This edited volume focuses on issues affecting women coming into contact with the criminal justice system. There are sections on women and drugs, HIV, and women offenders, as well as a section concerned with women in prison that covers a wide range of topics including the long-term incarceration effects on women in prison, the issue of three-strikes legislation and its impact on women, and the relationship between correctional officers and female offenders. As well, the issues of sexual abuse of women in prison and women on death row are given detailed treatment.

Price, B. R., and N. Sokoloff, eds. 1995. *The Criminal Justice System and Women: Offenders, Victims, and Workers.* New York: McGraw-Hill. 456 pages.

This edited book covers the field of women and crime beginning with theories and facts about female offenders, moving to address the subject of women as victims of crime, and concluding with some issues affecting women workers in the criminal justice system. It contains a chapter analyzing the conflict experienced by women correctional officers and has a strong focus on wife battering and domestic violence as well as drugs and racial issues affecting women and crime.

Rafter, N., ed. 2000. *Encyclopedia of Women and Crime.* Phoenix, AZ: Oryx Press. 361 pages.

As well as covering crimes by women and theories of female crime, this volume has sections on punishment and treatment of women, both in the United States and in Britain, Canada, and Australia. Each entry is supplemented by further reading lists, and an extensive bibliography is provided.

Zaplin, R., ed. 1998. *Female Offenders: Critical Perspectives and Effective Interventions.* Gaithersburg, MD: Aspen Publishers. 398 pages.

This edited volume addresses theoretical and applied aspects of female criminality and incarceration. There is an emphasis on treatment issues including mental health and childhood mistreatment, and a discussion of institutional programs for female offenders.

Criminological and Feminist Works

Bacon, M. 2000. *Abby Hopper Gibbons: Prison Reformer and Social Activist.* New York: State University of New York. 217 pages.

This book, by a historian who has focused on the contribution of Quaker women in social reform, traces the background and career of Abby Hopper Gibbons, who made a major contribution to prison reform for women in the United States in the nineteenth and early twentieth centuries. In discussing Gibbons's work she presents a history of the women's reformatory movement and shows how Quaker and non-Quaker women collaborated to change conditions for women in prison.

Butler, A. M. 1997. *Gendered Justice in the American West: Women Prisoners in Men's Penitentiaries.* Urbana: University of Illinois Press. 262 pages.

The author, a historian, explores the history of women's incarceration in men's penitentiaries in the West, focusing particularly on the experience of women in that form of confinement, their health, and the forms of violence they suffered prior to incarceration.

Enos, S. 2001. *Mothering from the Inside: Parenting in a Women's Prison.* New York: State University of New York. 176 pages.

The author reveals how women cope with motherhood from inside prison, showing how they find places for their children to live, manage relationships with their children's caregivers, demonstrate their fitness as mothers, and negotiate rights to their children in difficult circumstances.

Faith, K. 1993. *Unruly Women: The Politics of Confinement and Resistance.* Vancouver: Press Gang Publishers. 335 pages.

Taking a feminist approach to women's confinement, the author begins with a historical overview of women's "unruliness," discusses modern crimes by women with an emphasis on the connection between victimization and criminalization, and then moves to a discussion of the "pains of imprisonment" located against a review of prison programs and services designed to respond to the fact of imprisonment. Resistance is a focus of this work, which presents a comparative approach using material from Canada and the United States.

Freedman, E. 2000. *Their Sister's Keepers: Women's Prison Reform in America, 1830–1930.* Ann Arbor: University of Michigan Press. 248 pages.

This book is one of the leading historical presentations of women's imprisonment, especially in relation to the reformatory movement. It provides a comprehensive account of that movement and subsequent developments in women's incarceration.

Girshick, L. 1999. *No Safe Haven: Stories of Women in Prison.* Boston: Northeastern University Press. 201 pages.

Pointing out that incarcerated women constitute a largely invisible population because of their small numbers and their involvement in less serious offenses, the author draws on the life stories of forty women inmates at a minimum-security prison in North Carolina. In exploring their lives before incarceration, she asks us to see their criminality in the context of their childhood and adolescent experiences. Girshick argues that society's treatment of these women has led some of them to commit crime, and she makes recommendations for social change and community programs intended to reduce women's imprisonment.

Grobsmith, E. 1994. *Indians in Prison: Incarcerated Native Americans in Nebraska.* Lincoln: University of Nebraska Press. 205 pages.

The author's focus is the incarceration of Native Americans in Nebraska, and she argues that for Native Americans imprisoned there, adjustment to prison life involves more than acceptance of incarceration, bringing also a need for a process through which each Native American must determine how to merge being Indian with being incarcerated, where sacrifices in maintaining heritage and identity can be made, and where they cannot. Beginning with the historical framework, the author examines life in prison for Native Americans and focuses on alcohol and substance abuse as a particular aspect of the specificity of Native American imprisonment.

Hawkes, M. 1994. *Excellent Effect: The Edna Mahan Story.* Laurel, MD: American Correctional Association. 243 pages.

A history of the life and career of Edna Mahan, who for forty years was the superintendent of the Clinton Farms Reformatory for Women in New Jersey.

Heffernan, E. 1972. *Making It in Prison: The Square, the Cool, and the Life.* New York: John Wiley & Sons. 231 pages.

An early attempt to explore and explain the culture in a women's prison. The author identifies certain typologies within the prison culture that women adopt as a means of coping with the prison experience.

James, J., ed. 2000. *States of Confinement: Policing, Detention, and Prisons.* New York: St. Martin's Press. 368 pages.

This book contains a section on sexuality and confinement with a discussion of various aspects of incarceration, including fighting HIV and health care accessibility. There are also chapters on race, ethnicity, and culture.

Lekkerkerker, E. C. 1931. *Reformatories for Women in the United States.* J. B. Wolters, Groningen, etc. 615 pages.

An important historical resource on women's imprisonment, this book, written in 1931, describes the state of women's prisons and reformatories at that time and provides valuable historical evidence of the reformatory movement.

Martin, Susan Ehrlich, and Nancy C. Jurik. 1996. *Doing Justice, Doing Gender.* Thousand Oaks, CA: Sage Publications. 270 pages.

A study of women in the justice system covering police officers, lawyers, and corrections that reveals how gender informs and shapes perceptions of women and women's performances in the criminal justice system. The book is a standard in its field and explores the historical roles of women in the criminal justice system, the contributions that women have made and continue to make to the system, the barriers women encounter and the strategies and tactics they perform to counter them, and the effect that women have had on the system, on victims, offenders, coworkers, and the public.

O'Brien, P. 2001. *Making It in the "Free World": Women in Transition from Prison.* New York: State University of New York Press. 201 pages.

This book addresses the topic of how women return to the "free world" after the experience of incarceration. The author presents detailed descriptions of the experiences of women with a range of criminal histories, and she suggests policy changes particularly in terms of alternatives to incarceration. Issues such as the concrete establishment of a home and address after leaving prison, how relationships formed within prison affect the transition from confinement to freedom, and how parole supervision affects women's ability to sustain themselves in the "free world" are also covered.

Owen, B. 1998. *"In the Mix": Struggle and Survival in a Women's Prison.* Albany: State University of New York Press. 219 pages.

This book is a detailed exploration of the struggle and survival of women confined in the largest women's correctional facility in the world. Her research centers on the culture existing in a contemporary women's prison in California. She examines closely how imprisoned women learn about, negotiate, and shape the prison experience. The book is written with a feminist perspective and deals not only with the actual prison experience but family life before incarceration. Relationships inside and outside the prison, and race, figure prominently as aspects of the discussion, and the author identifies access to information about prison and interpersonal coping skills as two key factors in women learning to negotiate the prison world.

Pollock, J. 2002. *Women, Prison, and Crime.* 2d ed. Belmont, CA: Wadsworth. 258 pages.

Addressing women's criminality and women in prison, the author presents a comprehensive and comparative discussion of these subjects. The experience of living in prison, legal issues for incarcerated women, and programming for women in prison are addressed in addition to staffing and administration issues such as the position of men guarding women and the constraints faced by female correctional officers.

Rafter, N. 1985. *Partial Justice: Women in State Prisons, 1800–1935.* Boston: Northeastern University Press. 269 pages.

One of the leading histories of women's imprisonment, this book discusses both reformatory and custodial prisons and presents the theoretical underpinnings of women's incarceration. The author's focus is historical and criminological, and the volume presents material not found in other histories, including racism in state prisons and the special nature of women's imprisonment in the South.

Rierden, A. 1997. *The Farm: Life inside a Women's Prison.* Amherst: University of Massachusetts Press. 224 pages.

This is a study of the dynamics of a women's prison, the Connecticut Correctional Institute in Niantic, located in a rural area. The author studied the women prisoners from 1992 to 1995; her narrative focuses on several older inmates and on changes that took place within the prison as the population shifted from minor to serious repeat offenders.

Ross, L. 1998. *Inventing the Savage: The Social Construction of Native American Criminality.* Austin: University of Texas Press. 314 pages.

The author draws on the life histories of imprisoned Native American women to show how race/ethnicity, gender, and class contribute to the criminalizing of women's behavior. She reveals the violence in the lives of these women prior to incarceration and their responses and, through a comparison with the experiences of white women in the same prison, brings out the significant role that race plays in determining women's experience within the criminal justice system. Importantly, she presents a historical/colonial view of the Native American experience, showing how this extra dimension has played a role in the criminalization of the Native American population.

Shichor, D., and D. Sechrest, eds. 1996. *Three Strikes and You're Out: Vengeance as Public Policy.* Thousand Oaks, CA: Sage Publications. 290 pages.

This book comprehensively considers aspects of legislation providing for the three-strikes rule, including the historical, legal, economic, and social aspects. One section discusses the effects of three-strikes legislation on women and presents arguments opposing the use of this legislation for women offenders. A historical perspective on female offenders discusses their crimes, sentences, and imprisonment rates. The authors argue that the impact of three-strikes laws on women is problematic in view of evidence that women often commit violent crime in response to physical and emotional abuse.

Sommers, E. 1995. *Voices from within: Women Who Have Broken the Law.* Toronto: University of Toronto Press. 167 pages.

The author presents the voices of women confined in prison, describing what they feel led to their imprisonment, and identifies through a feminist analysis the ways in which oppression in the form of sexism, racism, and classism has rendered women powerless and isolated. The author's detailed focus on women's lives brings a multidimensional approach to the study of women in prison as she highlights the social context of their incarceration.

Watterson, K., and M. Chesney-Lind. 1996. *Women in Prison: Inside the Concrete Womb.* Boston: Northeastern University Press. 402 pages.

The book draws on candid interviews with over 400 women inmates and correctional officers to explore the experience of incarceration.

Popular Works

Atwood, J. E. 2000. *Too Much Time: Women in Prison*. London: Phaidon Press. 196 pages.

A documentary survey of the experience of women in prison by a photojournalist. The book presents photographs and interviews with women and correctional officers and produces an account of society's attitude to women's criminality and incarceration. The author visited about forty prisons, and the book contains striking photographs as well as the voices of the incarcerated women.

Furio, J. 2001. *Letters from Prison: Voices of Women Murderers*. New York: Algora Publishing. 240 pages.

This book concerns communications between prison activist Furio and incarcerated women convicted of murder. The author established relationships with thirteen women, and the book contains their letters and explores the backgrounds of these women in biographical essays. Using the women's letters, Furio draws attention to their humanity, their shared backgrounds of abuse, and the biases they encounter in dealing with the criminal justice system.

Jones, A. 1996. *Women Who Kill*. Boston: Beacon Press. 448 pages.

This book explores how and why women have killed throughout American history and what their circumstances reveal about society, its prejudices, and the criminal justice system. The studies are historical in nature and include explorations of the events concerning female murderers such as Lizzie Borden and Jean Harris.

Wojda, Raymond, and Judy Rowse. 1997. *Women Behind Bars*. Lanham, MD: American Correctional Association. 75 pages.

A vivid insight into life in prison that takes the form of women's first-person accounts of the circumstances that led to their incarceration and life in a women's prison. The photographs add an extra dimension to the personal accounts to bring the prison experience to life for the readers.

Book Chapters and Journal Articles

Banks, C. 2002. "Doing Time in Alaska: Women, Culture, and Crime." In *It's a Crime: Women and Justice,* 3d ed., edited by R. Muraskin. Upper Saddle River, NJ: Prentice-Hall.

Feinman, C. 1984. "An Historical Overview of the Treatment of Incarcerated Women: Myths and Realities of Rehabilitation." *Prison Journal* 63 (2): 12–26.

Koban, L. 1983. "Parent in Prison: A Comparative Analysis of the Effects of Incarceration on the Families of Men and Women." *Research in Law, Deviance, and Social Control* 5: 171–183.

Mahan, S. 1984. "Imposition of Despair: An Ethnography of Women in Prison." *Justice Quarterly* 1: 357–384.

McClellan, D. S. 1994. "Disparity in the Discipline of Male and Female Inmates in Texas Prisons." *Women and Criminal Justice* 5 (2): 71–97.

Raeder, M. S. 1993. "Gender and Sentencing: Single Moms, Battered Women, and Other Sex-Based Anomalies in the Gender-Free World of the Federal Sentencing Guidelines." *Pepperdine Law Review* 20: 905–990.

Schupak, T. 1986. "Comments: Women and Children First: An Examination of the Unique Needs of Women in Prison." *Golden Gate University Law Review* 16: 455–474.

Vachon, M. 1994. "It's about Time: The Legal Context of Policy Changes for Female Offenders." *Forum on Corrections* 6: 3–6.

Velimesis, M. I. 1981. "Sex Roles and Mental Health of Women in Prison." *Professional Psychology* 12 (1): 128–135.

Weston-Henriques, Z., and D. Jones-Brown. 2000. "Prisons as 'Safe Havens' for African-American Women." In *The System in Black and White: Exploring the Connections between Race, Crime, and Justice*, edited by M. Markowitz and D. Jones-Brown. Westport, CT: Praeger.

Zimmer, L. 1997. "How Women Reshape the Prison Guard Role." In *Workplace/Women's Place: An Anthology*, edited by D. Dunn. Los Angeles: Roxbury Publishing.

Government Publications

Bureau of Justice Statistics. 1995. *National Crime Victimization Survey.* U.S. Department of Justice, Washington, DC.

———. 1997. *HIV in Prisons and Jails, 1995.* U.S. Department of Justice, Washington, DC.

———. 1999. "Mental Health and Treatment of Inmates and Probationers." BJS Special Report, Washington, D.C.

———. 2001. *Prisoners in 2000.* U.S. Department of Justice, Washington, DC.

Greenfeld, L. and T. Snell. 1999. *Women Offenders.* Bureau of Justice Statistics, U.S. Department of Justice, Washington, DC.

Sabol, W. J., and J. McGready. 1999. 'Time Served in Prison by Federal Offenders, 1986–1997." U.S. Government Printing Office, Washington, DC.

U.S. General Accounting Office. 1999. *Women in Prison—Issues and Challenges Confronting U.S. Correctional Systems: Report to the Honorable Eleanor Holmes Norton, House of Representatives.* General Accounting Office, Washington, DC.

———. 1999. *Women in Prison—Sexual Misconduct by Correctional Staff: Report to the Honorable Eleanor Holmes Norton, House of Representatives.* General Accounting Office, Washington, DC.

U.S. General Accounting Office, General Government Division. 1999. *Women in Prison—Transition of District of Columbia Female Felons to the Federal Bureau of Prisons.* General Accounting Office, Washington, DC.

Core Periodicals

Corrections Today
American Correctional Association Publications
4380 Forbes Boulevard
Lanham, MD 20706

This is the magazine of the American Correctional Association and provides current information about the correctional scene with a focus on those employed in the correctional system.

Federal Prisons Journal
U.S. Department of Justice, Federal Bureau of Prisons
320 First Street NW, Room 738
Washington, DC 20534

This journal includes articles on management and policy issues concerned with the federal prison system.

International Journal of Offender Therapy and Comparative Criminology
Sage Publications, Inc.
2455 Teller Road
Thousand Oaks, CA 91320-2218

Covering both treatment issues for prisoners and alternatives to imprisonment, this journal provides a broad forum for research and discussion on offenders and incarceration. It also has a comparative focus.

Journal of Offender Rehabilitation
Haworth Press
10 Alice Street
Binghamton, NY 13904

This journal provides a forum for the publication of research studies and discussion concerned with the rehabilitation of offenders.

National Prison Project Journal
National Prison Project
ACLU Foundation
1875 Connecticut Avenue NW, #410
Washington, DC 20009

This is published by the American Civil Liberties Union and is a valuable resource for current information on litigation affecting prisoners' rights.

The Prison Journal
Sage Publications, Inc.
2455 Teller Street
Thousand Oaks, CA 91320-2218

This journal presents material on imprisonment in the form of research studies and discussions of penal policy, incarceration, and alternatives to imprisonment. It contains comparative material and is a leading periodical in its field.

Punishment and Society: The International Journal of Penology
Sage Publications
2455 Teller Road
Thousand Oaks, CA 91320-2218

The leading journal in the field of punishment, this periodical covers penal institutions as well as penal theory, punishment, and comparative penology.

Sexual Abuse: A Journal of Research and Treatment
Association for the Treatment of Sexual Abusers
10700 SW Beaverton-Hillside Highway, Suite 26
Beaverton, OR 97005–3035

This journal is an important source of information on this subject, dealing with the clinical, treatment, and theoretical aspects of sex abuse.

Nonprint Resources

Videos

Abused Women Who Fought Back: The Framington Eight
Format: VHS format

Length: 44 minutes
Date: 1999
Source: Films for the Humanities

This program explores the problem of domestic violence through the dramatic stories of women who became known as the Framington Eight. Each woman was imprisoned for killing a spouse or partner they say abused them repeatedly. Each claimed Battered Woman Syndrome as a defense. The program looks at both sides of this issue, speaking with women who say they would be dead now if they hadn't killed their partners, and to prosecutors and family members of those who were killed, who believe the use of Battered Woman Syndrome as a defense has gone too far.

American Justice
Type: VHS format
Length: 50 minutes
Source: A & E

This film focuses on women's experiences on death row. Women talk about their crimes, their life in prison, and their sorrow over not being able to see their children or grandchildren grow up.

Battered
Type: VHS format
Length: 56 minutes
Date: 1989
Source: Home Box Office and Ambrose Video Publishing

Battered wives, wife beating, abuse in the home. Includes interviews with middle-class white and educated women in prison who have been systematically beaten by their husbands and boyfriends.

Blind Spot: Murder by Women
Type: VHS format
Length: 87 minutes
Date: 2000
Source: Women Make Movies, New York

This documentary combines one-on-one interviews with six women murderers with reenactments of their background experience and visual recreations of their interior lives. The women describe their actions as perpetrators in detail and face the issue of having taken a life.

Breaking Silence
Type: VHS format
Length: 60 minutes
Date: 1988
Source: Future Educational Films and Aquarius Productions

A documentary film on incest and the sexual abuse of children.

Childhood Sexual Abuse
Type: VHS format
Length: 26 minutes
Date: 1990
Source: Films for the Humanities

Three women relate their experiences of being abused sexually as children. Two psychologists offer perspectives and statistics. A police officer also describes procedures used to question abused children.

Convicts on the Street: One Year on Parole
Type: VHS format
Length: 60 minutes
Date: 1990
Source: Ambrose Video

Follows a parole officer and his fifty charges. He makes surprise visits to the homes of those he suspects of violating their paroles.

The Correctional Officer: Recognizing and Preventing Closed-Custody Male Sexual Assaults
Format: VHS format
Length: 40 minutes
Date: 1996
Source: American Correctional Association

Sexual assault is the second most frequently committed crime in prison. Three out of every ten newly admitted inmates will be forcibly raped within 48 hours of their arrival. This training video teaches correctional officers how to detect these attacks and how to prevent closed-custody sexual assaults.

The Correctional Officer: Working with the Female Offender
Format: VHS format
Length: 22 minutes

Date: 1998
Source: American Correctional Association

Identifies the most common factors shared by female offenders and discusses how these issues will impact the offender's interaction with staff and other offenders. The video describes the key differences between the behavior and motivation of male and female inmates and demonstrates techniques for communicating positively with female offenders. It points out that staff professionalism plays an important role in helping female offenders achieve positive goals after their release.

Crack U.S.A.
Type: VHS format
Length: 42 minutes
Date: 1990
Source: Home Box Office

Focuses on Palm Beach County, Florida, which has seen entire neighborhoods wiped out by crack. Teenagers discuss the desperate measures they have taken to obtain the drug.

Cross Gender Supervision
Format: VHS format
Length: 20 minutes
Date: 2000
Source: American Correctional Association

As the national prison population grows, so do the number of female correctional officers and inmates, and therefore instances of cross-gender supervision. Consequently, new supervision issues have arisen such as violence and sexual misconduct. The video also addresses ways these problems can be avoided.

Defending Our Lives
Type: VHS format
Length: 43 minutes
Date: 1997
Source: Cambridge Documentary Films, Inc.

Shows the magnitude and severity of domestic violence in this country. Features four women imprisoned for killing their batterers and their terrifying personal testimonies. Each of these women tells her own horrific tale of beatings, rape, and torture at the hands of her husband or boyfriend.

Investigative Reports: Women in Prison
Format: VHS format
Length: 50 minutes
Source: A & E

A first-hand look at the daily life among gangbangers and drugs. For women inmates there is the added pain of worrying about their children. The film shows interviews with inmates, prison officials, and psychologists, and argues for changes in the current system.

Nine Hundred Women
Type: VHS format
Length: 73 minutes
Date: 2000
Source: Gabriel Films, Women Make Movies

The Louisiana Correctional Institute is located in the swamps of southern Louisiana in the small town of St. Gabriel. Built in 1970, it houses the state's most dangerous female prisoners and often exceeds its population capacity of 900. Seventy-five percent of these women are mothers, and one fourth are serving sentences of fifteen years or more. The filmmaker delivers a portrait of life in this deceptively peaceful atmosphere that is filled with stories of life on the streets, abuse, freedom, childbirth, and motherhood. Six women—a grandmother, a young high school student, a pregnant woman, a recovering heroin addict, a prison guard, and the only woman on death row—share their frustrations and hopes.

Survivors
Type: VHS format
Length: 32 minutes
Date: 1989
Source: MTI Film & Video

Documents the problem of child abuse in our society as it affects the adults who were victimized as children. It explores the damaging psychological impact of abuse on children and how it continues to haunt them as adults.

Suzanne Suzanne
Type: VHS format

Length: 26 minutes
Date: 1982
Source: Third World Newsreel

A documentary film that focuses on the tense relationship between a young black woman named Suzanne, a former drug addict, and her mother. Both were victims of the father's abusiveness.

To Love, Honor, and Obey
Type: VHS format
Length: 63 minutes
Date: 1980
Source: Third World Newsreel

This documentary about domestic assaults against women presents interviews with battered women and scenes of victims seeking or receiving help. It includes statements by doctors, lawyers, social workers, and police concerning wife abuse. It concludes with an update on one woman's case.

Internet Sites

Amnesty International USA–Sexual Abuse of Women in Prison
http://www.amnestyusa.org/rightsforall/women/

Drug War Facts
http://www.drugwarfacts.org/

Faces from the Human Rights and Drug War Exhibit
http:// www.hr95.org/hr95faces.html

Families Against Mandatory Minimums
http://www.famm. org/index2.htm

Prison Activist Resource Center: Women
http://www.prisonactivist. org/women/

The Sentencing Project
http://www.sentencingproject.org/

Women in Prison (WIP)
http://www.womeninprison.org.uk

Women in Prison: A Call for Feminist Action
http://www. rohan.sdsu.edu/~rbowman/essay1.htm

Index

209

About the Author

Cyndi Banks is Associate Professor of Criminal Justice at Northern Arizona University. She teaches courses on women in prison, juvenile justice, justice ethics, and comparative crime and culture. Her published work includes a study of Alaskan Native women in prison. She has also published numerous articles on gender, sexual violence, and comparative criminology and is the author of two books.